Re

Richie Sadlier is a former professional footballer, currently working as a television pundit and psychotherapist. He is a regular contributor to RTÉ radio and the Second Captains sports podcast, presenting *The Player's Chair*. He also writes regularly for *The Irish Times*.

Praise for *Recovering*

'You'll go a long way to find a better autobiography. It's raw, unfiltered honesty from start to finish, a captivating account of one man's story that will resonate with so many more.'

Irish Independent

'The bravest book I've read in a long time. A really quality read written by a man who happened to be a footballer, rather than a book necessarily about football.'

Damien O'Meara, RTÉ

'Storytelling of the highest calibre. Richie Sadlier's autobiography is a judiciously layered and thoughtful examination of how to live a life and develop as a person despite everything. It's also relentlessly entertaining. A rare and precious example of a sports book that has both story and stories in abundance.'

Malachy Clerkin, *The Irish Times*

Recovering

RICHIE SADLIER

with Dion Fanning

Gill Books

Gill Books

Hume Avenue

Park West

Dublin 12

www.gillbooks.ie

Gill Books is an imprint of M.H. Gill and Co.

First published in hardback 2019

First published in paperback 2020

978 07171 8954 0

Design and print origination by O'K Graphic Design, Dublin

Edited by Brian Langan

Proofread by Jane Rogers

Printed by CPI Group (UK) Ltd, Croydon, CRO 4YY

A CIP catalogue record for this book is available from the British Library.

5 4 3 2 1

To Mum, Dad, Jamie, Anna and Catherine

Many of the names in this book have been changed, along with other identifying details, to respect and protect the privacy of those involved.

Prologue

Once there was a way to get back homeward. Once there was a way to get back home.

'Golden Slumbers', LENNON & MCCARTNEY.

I t is the winter of 2016 and I am well.

If you were to ask me how I feel when I experience the lows we all go through, I might tell you that this will pass. I might even say everything is going to be OK.

I was once a professional footballer, but I'm not that any more.

I'm a football pundit, but I'm also a psychotherapist, a job which has given me more fulfilment than anything I've ever done.

I have a drink problem which, since 22 August 2011, I have treated by not drinking. I work in mental health. It's good to talk, I believe that. But I believe even more strongly that it's good to talk about the right things.

Life is complicated, but where I can I have simplified it and, yes, in the winter of 2016, I am well.

On this day, when I am well, I'm driving through Monkstown in south Dublin when a car crashes into the back of mine. It's not a serious incident, but when I get out to check the damage, I begin to feel a little dizzy. Somebody helps me stay on my feet and I walk off the road and over to the pavement where I sit down. I'm not hurt, my car is fine and I wait for the light-headedness to pass.

My hoody is pulled up as far as it can go but as the dizziness passes, I feel something else. I lean forward, putting my head between my knees as if I'm bracing myself for impact. Then it comes. It's like I'm under attack. I start sobbing: deep, frightened, threatened sobbing. The tears of a vulnerable and inconsolable child. I didn't expect them, but they don't surprise me. I know where they have come from. I know what I am afraid of. And now I know what I have to do.

I know there are things I'm still running from.

———

'Why are you here today, Richie?'

It is 2008, a year or so after I returned from England to live in Dublin. I am in a therapy session.

My professional football career is over. Every morning I wake up and I feel I am out of control. I don't know what each day will bring, but this prospect doesn't thrill me. I live in fear of the wreckage in my life. I add to the wreckage every day.

I am not well.

'Why are you here today, Richie? What was your reason for booking this session?'

Why am I here? I *know* why I'm here but I don't know how I can say it. I could say that I'm struggling with retirement, but that would just be a euphemism for saying I live a life in freefall.

'Why are you here today, Richie?'

The struggle of a sportsman's early retirement is not why I'm here.

'Why are you here today, Richie?'

The clocks stop.

I cut off eye contact and I scramble for the right words. I'm really struggling to say what I've come here to say.

Say it, you fucking wuss.

'It's OK, take as long as you need.'

Look at you. Mute little shit. Pathetic. What a man you are!

After a minute or so of total silence, I mumble my response as best I can.

From somewhere, I find the words.

I sob as I tell her, staring at the floor.

The therapist just lets me talk. She doesn't try to fill the silence when I can't. She is sound and supportive and really, really caring. The kind of person who would be perfect to speak to about this.

After the session, I sit in my car and cry on and off for about an hour. Her practice is in Dún Laoghaire and I can see the sea from my car. I know it wouldn't be wise to turn the key. I just sit there crying, not knowing what to do. I can't ring anyone to talk about what just happened. This is a secret and we can never be free of those.

I don't want to go anywhere because I can't face company. Sitting alone in my car is the best option. I suppose it's the only option.

Well, apart from going drinking for two days. Which is what I do next.

The therapist has booked me in for another session but I don't show up. I don't contact her to say I won't be showing up and I never go back. I turn on myself for wasting her time and not returning for the session, but I just want to put the toothpaste back in the tube. I want to keep my secrets where they belong.

I had a secret I believed I could never be free of. A secret I have tried to talk about over the years but which I have always tried to take back.

Don't ask me about myself.

Let's talk about you.

Don't get too close.

Why do you want to know?

I felt overwhelmed by shame for most of my life. I felt I had failed. I felt I had let people down.

For a time it seemed I could succeed and make this failure OK. I went to England to become a professional footballer and I also played for my country. For a time I had the promise of success, and then I had that promise taken away from me.

I spent a long time mourning this career, which I felt I was entitled to do. I drank and drugged my way through this mourning. If your life had turned out like mine, you'd be entitled to do this, too.

I spent a long time running. And as I ran I took this secret with me.

———

It's a winter's day in 2016 and I'm sitting in the Second Captains studio about to record a podcast.

'Jaysus, sorry about this,' I say. 'I'm all over the shop with this answer.'

'Relax, it's grand. Happens to us all,' says Eoin McDevitt. 'We can just go again when you're ready.'

These lads are my friends. I trust them and I'm entirely relaxed around them.

I had lost my train of thought almost as soon as I started to speak. I couldn't get to the end of the first sentence. I do my best to play down how rattled I am but I'm really worried that I won't be able to continue. It isn't the first time in my media career that I've needed a second attempt at an answer, but it's the only time I think I might have to abandon the recording.

These aren't nerves. This is something else. I feel the need to explain.

'Ah, it's just I have clients at the moment who have gone through shit like this and I just don't want to phrase things clumsily, y'know? Last thing they need is to hear me put my foot in it on a podcast.'

'Oh yeah, didn't think of that. No hassle, we'll go again whenever you're ready.'

The lads sit patiently while I get my shit together. Avoiding eye contact with Eoin and Ken Early, I try desperately to clear certain memories from my mind. It probably only takes me about a minute to compose myself, but again it feels like the clocks have stopped. I take an extra-long gulp from my pint of water and say I'm OK.

'Fuck's sake, lads,' I say, 'it used to be fun coming in here. Can we not go back to moaning about Ireland being shit?'

I keep it together for the rest of the recording and don't need another break, but by this stage I'm not short of practice in hiding my feelings. I have become skilled at pretending I'm grand at all times. I've had years and years of practice; years and years acting as if nothing ever happened.

———

Twenty-four hours after that podcast, a car collides with mine in Monkstown and every feeling comes pouring out.

I am sitting on the side of a road a couple of kilometres from the office of the therapist I had visited eight years earlier and I am sobbing again. The tears keep coming, but this is different. Everything is different now. I know what I will do. I will tell someone about this. I will lift the weight a little because I have learned there is no other way.

There is no escape and there is no way back home. Right here is where you live your life. This is where it's at.

1

15 November 1989

'If you could ask anything of your father, what would it be?'

It was a November morning, and we were trying to help our father defeat the disease which had overshadowed our lives.

I was two months shy of my eleventh birthday and my brother Jamie was twelve and a half. We had grown up as the children of an alcoholic and we knew nothing else.

I considered the question and decided to go big. The room was packed. I knew my words would carry a weight they might not in emptier spaces or at lonelier times.

I had nothing to lose. Fuck it, I'm going all in.

'I'd like him to take me to the World Cup next summer,' I said.

The response wasn't what I expected.

Instead of a ringing endorsement – a voice shouting 'Hell, yeah!' or 'Take him to the fucking World Cup, you bollocks' – the whole room just broke into laughter.

I desperately hoped the focus would shift to someone else.

The person who had asked the question was the facilitator for a group therapy session. My parents and Jamie were in the room too, along with eight other adults I'd never seen before. We were in a rehab centre in Wexford, visiting my dad, who was receiving treatment for alcoholism. My younger sisters, nine-year-old Anna and seven-year-old Catherine, had been sent to school as normal that day. They were too young, and probably too loose-lipped, to be told the full story. Kids that age shouldn't be burdened with knowing things they're not allowed to repeat. Our mother had shielded us from my father's disease, protected us and compensated for our dad when she had to, but reality always finds a way in. There is no escaping it.

I wasn't mad on reality myself. I was happiest when I was daydreaming. Whether it was imagining myself scoring at Wembley or Lansdowne Road, there was always another world I could go to. Dad taking me to the World Cup might have been a fantasy, but I thought this place, on this day – 15 November 1989 – was where I could share those dreams.

The reason I remember the date is not because it was a pivotal moment in our lives. I remember it because it was the day Ireland played Malta in their final World Cup qualifier. A win and we'd qualify for the first time ever. And if we did win, I wanted my dad to take me to Italy for the tournament.

It's already tricky enough to talk to a room of adults when you're only ten, but the laughter made me want to disappear. Noticing my anguish, the facilitator jumped in to help me.

'What would you ask of your father, Richard? What would you most like him to do differently?'

I went for the honest answer this time. I asked for the thing I wanted more than anything else.

'I just want him to watch me play football.'

If I hesitated about this, it was because I felt I was asking a lot of a man who did so much. Maybe I was asking too much from my dad. After all, he was a man who could do magic.

My dad was always my hero. John Sadlier might not have been winning All-Irelands or saving babies from burning buildings, but he could make chocolate appear from bushes. He could take us into a magical land of wonder where everything could change at any moment. A flower was not just a flower. A shrub in Marlay Park was not just a bit of greenery on the side of a path but an unending source of sweets and chocolates.

At Christmas, he was able to sneeze a fistful of Quality Street straight out of his nose. In St Enda's Park in Rathfarnham, he could make bananas appear in the flowers. Sweets would fall magically from his woolly hat as we were walking up Three Rock.

When he took us to these places, we knew that everything could be overturned at any second. We just had to believe in magic. And I believed. I believed the magic was real.

If we were good, he would let us in on his magician's world. If we all said the magic words together – 'Alacazam', 'Hocus Pocus', or whatever the magic required – the treats would appear. It worked every time.

He was my idol. For as long as I could remember, I'd wanted his approval and it was a long time before that changed. If it ever really did.

He could be as giddy as a schoolkid some days, playful and great fun to be around. He was very ticklish, too, and my sisters could have him in stitches in no time. When all my mum's side of the family would meet in my granny's farm in Cork, he was the adult who took all the kids on adventures in the woods. Like the Pied Piper, he was the one we followed wherever he went, always sure it would be an adventure we'd remember. And when it came time to build human pyramids, he would always be the one at the centre on the bottom row, laughing hysterically every time we came crashing down. I had the coolest dad of all.

But there was the other side, too. There were the times when the magic wouldn't work. At those times, no spell could make the darkness go away. Then it wasn't a land of wonder: it was a grey, miserable land. On those days, he was an angry no-go zone.

I desperately wanted the magician to come through the door each night, but we never knew which version of my dad would arrive home.

Hungover, drunk or sober, take your pick, you'd know who it was before he said a word. His mood came in the door before him.

One night, he wasn't happy to find the gas fire on in our sitting room when he arrived home. The room was too hot so he had a go at Mum for wasting money. In a tantrum, he stormed out to the pub. The following night he came home to a house with no fire on. It was colder than he liked it, so he had a go at Mum, using the temperature as his reason for spending so many nights out of the house. In a tantrum, he stormed out to the pub.

Some nights we wouldn't see him at all, and Mum would be left to explain why his plans had changed.

I could never understand how he could change so much. I'd be afraid to make eye contact with him when this version came home. At those times, I'd silently leave the house with a ball and head for another world.

———

My dad came from a world of drink and drinkers. His parents, Dick and Aggie, ran Sadlier's pub in Limerick city and their family of six children lived above it. Granda Dick bottled his own Guinness, sherry and wine, and he drank each evening on his own after hours. Dad was sampling the stock from the age of ten, swigging out of bottles he would deliberately overfill.

He'd pilfer from the till when the opportunity arose and head off swimming and fishing in the Shannon with his brothers. He told us he would mistakenly drink cider, thinking it was Cidona, before he hit his teens. I find that hard to believe as he was a bright kid, and an even brighter student.

He had to report for work in the bar within five minutes of school finishing every afternoon. Even if the bar was empty, he wasn't allowed to be idle. Drinking on the job was frowned upon, as the more the customers drank, the more alert he'd have to be.

My mum, Mary O'Reilly, was from a pretty tough background herself. She was brought up in a sparse farmhouse near Kilbrin in north Cork with no running hot water, no central heating, no TV, no telephone, no luxuries – just cement floors and an open fire.

Mum and Dad met in their third year in UCC, where Dad was elected president of the Students' Union. Granny Aggie suggested Dad apply for a job in the civil service, which brought them to Dublin. In November 1974 Mum went home to tell her parents that Dad and herself had bought a house in Dublin and were planning to get married, to which her father responded, 'Best of luck to you, my child.' She didn't realise that those were the last words he would ever say to her. He died ten days later from a massive coronary.

Mum and Dad got married on St Patrick's Day, 1975. It was just four months after the death of her father, which upset her mother Kate – known as Granny O to us – who did not want the wedding to go ahead so soon.

When my parents moved to Dublin, they settled in Ballinteer, later buying the four-bedroom semi-detached house in Broadford, a housing estate in the area, where we would all grow up.

By the time he turned thirty, Dad had four kids and a drinking problem. My mum held it all together in those early years. In addition to raising the four of us, she used to mind other children in our house during the week while their parents were at work. Our home was a lot of things, but it was never quiet.

Jamie and I would transform our house into a sporting arena. We would rearrange the sitting-room furniture to replicate a football pitch and wreak havoc with a tennis ball. Any breakages were blamed on neighbouring children who weren't even there, but no matter how hard Mum tried to stop us playing, we persisted.

When we became obsessed with WWF, our parents' bed became a wrestling ring. Jamie would give it the full Vince McMahon in the introduction and then we'd essentially beat the shit out of each other on the bed.

Every summer, my parents would take in foreign students for extra income. One year three bedrooms were needed for our Italian and Spanish guests, leaving all six of us to sleep squashed together in one bedroom – Jamie and me in bunk beds, Anna and Catherine on a sofa-bed, and our parents in the double bed. Mum told us it was a scheduling error, but I assume we needed the cash.

For Jamie and me, this was a great development. Now we could launch ourselves from the top bunk towards our parents' bed, trying to bodyslam each other in true Hulk Hogan style.

We never had that kind of living arrangement again, but myself and Jamie would have been happy enough if the set-up had continued.

In many ways, we were happy. I had an older brother to play with, sisters I adored and, when I discovered football, something I loved, something I was good at.

But there was tension too, and much of that tension came from the uncertainty of wondering which version of our dad would walk through the door every night.

If you met me, you'd say I was a good kid. Certainly I was no trouble, but I didn't feel like a good kid. I worried all the time and thought calamity was around every corner. I was a bed-wetter, something that continued into my early teens. I'd lean my mattress, covered in piss, against my bedroom wall to dry during the day. When friends called around, everything would be fine if we were playing downstairs. But if they wanted to go upstairs to play in my room, I'd have to disappear like a ninja to put the mattress back on my bed. They never understood why, even in winter, I'd leave my window open when we played up there.

When he hit his teens, Jamie rebelled. He kicked up a fuss about everything and ran amok. Being the eldest, he took the brunt of things in ways the rest of us didn't. He was the first to stop believing in Dad's magic.

At the age of fourteen, he ran away from home twice – three days the first time, six days the second. When I think about it now, it was a perfectly reasonable course of action in the circumstances. Back then, though, I hated him for the extra hassle he was causing Mum, who had enough on her plate without him piling it on. We went from playing together all the time to barely speaking, something which continued well into our teens. Looking back now, I realise we developed different ways of coping, but I also feel sad that my brother and I, who had together built an imaginary world, grew so far apart.

While Jamie rebelled, football increasingly became my retreat. It was the most reliable way I knew to get away from trouble. It was a means of escape but also a way to get my dad's attention. I couldn't exactly do magic when I played football, but I was good – good enough that, just maybe, he'd notice.

I was always close to my sisters, even if they developed their own ways of surviving as well.

Anna was just under two years younger than me and she always did her best to keep everyone smiling. She still does. As a child she was funny, lively and everyone loved her. We were allies from the very beginning and I can never remember us fighting. In any family row, we were always on the same side.

We spent hours together. If we weren't playing, we'd chat about anything and everything. Our relationship has never really changed, even if I would test its strength in later years.

Catherine, the youngest, lost herself in the lives of her pets. My dad played his part in this too. Every time one of them died, he would preside over a funeral service at the patch of grass next to the shed in the back garden that was reserved as a pet cemetery. He would find a cardboard box and pad it with cotton wool for maximum comfort. Then he would stand next to Catherine at the graveside for as long as she needed. There couldn't have been a more dignified send-off for Kevin the hamster and Erica the rabbit. And Catherine would be comforted through the loss of her most recent best friend.

Like Catherine, I loved animals. When I was eight, we got a dog and I called him Shambles. A week before his first birthday, Dad took him out for an early-morning walk, but Shambles was knocked down and killed by a Garda car on the newly built, unopened road behind our house. I remember Dad sitting at my bedside to deliver the news. I was heartbroken but I wanted to see Shambles. Dad brought me out to the car where the poor thing lay in the boot; thankfully his wounds weren't visible.

I badgered my parents for a new dog almost straight away, and the following year we got a bearded collie named Bella. She was a very nervous dog: if you opened a can of Coke in her company, she'd run out of the room with the fright. I hope I never experience the terror she felt every Halloween night.

———

Football consumed me all the time. From the age of six, I was involved with teams, but that was only the official part of my relationship with the game. I didn't go anywhere without a ball. If Mum sent me to the shop for milk, I'd have a ball at my feet for the journey. We weren't allowed footballs in the schoolyard so I'd bring in a tennis ball every day to use in matches. While visiting my grandparents in Limerick, I'd dribble a ball through the streets on the walk to the local chipper, Krank's Korner. When we visited Granny O in Cork, I'd be dribbling round the cow shit and potholes in the farmyard. I'd lob a ball in the direction of the odd cow when we were getting them from the fields in the evening just to see if I could get a rise out of any of them – first of all making absolutely sure Uncle Dan couldn't see me. There are an endless number of ways a kid can find amusement on a farm, but kicking a ball against the wall of the derelict creamery across the road was all I needed.

My pocket money always went on *Shoot!* magazine. I wasn't one of those kids with the best boots or the latest football strips. For two years I wore a pair of boots my parents had picked up in a car boot sale: they were too big, weren't any brand and had cost £2. To make a point about how little football gear I had, I once reserved a shelf in my wardrobe for it, which was more or less empty all the time. My parents were amused but unmoved. Just get on with it.

Most of my childhood was spent playing ball in front of or behind my house. Good or bad days, alone or with mates, that's where I wanted to be. I wasn't meek or shy or timid on a football field. I didn't feel subordinate to anyone. When matches weren't going our way, I knew teammates would look to me to find solutions. I loved that responsibility. On my best days, I swear to God I felt invincible. I felt like nothing was beyond me – something I rarely, if ever, felt away from the field.

If we played football at lunchtime and it was a draw, I'd spend the afternoon going through the order of the takers for the penalty shoot-out after school or compiling reports of the game in my head. I didn't get side-tracked by computer games or schoolwork because none of it could make me feel like football made me feel. I had my eyes on the prize. Sometimes the prize was becoming a professional footballer; sometimes it was anything that meant I didn't have to think about what was going on at home.

Using the pillars of our driveway as goalposts, I'd be in my element, raining in shots on anyone who'd stand between them. And when nobody else was around, my imagination turned those pillars into Wembley Stadium with the crowd stunned at how incredible I was. I could transport myself to another world with a ball at my feet. And in that other world – relentlessly practising, relentlessly obsessing about who I could be, what I could do, how proud my dad would be when he finally saw what his son had become – everything was going my way.

This fantasy world was where I lived.

I knew I was good, which got me out of a few scrapes. One day my teacher, Mr Casey, a no-nonsense type, decided to punish me for laughing in class. The punishment was to write 'I must not laugh in class' two hundred times. However, we had a Gaelic match that afternoon and Mr Casey told me, 'If you score five goals today, I'll let you off'. He said it in such a way that he obviously didn't think I could do it. I always wanted to prove people wrong, so I went out that day, scored five goals and got off.

I tried to ignore everything that bothered me at the time, no matter how impossible that was. If football could solve all the problems in my life, then nothing else could get in its way.

Once I started to play organised games it mattered even more. My mood at home was dictated by how I had played in my most recent match, and my focus would be on the next one. There were, of course, other things influencing my mood, but I had no control over them. Football was different.

As I progressed I really wanted Dad to come to my games, but he rarely did. Every time I played, I wanted to do more, to score another goal, to reach another milestone so I could tell him about it and maybe I could entice him to come and watch me.

There were lots of good explanations as to why he couldn't make it. He worked late. He worked long hours. He was a busy man. He stayed late in the office – although I was soon to discover that 'the office' was a catch-all term for anywhere that served drink.

So I spent my time hoping he would come but I would never risk a confrontation or ask him to come and watch me. The idea that I would tell him how I was feeling was ridiculous.

I was lost in a world of football. The first game I watched on TV from beginning to end was Ireland v England in Euro '88. The first time I saw Ireland play live, I took another step into this magical land. A neighbour brought me to the match at Lansdowne Road at the end of May 1989. The Ireland players were superstars in my eyes. Gods on

Earth. Standing on the South Terrace that day was an experience that blew my mind. When Kevin Moran scored at that end in the victory against Malta, I knew what I wanted to do with my life.

The return game on 15 November 1989 would be even bigger and I could think of little else. But I had a dilemma: how could I get to see the game on TV when I would be at school when it kicked off on a Wednesday afternoon? I came up with a few plans, but would immediately spot a flaw.

Then, the night before the game, I had a stroke of luck when Mum took me to one side and told me my father was an alcoholic. We would be visiting him in the treatment centre on Wednesday afternoon, which meant I would miss school and, amazingly, see the game.

The wider implications of my dad being in rehab didn't concern me. By that stage, Mum had been going to a support group for people impacted by other people's drinking for three years. Dad didn't think she needed to go. At one point, he'd asked her why she didn't take up knitting if she was looking for a hobby.

Jamie had been exposed to a lot more than me by this time, and had already been to support meetings. I was too young for that, but I didn't need to see Dad in rehab to realise he had a problem. He used to brew his own wine at home but he was his only customer. Dad, as is so often the case with alcoholics, was the last to see it.

When Dad went into rehab, Mum had initially told us he was away on business. I'm sure she resented being left to look after the four of us on her own, but there must also have been relief that he wasn't there. When she told me the truth, I was sworn to secrecy. Jamie and I were told to stick with the business trip story to everyone, even our sisters. We weren't to inform the school either. We both said we were sick. Mum didn't even tell the neighbours. I didn't understand alcoholism – I'm still not sure I do – but I copped that it was something to be ashamed about.

My dad, my hero, was an alcoholic. And nobody in the world was to know about it.

I did as I was told. I didn't tell anyone about it at the time. There's nothing to be gained by ruining your dad's reputation or embarrassing your mum by telling people she's married to a drunk. It was to remain our dirty family secret for years.

Mum had offered another woman a lift to the treatment centre and I overheard some of their conversation on the way down. She was going to visit her son. I vividly remember hearing her say he was a talented footballer that some of the top clubs in Dublin had wanted to sign, but drink had taken over and he had lost interest. This shook me. I knew drinking changed your mood and made you unreliable. I knew it destroyed families and ruined relationships. But I was stunned to hear it made this talented footballer turn down one of the top clubs. I took note and promised myself that would never be me. I had seen what it had done to my dad and I swore I would never drink. When I took the pledge at my Confirmation two years later, I really meant it. (Unsurprisingly, I chose my father's name, John, as my Confirmation name.)

Naturally, I had a ball with me at the rehab centre. After we'd watched the Ireland game, the son of the woman who'd travelled with us showed some interest in having a kickabout in the grounds outside. I didn't need to be asked twice. Jamie played too and, amazingly, so did Dad. For the first time ever – maybe the only time – the three of us were laughing and playing football together. Ireland had just qualified for the World Cup, but this game on a patch of grass outside the rehab centre mattered just as much. It certainly mattered more to me than what I had been hearing about alcoholism.

While my determination never to drink was sky high by the end of that day, my desire to be a professional footballer also increased. I now had some specifics, though – I wanted to play for the Republic of Ireland in the World Cup Finals, and I wanted my dad to watch me.

2

Walking on Eggshells

Dad came home from rehab after six weeks, but that wasn't the end of things. It turned out it was just the beginning.

We were asked to come to the kitchen table. All the important family discussions took place there, but on this day Jamie and I braced ourselves for something big.

'I can promise you both, I won't ever drink again,' Dad said. 'I'm done with it all.'

Jamie said nothing and neither did I. I had loads of questions, but it wasn't the time for probing. My questions were probably stupid, anyway; that's what I told myself. Dad said he wouldn't be drinking again, so we'd go with that.

We were reminded to keep quiet about it. I told Dad I was glad he was home and I went outside with my football.

But those unspoken questions, stupid or not, stayed with me. When my dad came out of rehab, I would torment myself with them.

How do you stop an alcoholic from drinking?

Why do they start in the first place?

Why does he want something that he knows is bad for him?

I still don't know the answers, but they were the questions I was asking at the time. There was too much at stake for us all. Life may have been better than before, but it was still complicated.

I had no idea how to behave around him. None of us did. If he drank again, we were screwed. I knew that much. My parents' marriage wouldn't survive another blow-out and nobody knew where that would leave us.

I promised myself I'd never be the reason he drank again. The problem was, I had no idea why he might drink again. That was confusing. I didn't want to do anything to tip him over the edge. But where was the edge? I had no idea what behaviour I was trying to avoid.

Dad didn't drink again after leaving the treatment centre, but that's not the only measure that counts in these matters. As he adjusted to his new way of living, we did our best to get to know our new dad, always afraid the old one could return at any time. We didn't know why he might come back, but every time Dad walked in the front door, we knew it was possible.

I was sure of myself when I played football, but I couldn't say the same for life at home. Dad's demeanour still influenced everything in the house. If he was quiet, I thought it was better to stay quiet too. If we were watching TV together, I'd look to him for guidance on what I found amusing. If he wasn't laughing, I wouldn't laugh. I thought my mood could affect his, but the way his mood affected mine took me a lot longer to appreciate. I felt conscious at all times of what he might be feeling, as if I was fitted with some kind of sensor.

The truth is, I was afraid of him, and afraid of the impact his drinking could have on the rest of us. Everything would come crashing down if he drank again. I didn't know it at the time, but Granny O's house in Cork had been put on standby for Mum and the four of us to move into if we had to leave.

I realised later how all of this turned me away from confrontation of any kind. I was always the one in the wrong, always the one apologising, although, ideally, I would have quietly removed myself from any situation before there was any apologising to do.

When Dad stopped drinking, we all had to develop coping strategies for this new world. The fact that he had quit was treated as shamefully as if he was still the unpredictable, drunken father. Maybe more shamefully. But secrets have a way of revealing themselves.

Catherine was eleven when she found a book about alcoholism in the house. She had just watched an episode of the American sitcom *Family Ties* in which alcoholism had been discussed. When she started to ask too many questions, my parents sat her down and explained everything to her.

Anna's way of learning was a bit more abrupt. We were all down on the farm in Cork and Dad had just left for Dublin with Catherine, having had a big row with Mum. Jamie was already successfully dodging family trips so he wasn't there, but Anna and I stayed on the farm with Mum. The three of us wandered off into one of my uncle's fields and Mum told her the whole story. Or as much of the story as is appropriate for an eleven-year-old.

They would eventually find their own ways of dealing with it, but I had already found mine. At the end of our garden at home, over the back wall, was a field. This was where Broadford Rovers played and this was where my football career began.

I started there when I was six. When I left after seven years to join local rivals Leicester Celtic from Rathfarnham, I was in tears. I was only thirteen and I didn't want to leave, but I knew if I wanted to make it as a pro, I needed to step up a level. But I didn't want to take too big a step.

My manager at Broadford Rovers, Gerry Fitzgibbon, didn't want me to leave either. Well, he did; he just didn't agree with where I was going. He was perplexed that I was leaving for a club in the C league, and with only the desire to play for their B team.

'You know you're far better than them,' he told me on the doorstep of our house. 'You could go to the A league right now.'

I'd been Broadford's top scorer every year and player of the year twice. One year I'd received the award from Andy Townsend, who was club patron. It was like shaking hands with a Hollywood A-lister. In the photo, my face says it all: I'm looking at a god.

Despite all this, I had a nagging voice in my head holding me back. Gerry tried to silence it.

'Any of the big clubs would sign you straight away, you know that, don't you?'

'Oh, I dunno about that, Gerry, but thanks for everything.'

I wasn't prepared to consider such a thing, even for a moment. It would have taken more than a pep talk to convince me I was worth that much.

And so I left to join Leicester Celtic B's.

Leicester played a mile and a half down the road, but it felt like I was moving continents. Damien Duff was on their A team, playing in the A league. I didn't know him and I had never met him, but, even then, everyone had heard about him. I figured if things went well in the B's, I'd get noticed and would move up.

And that's how it played out. I was up with the A's the following year, by which time Duffer had moved on to Lourdes Celtic. I knew some of the players and I knew I was at least at their level, so it didn't feel like too big a jump at the time. I continued to score regularly, which meant I had further options before long. Managers from the top clubs had started to ring me. I scored six goals in one A-league game, which was pretty unusual, especially for a mid-table team. People were telling me I could go places, but I wasn't convinced. None of it was as powerful as the voice in my head telling me they were wrong.

Then one day when I was fifteen, Gerry Mooney of Belvedere FC knocked on our door.

He started to sell me the idea of joining the club. Gerry's pitch was spot-on. There were no inducements, just the promise of good coaching and the opportunity to play regularly in front of scouts from English clubs. Nothing else mattered to me. Leicester had offered me the possibility of trials with Stoke City and Hearts if I stayed. The manager said he knew the scouts there.

Belvedere was another step up, but I still had my doubts. I wanted to be a professional footballer and play in England, yet I didn't think I'd be good enough for Belvedere. Fairview Park was a long way to travel from Ballinteer just to stand on the side-lines, which I reckoned was what would happen once I was found out. I knew what to do, so I stayed at Leicester Celtic.

When we were heavily beaten in our first few games, I realised I'd made a mistake. I rang Gerry Mooney in the hope he hadn't signed someone else in the meantime. If I wanted to be a pro, I needed to play at their level. If I wasn't good enough for them, that would be the end of it. Better to find out once and for all. Thankfully, they still had room for me and wanted to sign me. Without that move, I'm sure I would never have become a professional.

Mum was always at my games, supporting and cheering my every move. Dad still didn't come to my matches, but I was starting to understand why he couldn't make it. People need additional support when they come out of rehab. I wasn't his only child, he had his recovery to tend to and he didn't really like football. I knew all that. But, as per my masterplan, I thought he'd eventually come if I kept scoring. So that's what I did.

———

As I entered my teens, my opinion of myself was being shaped by how I did in my matches. I was OK if we won and I scored and played well. If we lost and I played badly, I was in trouble. On the good days there was nothing I couldn't do, but the bad days were tough to bear. If I missed a chance or miscontrolled a ball, it would stay with me for a long time.

I can still recall specific moments when I should have done better in games. In one match against Wayside Celtic when I was eleven, I was clean through on goal, but instead of shooting early or deciding to go around the keeper, I ran straight at him. He dived to the ground and smothered the ball. I still remember the groans of disappointment, but they weren't as loud as the voice in my head hammering me for being so shit. I can also still see a game for Belvedere against Joey's when I was sixteen. I rounded the keeper and delayed a fraction too long before shooting, by which time the keeper had recovered his position and blocked my shot. Even in games where I played really well, such were the moments that stayed with me.

When I joined Belvedere, like a lot of kids, I just wanted to fit in. To help me along the way, I began speaking with a stronger Dublin accent than I actually had. Belvedere was an old Dublin football club and I guess I thought the accent made me more believable as a football man. I would leave home as the good son with a soft Ballinteer accent and by the time I got to Fairview Park for training I was speaking like Rats from *Paths to Freedom*.

———

Around the time my dad came out of rehab, I started going to watch St Patrick's Athletic in their temporary home in Harold's Cross. Brian Kerr was the manager of St Pat's at the time and the club were league champions. In my memory Dad brought me many times. Maybe it was to make up for not bringing me to the World Cup – a League of Ireland game is a lot more accessible than Italia '90. However, my friend Ed, who was there every week, said Dad very rarely came. I must have spent so much time thinking about going to matches with him that my memory has transformed them into something that never was. Like a lot of things, though, what was real wasn't as important as what I imagined to be real.

Ed's dad was from Inchicore so he had St Pat's in his blood. Ed and I originally bonded over a shared love of Arsenal. Along with our mate Rochey, we went everywhere together. Ed had been one of the first to spot my potential to be a pro. When we were nine years old, he made me sign a contract saying that when I made it as a footballer, I would give all the credit to him in my first post-match interview. He lost the document, though, so I was in the clear when it eventually happened.

My friends were playing GAA with Ballinteer St John's so I took that up too. I was a full-back and enjoyed it every bit as much as playing football. One of my best mates, McGrath, played in midfield. My mate Johnny played half-back and is still one of the funniest blokes I know. I eventually had to leave St John's because my back couldn't sustain doing both GAA and football at a high level.

I tried guitar lessons, too, but my teacher, Tom Kitt, was elected to the Dáil and moved the classes to Saturday mornings. It clashed with football training so my music career died an early death. But my friendship with his son, Thomas, has never ended.

While my mates were discovering drink for themselves in their early teens, I kept my vow not to touch it. I had seen what Dad's drinking had done to our family and that was one of the reasons I stuck to my promise.

The fact that my dad was now sober hadn't changed that. I was still walking on eggshells, so I knew drinking was no life. I was adamant I'd never succumb. There was no way I was going to expose myself to the carnage. Whenever I was out with my mates, I was the quiet one, the sober one on the periphery, not really involved.

Then I tried it. And everything changed in ways I couldn't have imagined. I tried it because, well, what else was there to do?

There was no turning point, no big change of heart. We were on a family camping holiday in France, only our second trip abroad together. It was in the middle of USA '94, and I was fifteen. I remember watching the Holland game in the bar area of the campsite with a load of Dutch and Irish fans mingling together. The following day, Jamie and I scrambled together enough lads from Dublin to enter a team in the campsite five-a-side tournament. We managed to win the whole thing, so I celebrated by having a few beers with my teammates that evening.

It didn't feel like a big deal at the time, because it wasn't a big deal. My parents were in the bar with us so it was all above board. A few beers, nothing more. I wasn't sitting there cursing my poor willpower or hammering myself for abandoning the promise I had made when I was ten. I thought it was time to see what all the fuss was about, and straight away I knew I'd made the right call. I wasn't awkwardly sitting on the periphery anymore. I was just one of the lads, enjoying a beer after winning a football tournament.

It quietened my mind too. When I was about twelve, I had become obsessed with the idea of death, specifically my own death. This thought became a constant companion. If I wasn't directly obsessing about it, I was always aware of its presence, an uninvited guest in the room that could rear up and make an unpleasant intervention at any time. I don't know where this came from but I was sure I was going to die young. There were simply too many ways to die for me to avoid them all. I would spend hours thinking about the way I would die. I lived in constant fear of some disaster that was about to strike. When the family threw a surprise fortieth for my mum, I ran upstairs and burst into tears, devastated I would never reach that landmark.

Drink worked and my old promises were easily forgotten. Years later, I would be baffled when I would vow that I wouldn't go out or that I would only have one or two drinks if I did. Or vow after two or three that there would be no chaos this time, only to wake up surrounded by the familiar wreckage. Then I would wonder why the promises I made had no effect, but my childhood version was easy to forget when I started drinking. And now that I had started, it was too much fun to stop.

From then on, Friday night was all about drink. The week would be spent trying to scrape together the few quid needed to buy cans for the Friday night. It turned out girls were way less intimidating when you're drunk. And I was more sociable and, incredibly, more kissable. I felt, at last, that I belonged.

Outdoor drinking was all there was in those days. The grounds of the closed-down youth club in the estate provided both privacy and the possibility of getting a chase from a wandering guard. Rebel songs would be blaring from someone's ghetto blaster and scraps would often break out among the older lads. And if you blacked out on the ground – a common enough occurrence – you were relatively safe. My worst nights came when I was drinking cider, so when I was around seventeen, I decided to lay off it for good. It was best to stick to drinks that agreed with me.

Saturday nights were a no-go for boozing, though, as Sunday was when I had my games with Belvedere. Nothing was to interfere with that. I would ring-fence those nights, mark them down and be clear that on Saturday nights I never drank. This was the dedication I felt was needed to become a professional – something which was beginning to seem like a real possibility.

3

Going Pro

When I was sixteen, my dad started to regularly watch me play at Belvedere. Nobody said anything. I didn't know what had changed and he only ever came if Mum was coming too, but I noticed. Of course I noticed.

I was playing the best football I'd ever produced at the highest level I'd ever played and now, each time I looked to the side-lines, Dad was there. He never once criticised my performances or grilled me about anything. There were no post-game dressing-downs that other lads got from their dads, no input from the touchline that overstepped the mark. He didn't mouth off at referees or tell the manager what team to pick. He just asked if I was happy with how I had played, and he left it at that. I never once told him how much it meant to me that he was there.

If I craved Dad's approval, it was Mum who kept things going. I would talk to her about everything and if I needed something, she would find a way of getting it for me. As football became serious, she managed to scrape together £65 for a new pair of Mizuno boots, which was a lot back in 1994 and a far cry from the £2 boots I wore when I started out. There was one condition: I couldn't tell anyone she'd paid for them. When Belvedere were playing in a summer tournament in

Wales, it was Mum who found the money and it was handed over again on the basis that nobody ever know it came from her. After I signed my first professional contract, one of the first things I did was pay my mum back the money she had spent to help me get there. I'd kept a record of all she'd paid for and when she came to visit, I gave her a cheque for £800. I owed her a lot more than money, though.

The possibility of moving abroad was also starting to emerge. While at Leicester or Broadford, I had never played against a big Dublin club with expectations of winning, but now I was the main striker for one of them. And I wasn't just being picked to start every game, I was playing very well and scoring all the time in a team that was chasing trophies.

Before Belvedere, I had never even spoken to anyone who had been on trial with an English club, but now I had teammates who could tell me what was involved. And my Belvedere managers, Gerry, Peadar Behan and Vincent Butler, were telling me I should set that as my target. This was different from being encouraged by Mum or any of my teachers in St Benildus College, my secondary school in Kilmacud. This was praise from people who knew what it took to play at that level.

One night, in February 1995, Gerry Smullen, the Millwall scout in Ireland, called to our house to invite me over on trial. It was barely six months since I had joined Belvedere. Mum and Dad were with me when he outlined what would be involved. I can still remember the buzz in the room that night. It wasn't what we were saying, it was the looks we were giving each other. The 'play it cool but, Jaysus, is this really happening?' kind of look. None of us really knew how to react, other than to just say 'Yes'. For me, this was a major step on the ladder towards life as a professional, but my parents had to consider that I might soon be emigrating.

Millwall weren't the only club showing an interest. I went on trial to Bolton Wanderers when I was sixteen, but I totally froze. Unsurprisingly, I wasn't asked back. I remember walking through the first-team dressing room after training and Alan Stubbs, eight years my senior and an established player, fired a pair of dirty socks at the back of my head as hard as he could. It wasn't the time or place to show him who was boss, so I kept going.

I was due to go to Sunderland that same year, but I got tonsillitis and couldn't travel. But once I went to Millwall, my mind was made up. Millwall, it's fair to say, probably took a bit longer to make their mind up about me.

I first went over there for a week at Easter when I was in fifth year. I told the lads on the team my name but maybe they didn't catch it, they seemed happy to call me Paddy. I wasn't pleased about that, but I was sixteen and there were a lot of them. Let's go with Paddy for the time being.

On the field, with so much at stake, I froze again. I thought I would have to impress with every touch. I worked myself up too much and completely flopped. In a practice game against Watford, everyone was bigger, faster and stronger. I felt completely out of my depth.

I have the generosity of Millwall's youth development officer to thank for not calling a halt to everything there and then. He must have realised that what I produced couldn't have been my normal level or I wouldn't have got that far. I was told to keep working on my game because they'd be keeping an eye on my progress. I was encouraged by this, but also knew that it could be just what clubs tell players they know they'll never watch again. On this occasion, they were telling the truth.

Millwall offered me a two-year deal that summer after seeing me play for Belvedere in the tournament in Wales. Signing it would have meant not sitting my Leaving Cert. Amazingly, and for that reason, I turned it down.

Over fifty players had moved to the UK from Belvedere by that time and only two went on to have careers in the game. Despite obsessing about an offer like this for as long as I could remember, I said no because I felt I needed a plan B. Maybe part of me just wasn't ready to take the plunge.

Either way, I decided that if they wanted me then, they'd still want me in a year. But in professional football, that's exactly how things don't work. Managers can leave and other players can be signed in your position. You can pick up injuries or lose form. A year is an awfully long time in youth football. It certainly turned out to be that way for me and Millwall.

The youth development officer who rated me left the club and his successor had never seen me play. A new coach was put in charge of the youth team and he didn't know me either. That February, first-team manager Mick McCarthy quit to take the Ireland job. I would have to go back and impress an entirely new regime. Thankfully, that's what I managed to do.

I returned to Millwall on trial a fortnight after the Leaving Cert and they offered me a one-year deal at the end of that week. Money had never been part of my dreams, but now Millwall had made me an offer that was going to make me rich: £175 a week plus £160 to pay for my digs. Some might have looked at the offer and pointed out there was no signing-on fee or that the deal was just for one year. But that wasn't what I saw. I saw something else: *Three-hundred-and-thirty-five pounds sterling every fucking week.* This was incredible.

There was little room for haggling – not my greatest skill anyway – so I grabbed the pen. They told me I would be rewarded with a much better deal the following year if I performed at the club. I took them at their word, but then again I didn't have any other options. I went home for a week to do whatever you're meant to do to get ready to live out your dreams.

My parents wanted to do something to mark the occasion, so on my last night at home, they invited people to the house for a party. Neighbours, relatives, mates, former managers and some of my old teachers showed up to say goodbye and good luck. I was put on the spot to give a speech.

'Thanks for all the support, it means a lot. Special thanks to Granny O for coming up from Cork to be here. I'm just gonna go over and give it my best and hopefully do yous proud.'

Dad had spoken just before me and had started to choke on his words a little. I knew if I said much more, I'd get emotional too.

I promised my sisters I'd write them letters. There was no social media or mobile phones in 1996. None of us had been away from home for more than a week or two at that point. I didn't know what I was getting into any more than I knew what I was leaving behind.

'You may as well be dead,' my mate Sketts drunkenly told me.

I was leaving my family and mates behind and while it wasn't always a safe world, it was all I knew.

There'd been many times I hoped I'd never leave, certain my role in the house was to help others get by. In any case, I had dug my own escape tunnel for whenever it was required, accessible at a moment's notice by having a ball at my feet. I was on the doorstep of my own little world everywhere I went. I suppose when you've got that, you'll be OK wherever you are.

That was how I felt as I headed for the airport the following day, into a new life as a professional footballer. The coaching I got in Belvedere had helped to prepare me for the football stuff, but the off-the-field challenges were an entirely different matter.

Jamie was in America at the time but the rest of the family came to the airport with me. I kept it together until the lady at the check-in desk asked me to confirm it was a one-way ticket.

I couldn't hold it in after that. I'd only ever seen my dad cry properly at Granda Dick's funeral when I was thirteen. And now he was in tears again. He couldn't get the words out at the departure gate, but he did his best to wish me well and hugged me tightly. It was the kind of hug we'd never had before.

I hugged my sisters and then my mum. My mum was the only one not in tears. She was strong and that's why I'd always turned to her. But she told me later that she cried on and off for months afterwards.

I spent the entire flight to London in tears. I'd obsessed for years about being on this flight, about heading to England to be a footballer. Now it was happening and it was nothing like I'd imagined. Escape wasn't as simple as it appeared to be. I thought I was ready, but there was fear and uncertainty where I was headed. And, as I would quickly discover, nothing could prepare me for life at Millwall.

4

We Are Millwall

I had been in London a week when I was in a pub with one of the Irish lads from the Millwall youth team and two mates from home. We were talking, laughing, minding our own business, and then we became aware that somebody was shouting in our direction.

'Fack off, Paddies!'

It took a minute to work out what was going on. I picked up some phrases like 'potato-pickers'. One of my mates took exception and squared off with the loudest, most obnoxious guy. One of the others, the most reasonable of the bunch, explained to me that this obnoxious guy hated the Irish because his friend had been killed in Northern Ireland while serving with the British Army. I tried to make peace while the rest of his mates unburdened themselves with lots of anti-Irish sentiment.

'Paddies, fack off. And don't facking come back.'

They let us know their feelings, but I genuinely had no idea how we were meant to respond. Apologise? Sympathise? Fight? In any case, there were eight of them and they were raring to go.

The landlord came over and we relaxed a little. He was the authority in these parts, and he could see that we'd been minding our own business and would calm things down so we could go back to our quiet drink.

Not exactly.

'You heard them, boys. Fack off!'

He was throwing us out.

'And don't come back.'

Six months earlier the IRA had bombed Canary Wharf in London.

'Facking Paddy cunts,' one of them said as we headed for the exit.

My work environment at Millwall was just as challenging. When I arrived at the club it was quickly established that the chances of making it beyond the youth team were slim. In our youth squad of eighteen players, we knew four at most would be offered professional contracts. And of the four, probably only one or two would be offered a second one. *Be one of the four.* We heard that all the time. Be one of the four, impress us. Stand out but do it by fitting in.

We were being coached into becoming better players but, more important, we were being moulded into Millwall players.

I kept hearing the term 'Millwall player' by staff and fans, as if being a 'Millwall' type of player made you superior. At the time, I thought it was self-praising bullshit. Imagine a club as small as Millwall making out that players who played for them were in some way special. I would come to understand it differently over time, but at youth team level, the coaches understood it better than most.

They had been around the club a long time and knew why the distinction was important. We would all learn it, too. Technical ability will only get you so far in The Den. You needed a whole lot more to thrive in that place.

The reason for this was the Millwall fans.

Minutes after I came on as substitute to make my Millwall debut at The Den, a fan tried to confront the referee, but a couple of players got in his way. Then a fan ran on to the pitch to attack our manager, only to be stopped by a ring of police surrounding the dugout. The fan who tried to get at the ref was a Millwall fan. The one who tried to attack Millwall's manager was a Millwall fan. I knew then the club I'd joined wasn't like all the others.

One night, Joe Royle, then manager of Manchester City, was walking down the tunnel at The Den after another routine game between the two clubs featured aggro, unpleasantness and violence.

'Horrible club, full of horrible people,' he said to anyone who was listening. 'This is England's answer to Beirut.'

I was standing in the tunnel at the time and when I told a few people at the club what Royle had said, they didn't know whether to be outraged or proud.

But they knew they were different, there was no escaping that. Millwall was different from other clubs, it was different from other places. I'd hear stories from Irish players at other clubs when I went away with underage Ireland sides and they'd all have a sameness about them. Not Millwall. They did things their own way.

Whatever you think you know about football supporters and how they behave, Millwall's fans would make you think again. I hated them and I loved them simultaneously.

When I was in the youth team, the fans would never usually see me play, so I was OK. Meeting them on nights out was no big deal. They'd brag about being in tear-ups with other fans and show us their scars for good measure. That was their way of impressing us, of letting us know the level of their devotion to the club. Once I got into the first team, though, interactions were dictated by my recent form or the team's recent results, or the fans' consumption of drink or cocaine or a combination of the two.

Millwall didn't feel like other parts of London. Nobody worked on the docks by the time I moved there and the club didn't play on Cold Blow Lane anymore, but the spirit and defiance remained.

It was a forgotten place in one of the greatest cities in the world. We could see Canary Wharf in the distance, the City of London growing and prospering around it, and Greenwich's big, grand houses to the south. In the main, the fans didn't come from those places, though. Millwall had nothing in common with the places around it. Nobody liked them and they didn't care.

Millwall was different: warmer and funnier, but sharper and scarier too. It was an hour on a plane from Dublin, but it could feel like six thousand miles away on some days, and a home from home on others.

The club traded on its reputation, because its reputation terrified so many people.

If you go to Millwall as a young player, survival is the only game in town. And it was survival on Millwall's terms, a code passed from group to group. Every dressing room in England is suspicious of difference, of a player who might want to do things his own way, but at Millwall there were harder rules and harder men.

On the day I got my Leaving Cert results, I learned to understand that.

'Well done, son. Now go out and train because they're fuck-all use to you now.'

This was player welfare in the Millwall universe on a day built up for years at home as a significant event in my life. My original plan had been to get the train from Dublin to Cork with my mates to see the Prodigy and Oasis in Páirc Uí Chaoimh and get hammered, but I was more than happy to be where I was, with first-team manager Jimmy Nicholl telling me to get on with it. My old life was meaningless here.

But for all that, I loved the life of a young professional footballer. We would train until lunchtime and sit on the couch for the rest of the day. I don't think I'm missing any details. Footballers are discouraged from doing much of anything once they finish training. The job involves a lot of resting and taking it easy, which is hard to do at that age. Restlessness is almost impossible to avoid, but it's up to you to come up with your own way to handle it.

And weirdly, everyone seemed to treat me a little differently, as if I were already an adult or a person of status. Seventeen-year-olds weren't treated like that where I came from.

I remember walking through the local shopping centre and a group of girls stopped to flirt with the Millwall youth players I was with. Girls approaching lads? At seventeen? Sober? I hadn't seen that before either.

I was moving into an adult's world, but I was there to do the most juvenile thing – to play football. I was doing well – well enough that I went from being called Paddy to being called Sads. I was making a name for myself, literally.

———

Playing for Ireland had been my dream from the day I knew Ireland had a team, and within a month of moving to Millwall, I got the call. I had never caught anyone's attention scoring goals every week for Belvedere, but now that I had signed for an English club, apparently I was ready.

I remember the exact spot I was standing in when I was first told. I had just walked out of the canteen when Micky Beard, one of the youth development officers, told me he wanted a word. I assumed it would just be a general chat about how I was settling in or, more likely, an apology saying there had been a mix-up and they realised signing me was a mistake. I hadn't done anything wrong and was doing well in training and games, but a voice kept piping up in my head saying I was going to be found out. If they knew what you were really like, you'd be gone.

You don't belong here, and you fucking know it.

That feeling was starting to become familiar. Like travelling on a train without a valid ticket, I was constantly looking over my shoulder, expecting to be caught.

Sorry, son, your time's up.

Perhaps they'd scouted a much better striker my age from elsewhere. Maybe there'd been another change of staff and the new lot didn't rate me. I followed Micky to the office at the end of the corridor and braced myself for the news, whatever it might be.

'Congratulations, son, you've been called up. The FAI have sent over the fax. You're going to play for Ireland.'

I was shocked and delighted but this was Millwall so I played it cool, or at least I tried. I misinterpreted Micky's outstretched arm as a desire to hug me. I had committed to the hug before I realised my error, but I was all in by then. I rang home immediately to tell them the news.

I was named in Maurice Price's under-18 squad to play against Finland in Tolka Park. I came on in the second half. We won 2-0 but I don't remember much about the game. I do remember how I felt afterwards. I flew back to London feeling a few feet taller. I was an Ireland youth international and a professional footballer living in England – exactly the course I had set for myself years earlier. I was particularly pleased we were allowed keep our playing kits. I still have mine today.

———

Millwall gave me a week off to attend my St Benildus debs that October. The debs was on the Thursday of that week, after which I had only an hour's sleep before Dad brought me to the airport. Someone woke me up at the boarding gate to tell me it was time to go. I showed up at the training ground at noon that Friday, still drunk from the night before. I was told to put on my gear and run a few laps of the local park to sweat the previous night out of me. I ran behind some hedges, fell asleep and returned an hour later.

I still got selected to play against Portsmouth on the Saturday morning. This caused uproar among the other three strikers, who were furious I had been selected ahead of them, despite missing a whole week of training and then showing up drunk. But I took it as a sign that I was doing well.

I had no problems being selected for the under-18 team. We played in the same division as the top London clubs and I was more than holding my own against them all. I scored my first hat-trick for Millwall in a game against QPR. I went into every game thinking I would do well. And in most cases, I was right.

The youth team coach, Ian McDonald, kept telling me the same thing, over and over.

'You've got a chance, Sadlier. I'm tellin' ya.'

A chance at making it. A chance at being something. It's not about what you are when you're eighteen and playing in the youth team. In professional football, it's about what you could turn out to be.

There was a lot I had to get used to. Fans – girls and lads – would be waiting outside the training ground, hoping for a conversation. It would usually start with a request for an autograph. Everyone wants to be your mate when you're a footballer. I was always friendly and polite but I wasn't mad on being in the company of people who thought I was something special. It just felt weird. I'd be asked my view on the footballing issues of the day as if my opinion mattered.

———

At Millwall, everything was a test of some kind, or at least it appeared that way. If you didn't understand that, then you didn't get the club, you didn't understand Millwall.

Everything we did or didn't do was logged somewhere. Not in any formal way, but everything was noticed. Your character mattered as much as your ability. And at that football club, only certain characteristics were deemed important.

When a youth team game away at Chelsea was called off at the last minute due to snow, the senior pros mocked those of us who had agreed with the decision, even though the pitch was frozen solid.

'Heard you didn't fancy it, son. Fucking soft twat.' We are Millwall.

Another time, after a game at Fulham's training ground, we discovered that the showers were broken. Ice cold water on a freezing day.

'Let's see who the tarts are, eh?' announced the coach.

Any sign you were hesitating would be held against you. We are Millwall.

You want to wear gloves because it's cold? Fucking no chance. We are Millwall.

I used to prefer long-sleeved shirts all year round, but that was used against me in the winter months.

'Long sleeves again for you, Sadlier, yeah? You puff.' We are Millwall.

When it came to declaring yourself unfit for training, the response was always suspicion and derision.

'Fancied a morning off, eh?' Support or sympathy didn't feature. We are Millwall.

This was the deal we'd signed up for as Millwall players. It was tough, a pain in the arse and sometimes fucking exhausting, but I loved every minute of it.

One Friday morning I was told I was to go straight to The Den the following afternoon to be with the first team. I wasn't going to be in the matchday squad, so I knew I wouldn't be playing, but I was told it was a sign I was making steady progress. They wanted me to get a feeling for the occasion without the pressure of being involved. It would mean I'd miss our youth team game against Arsenal, which kicked off at eleven that morning at our training ground, but the manager didn't care about that. I did, though.

Now I had a dilemma. I was a kid, and kids don't tell first-team managers to change their decisions. Not this kid, anyway. I was keen to be involved with the first team but this wasn't the involvement I was looking for. Standing around just observing them was of little interest to me, so I knocked on the manager's office door at the training ground that Friday afternoon.

'Yes,' he said.

'Gaffer, it's Sads. Any chance of a word?' I said, scratching my head and looking at the ground. My stomach was in knots. The assistant manager was there too. It was probably the first time I'd been on my own in a room with the two of them. I made my pitch.

'Just thinking, if I go to The Den for one, that'll mean missing the Arsenal game. I don't wanna be calling the shots here, and obviously I'm buzzing to be involved in any way, but any chance I could play the game and arrive a little later? I should be there by 1.45. But obviously it's, eh, your call, em, obviously.'

The two of them looked at each other and smiled.

'Well done, son,' said the boss.

'For what?' I said, a little bemused.

'That was a test.'

'Really? Jaysus. Eh ... did I pass?'

Of course it was a test. How did I not know it was a test? This was their way to see if my priorities were in the right place, their version of a psychometric assessment, an attempt to weed out the personalities who didn't suit the role. A Billy-big-bollocks would have tossed off the youth team match to be part of the first team. They didn't want any of that sort at Millwall. I'd cleared another hurdle.

———

Despite the occasional 'fack off, Paddies' run-in, having an Irish accent was, a lot of the time, an advantage. It turned out the English girls loved it. I'd only stopped wetting the bed a few years earlier, but now I was an exotic creature, albeit an exotic creature who got asked to say 'thirty-three and a third' a lot.

As someone who had never lived away from home before, I enjoyed the stability of living in digs with Carole and Keith, a married couple with a dog called Oscar. I had stayed with them when I was on trial and the club arranged for me to live with them when I moved over. Friendly, easy-going and good-natured, Carole and Keith were the perfect hosts.

Several other academy players were put in houses in south London, but we weren't all given the same service. In one house, the landlady ended up sleeping with a nineteen-year-old player in her care, narrowly avoiding being caught in the act by her husband. Another landlady was a repeat offender in this area. Years later, the club was forced to initiate an inquiry into her behaviour after one player's parents informed the club she had slept with their eighteen-year-old.

Sex wasn't the only thing on offer. One lad ended up being housed with a drug dealer, so he got discount weed in the comfort of his own home. Things took an ominous turn when the player was randomly drug tested one Monday morning. He thought he was doomed and rang his parents to come clean, claiming he was just doing his best to deal with the pressures of the job. He thought he had outsmarted everyone when they reacted with sympathy. Then the test results came back. Despite smoking weed the day before he gave his urine sample, he was given the all-clear by the FA testers. I've questioned the merits of dope-testing in football since.

Most of my wages went on my monthly phone bills rather than weed. I'd spend almost every evening hogging the house phone, listening to friends in Dublin talk of how much they were enjoying college life. As promised, I kept in touch with my sisters by writing them letters. Every couple of months I got home for a weekend.

I spent a week in Dublin that Christmas, which gave me an idealised version of life at home. Where was I going? What was I doing at Millwall? My chances of getting a contract were slim so I had begun to look at all I had left behind in a romanticised way.

On a previous visit home, I had sneaked into a college lecture with McGrath, who was studying business management in IT Tallaght. I'd no interest in the lecture, I just wanted to see what the fuss was all about. It seemed you could show up when you wanted, pay as little attention as you liked and spend the year on the piss, as long as you passed your exams. It sounded like something I could handle. It's odd for a seventeen-year-old to say, but being in the same room as girls in a setting like that was also a novelty for me. I had been in single-sex schools all the way up, which isn't the ideal preparation for life ahead. Certainly not for the life of a footballer.

In any case, I was well aware that I'd probably be in college for real the following year. I had got enough points in the Leaving Cert to go to college. That had always been the fallback plan. I would have gone for something vague like Arts, as I had no specific interests in anything career-wise. But I figured being in college was better than not going.

Back in London after Christmas, things got worse. Training and games were being cancelled due to the weather and the coaches were starting to single me out for criticism. They were preparing me for what was to come, but I wasn't sure I could handle it any more.

I started to focus more on the chances – or lack of them – of getting a new contract. I convinced myself I was wasting my time staying there. The voice in my head that told me I didn't belong, that anything less than perfect meant I was a failure, was having a field day.

One night, I waited for the cheap rates to kick in, rang home and said I was done. Without any warning, I told my mum I wasn't going to make it and had decided to leave. I rambled through the reasons I didn't enjoy being there, but my main point was that I knew it would all be for nothing. Life's too short to be wasted on chasing pipe dreams, I said. I didn't know why I ever thought I'd be good enough to make it.

Mum talked me down and wondered why I hadn't said any of this before.

'You'll feel differently in the morning,' she said. 'Don't do anything tonight.'

Instead of booking a flight as I'd planned, I went to bed.

A couple of days later, Jimmy Nicholl said he wanted me to train with the first team because I was in line to make my debut that weekend. He called me into his office after training on the Friday.

It turned out my behaviour was among the many things he'd noticed. He said he was pleased I'd kept my nose clean despite some of the company I'd been in. He also baffled me a little by telling me he was impressed by what he'd seen in training. But what did I know?

I was thrilled. But I also used it as an opportunity to remind myself what a useless prick I was.

Forty-eight hours earlier, you were ready to quit. How could you be so stupid?

I was going to make my league debut in twenty-four hours, when I had been so close to walking away from it all.

Years later, I'd find out the truth. After my call home, my mum had called my old Belvedere coach, Vincent Butler. He then rang Millwall's chief scout, who rang Jimmy. They felt something needed to be done to keep me there, so why not throw me into the first team to lift my spirits?

It wasn't my brilliance at all, but a desperate phone call to my mum which had changed everything. Mum was protecting me once again.

I survived those early years in my own way, which at the time was the only thing that mattered. The coaches thought they were giving us the best chance for survival with their tests and their initiation ceremonies. I can't judge them for it. Looking back now, I can see that it was nuts, but they knew one thing and it informed all the others: Millwall was different.

5

Last Train to Bromley

The night before my Millwall first-team debut against Bristol City in February 1997, I had something planned to take my mind off the match. I'd met a girl over Christmas, and she and a friend were coming over from Dublin for the weekend.

I went to meet them at the hotel the night before my debut, but their flight was delayed so they arrived in London a few hours later than planned. As a result, I was out longer than I should have been. It's frowned upon to be out of your house the evening before a game. I knew I'd be in big trouble if I was caught, but there was little chance of that.

I was sitting on a train at Victoria Station just after 11pm. The whistle had already gone when two men rushed towards the closing doors and bundled their way on. They were delighted with themselves for making it on time. When I saw who it was, I was a little less pleased. One of them was Gerry Docherty, the Millwall physio. And with him was my manager, Jimmy Nicholl.

There was nowhere to run or hide. Gerry walked past without noticing me, which momentarily raised my hopes of a daring escape. Jimmy saw me straight away, though.

'You're in the doghouse, aren't you, son?' he said and just walked on. I thought I'd really blown it this time. I needn't have worried about being kept awake with nerves, as I was pretty sure I wouldn't be playing. All that talk about me being a good pro was completely undone in that moment. Back to the youth team for me.

I was wrong again and was named among the substitutes. I even did my bit for team morale by telling some of the lads in the dressing room beforehand what had happened the previous night. I was beginning to be accepted in the dressing room, even if a lot of the acceptance was because the players saw me as a reliable source of amusement.

But the morale among the squad probably needed more boosting than news of my mishaps could provide at the time I came into the team.

Having won only one of the previous nine games, there were rumours that Jimmy's job was on the line.

I came on for the last fifteen minutes of that game against Bristol City and won the crowd over with a mistimed, thundering, clumsy tackle as soon as I was on the pitch. I continued to bound around like an enthusiastic Labrador, but the team wasn't playing well, the crowd had turned long ago and the manager was hanging on to his job by a thread. Not the ideal scenario but on the day of my debut I didn't care. It was the greatest experience I'd ever had in my life.

But we lost 2-0 and the mood worsened. After the game, the security staff advised us to linger for a while in the players' lounge. A demonstration was taking place in the car park outside the main entrance, so it wasn't safe to go outside. At Millwall, 'demonstration' doesn't necessarily mean what it means elsewhere; it's a catch-all term for pretty much anything.

I knew there would be no bad blood towards me, but I didn't risk it. This wasn't the time to go mingling with the fans, to bask in their congratulations on my debut. A few cars were damaged, the chanting was pretty ugly and the atmosphere around the place was fairly toxic. As we waited to leave the stadium, our manager Jimmy Nicholl looked like a man longing for the safety of a police-protected dugout.

A week later, I kept my place for my first away game. It was my first overnight trip and my dad said that if I was going to play, he'd make the trip to see me. The idea that my dad would watch me play still mattered hugely. I would have to ask Jimmy Nicholl if I stood a chance of playing, which seemed a little cheeky for an eighteen-year-old, but if it meant my dad would be there, I didn't care if it went against the hierarchy of the dressing room.

Jimmy said he hoped I'd be used as a sub, but I wasn't given any assurances. My dad made the trip over on the boat with my sisters anyway. Anna said that when I came on he had tears in his eyes. It is the thing I remember most about that game.

Our 2-1 defeat brought an end to Jimmy's time in charge. He was sacked on 10 February 1997, nine days after I made my debut. And he wasn't the only one to lose his job.

The highest point in my sporting life at the time coincided with one of the lowest points in the club's history. Because of its financial plight Millwall was placed in the hands of receivers, its existence in jeopardy. Along with the manager, all the coaching staff were let go. The CEO went too. Twenty-two members of staff were culled in one day. If someone didn't come forward to save the club, there would be no club.

Players generally don't care about stuff like this. Despite public comments, they believe they'll always find another club. Some of the senior lads were just pissed off they wouldn't get money owed to them. They could forget about any outstanding bonuses or signing-on fees. The club asked us all to do our bit and take a voluntary wage cut of ten per cent. Senior players call the shots in times like this. Eighteen-year-olds with a couple of substitute appearances didn't have a say. We would answer as one, and it was a firm no.

Everyone was put up for sale, and a transfer embargo was put on the club. They could offload players but couldn't sign anyone. This was before transfer windows were introduced, so you could be gone at any time. If I had had an agent back then, I'd have been ringing him daily. Nobody wanted to go down with the ship.

One of the club's former managers, John Docherty, returned to take charge of the first team.

Docherty was old-school. He didn't allow us have water during training because it 'wasn't a fucking holiday camp'. But he liked me and he kept picking me, primarily because I was the only six-foot striker fit at the club. You can't play long-ball football without a target man up front. I was nowhere near ready physically, but they weren't allowed to sign a replacement, so I was in. I was so scrawny and so self-conscious about it that I always wore a training T-shirt beneath my shirt during matches. Some lads in that situation would do loads of weights, but not this genius.

The club was in crisis so the fans were not in a patient mood. The senior players took most of the flak, as you'd expect. At some clubs, youngsters are given nothing but encouragement, but I wouldn't get away that easily at Millwall.

I wasn't seen as part of the solution, so I became part of the problem. And I knew what Millwall fans did with problems. The honeymoon period I had been looking forward to lasted about two games.

I was playing regularly in a team that was losing games and couldn't score goals. In nine of our last eleven games that season, Millwall didn't score. And scoring goals was my job. So I was one of the reasons the crowd were unhappy and they let me know.

As I ran on to the pitch to warm up, they'd boo me. When the PA read out the team, they'd boo my name again. When I touched the ball – usually before giving it away – they'd boo me once more. Within six months of moving over from Dublin, I'd made my first-team debut. A month later, I had an entire stadium chanting 'Shit, shit, shit' whenever I caught their attention.

Soon the thought took hold: don't catch their attention. I started to hide in games, making runs to areas where I knew teammates couldn't find me with a pass. You can hoodwink a lot of people with that, appearing as if you're being positive and energetic. I'd get involved in physical battles too easily – because you can win those without having confidence or showing technical ability. Unfortunately, in order to get the upper hand you need some upper-body strength, which I didn't have. The T-shirt didn't really add power.

A player can still wreak havoc without strength if he has the experience to know how not to get caught – Dennis Wise gave us a masterclass in this when he arrived at the club years later – but I didn't have that either. If the ball came to me, nine times out of ten I would be dispossessed or concede a free kick. And the boos and jeers would get louder.

In small-sided games in training, I would continually give the ball away. I was so nervous playing with the older lads and had virtually zero confidence in myself at this stage. It was like being the shit kid in PE who is always picked last. You know nobody wants you in their team, but they've got to put up with you.

My teammates weren't much help. This is a truth about football: it's a team game, but every player is trying to protect his own reputation. Supporters can destroy that more quickly than anyone and every player thinks he can be dragged down by their weakest man, which was often me.

'Fucking hell, son, you're killing us,' one of them would say every time I gave the ball away. As soon as the ball got to me, the move would break down.

That feeling was bad but it was far worse when they stopped doing it, when all I heard was silence as my teammates resigned themselves to the inevitability of what would happen if they gave me the ball.

Before one game at The Den, I went through the whole warm-up without touching a ball. I was so convinced my first touch would be awful, I figured I'd avoid the ball and not catch anyone's attention. I was hiding in the warm-up, a grim state of affairs. As you'd expect,

I played terribly and was eventually substituted. The whole stadium cheered.

I was the player everyone hated in the team no one liked. Still only eighteen years old, this wasn't exactly how I'd always dreamed football would be. The imaginary crowds in my head as a kid had been far more appreciative.

It was hard to see the bigger picture at the time. Overall, I was making the kind of progress most young Irish players only dream of. The majority don't make the first team once, let alone several times. And even if the crowd didn't think much of me, the manager and coaching staff obviously did. I wasn't enjoying it, but footballers aren't meant to enjoy losing almost every week. I liked virtually nothing about being a Millwall footballer during that time. The mood in the club was awful, but that's the way it's meant to be when you're close to extinction. Being singled out for abuse from your own supporters comes with the job when you play for Millwall. It just wasn't something I was prepared for when I was eighteen.

It was always worse on days when family or mates were over from Dublin. It hurt more. It was more embarrassing. I knew they could hear a lot more in their seats than I could hear from the pitch.

Four games from the end of the season, I exaggerated the pain I felt in my foot and came off early. Or, to put it another way, I faked injury just to get the hell off that pitch and out of that stadium. I was doing no good for the team and the crowd were doing nothing for me, and I don't think anyone would have been disappointed by my unavailability. A win for everyone.

My uncle Jack was over from Tipperary with my younger cousin Niall to watch me play that day. Bruce Grobbelaar was in goal for the opposition, Plymouth Argyle. In the players' bar afterwards I went through the motions with Jack about being gutted that I'd been injured and frustrated I was taken off so early. Bullshit, but he didn't suspect a thing.

Being injured doesn't shield you from everyone, though. On nights out, some drunken fans would always be keen to have a go. In those scenarios, you couldn't do a thing. Retaliate, even just verbally, and you'd be vilified if things got physical. It's lose-lose. You'd just take the abuse and hope that nobody would throw a dig. And even if someone did hit you, there'd be nothing you could do. There's no way to spin positives from getting into drunken brawls with your own supporters. You'd be heavily fined and publicly hammered. So you would just stand there and take it.

'I pay your wages, mate, and you're facking shit.'

Good point, well made.

In every interview I gave at the time, I would have said that fans had a right to say what they liked because they did pay my wages. I probably added that my performances deserved some stick.

What I wanted to say was that they were fucking pricks who didn't deserve to be called supporters. That they were doing no good for the team by turning on us so often in the way they did. And that I wondered what they were hoping to achieve by rounding viciously on a kid like me.

But I held my tongue. This was what was expected of a footballer, but silence was also how I had learned to survive. I wouldn't tackle an issue head on. At home in our family dynamic that was the role of my eldest brother. Instead I would try to find a way to escape, like I always had, away from the confrontation. It was just that football wasn't much of an escape at that stage.

After a couple of appearances under Docherty, I was offered a one-year extension to my deal. It was a no-brainer for the club – the transfer embargo probably strengthened my case – but also no indication I'd made it. I was young and cheap, and the club had always relied on a number of youth players coming through every few years. I was raw and had a lot to learn, but they figured I had potential and, if it wasn't fulfilled, it wouldn't cost the club much.

I was about to become one of the four who would survive, but only just.

Yet again there would be no signing-on fee and just an extra £50 on my weekly wage. What the fuck? That wasn't in keeping with their promises the previous year. They told me their hands were tied because of the club's financial plight. They made out they were breaking the rules by even offering me the deal while the club was in receivership. In those situations, you've no way of knowing what to believe, but it's usually right to assume you're being lied to. I decided to say no, because surely they'd come back with an improved offer? I knew they were broke, and yeah, I suppose they were potentially about to go out of existence, but an annual jump of £2,600? I felt I deserved more and I let it be known – I turned it down politely and apologetically, saying it was a little on the low side.

The mood shifted. The chief scout started to blank me as he walked past. The manager summoned one of the senior players, Keith Stevens, known as Rhino, to give me a dressing-down about having the wrong priorities. Rhino was one of the hardest players in the history of the club. In other words, someone you don't fuck around with.

We had a good chat, I put my side of things to him, he gave it to me from the club's perspective. We saw each other's point of view. Actually, none of that happened. He just sat down and gave me a message.

'Sign the deal and get on with it, you flash Paddy cunt. It's not about money at your age, son, sort your head out and get back to thinking about football.'

The chief scout then started to speak to me like I was on my way out.

'Disappointed in you, son, thought you were one of the good ones.'

The club wasn't flinching. I didn't like how things were going, so I found a more reliable escape.

I went to the pub at lunchtime and settled in for the day. That was how I spent every Saturday when I was in the youth team if the first team had an away game. If they were playing at The Den, we would have to be there to clean up the dressing room after them. I was now in the first team, but I had a slight groin strain, so I wasn't fit to travel. I remember speaking in the bar to mates about the injustice of it all. Do well and we'll sort you out, they said. I had made the first team within six months and all they did was offer me an extra fifty quid a week. I went on like this for a while, or at least I think I did.

Next thing I knew, I was waking up in a padded police cell with the taste of vomit in my mouth and absolutely no recollection of where I had been, what I had done, who I was with, or how I had got there. There was vomit on my shoes and on my jumper. I was in a cell somewhere in London without any recollection of what had happened.

I swore I'd never get pissed again. No chance. Waking up with no memory of the night before wasn't a new experience. I had had plenty of nights like that in Dublin before I left home, and umpteen others since arriving in London. But this was a step too far. Negotiating furiously with God or whoever might be listening, I swore I'd calm things down if I got away with this one.

A police officer slid open the hatch on the cell door and noticed I was awake. Then he offered me a glass of water.

'Had a few too many last night, eh, son?'

I took his friendliness as a big positive. He'd hardly be sound if I'd killed someone, so I struck murder off the list of possibilities. I wasn't sure what the right move was. Should I come clean about not knowing why I was there? Probably not, as that would lessen the impact of any later pleas of innocence. Say nothing.

As it turns out, I had just been put in the cell to dry out. Three of us thought the pub at the top of my road was having a lock-in. It was after midnight and we were trying to get in. The eleven hours of drinking earlier that day, it seemed, hadn't been enough. The neighbours thought we were burglars and rang the police. The mix-up was sorted out as soon as they got there, but as I was too drunk to spell my own name, I was brought to the cell to sleep it off.

It turned out there was no reason to even consider taking it easy next time. Now I just needed to make sure the club didn't find out.

The following day, the chief scout rang with a very serious tone in his voice.

'I'm going to ask you something, son, and I want you to give me an honest answer.'

I didn't think they'd sack me over the night in the cell, but I knew they could heavily fine me. More importantly, it would hardly strengthen my negotiating position on the contract. I was screwed.

I braced myself for the question. I thought that if he was at the point of asking about it, he knew about it, so coming clean would be the right play now. Maybe I could play the mental health card. *Sorry, my mind just went. Sorry, my head is gone. Sorry, I'm just homesick and I feel alone.* Anything to get away with it.

'Tell me the truth, son ... has Tom Walley from Arsenal spoken to you this week?'

He didn't have a clue. What was all that worry for? Tom was the former Millwall youth coach, now working at Arsenal. The club were worried Arsenal would take advantage of my contract situation and make a move. I had played well against them in the youth league and supposedly Tom rated me highly. It's funny; in all my days wondering what it would feel like to have the club I supported as a kid express an interest in me, I never once imagined I'd react the way I did – by just being thankful nobody knew I'd been a drunken mess.

I ended up signing the contract later that week. One more year, and an extra fifty big ones to play around with. Now I was up to £385 a week. I would have been happier with more, but I wasn't exactly setting the world alight with my first-team performances. I had made a lot of friends at the club and I knew they gave younger players opportunities. That's what really mattered at the time.

Rhino found out the specifics of my contract the following week and told me I had been nuts to sign for so little. He said he wouldn't have insisted I sign if he had known the figures.

Docherty left the club before the final game of the season. We were safe from relegation but the dressing room was a toxic place by then. He had been in charge of Millwall when the club was in top flight in 1988, something he often reminded us of, which didn't help anyone. We were in the shit and didn't need to hear him waffling away about past glories.

A week later Billy Bonds was named his successor. The club was rescued by businessman Theo Paphitis and my phantom foot injury had recovered well. The future was starting to look brighter on many fronts, particularly now that I was heading home to Dublin at the end of the season.

This was everything I wanted a summer in Dublin to be. I had nearly two months to do what I wanted with people I liked. I met up with all the mates who'd been over to visit me in London, but we were all together and we went to all our old haunts.

It was also my first summer back home as a professional footballer. Everywhere I went I was congratulated on my progress, with people saying they were following Millwall excitedly on Ceefax. On paper, it had been a great first season. I'd broken into the first team within six months and established myself as a regular starter by the end of the season. With a new contract and some underage international appearances thrown in, it looked like I had it made. I wouldn't have summarised things the same way, but I didn't correct anyone. Neither the financial plight of the club nor the mood of the fans was relevant to anyone in Ireland. I had done enough to get a second contract, which was all that mattered.

One night we found ourselves in Club Sarah in Rathfarnham. They were selling shots for £1.50 all night. Who was I to pass up a promotion like that? Unfortunately, McGrath had to put me in a cab around midnight, pay the taxi driver and tell him my address. The cab ride should have taken ten minutes but, somehow, I rocked in some time after 5am. I only know this because I woke my parents by undressing in front of them in their bedroom. I've no idea what happened in the missing five hours. My mum ushered me into the right room, but my dad found me naked and asleep on the toilet an hour or so later. He woke me and pointed me in the direction of my room, where I woke up several hours later, having wet the bed.

There were no lectures from my parents. I could pass it off as a rare occurrence because they weren't around me all the time. I had no real sense at the time that alcohol was becoming a problem for me, because I knew plenty of others who had similar tales from their nights out. I figured this was what weekends entailed for anyone my age, and I honestly can't remember thinking anymore about it.

I put it down to the difference between the size of measures in London and in Dublin, and added shots to the list of drinks that didn't agree with me.

To cap off a great summer, I was named in the Ireland squad for the U-18 European Championship finals in Iceland, with newly appointed Brian Kerr in charge.

I had always dreamed of playing for Ireland. I had an idea what that would mean, but I had no idea what playing for Ireland under Brian Kerr would mean.

I'd never worked with Brian and his assistant Noel O'Reilly before. In fact, I had never met Brian before, but I had watched him from the stands in Harold's Cross when I was a kid supporting St Pat's. I might have joined the squad with a huge, if vague, sense of pride, but I left with a feeling closer to infatuation.

Brian and Noel were incredible. They had authority because they'd just taken Ireland's U-20 team, featuring a young Damien Duff, to the semi-finals of the U-20 World Cup in Malaysia, but they had something more than that as well.

You wanted to be around them. Noel had a way of making you feel this was the best place in the world to be. They both came from the world of Dublin football, but they weren't insular; they were worldly and open. Noel had been a coach at Belvedere so he knew everything about me, but then he seemed to know everything about every player. Noel had a magic about him. Amazingly, we all felt we were part of his gang, living the dream, the envy of every team in the world.

They played on this aura. Along with every other team in the competition, we were invited to the Blue Lagoon spa, half an hour's drive outside Reykjavik. It was surrounded by a black lava field and a barren, lunar landscape.

Brian said we should get out and walk the last mile of the journey to stretch our legs while the coach drove on ahead to the spa. Brian knew the other teams would be arriving at the same time so he told us to start running when he saw each bus approaching from the distance. As they drove by, they would think we had run the whole way from Reykjavik, so we grimaced and puffed our cheeks out for maximum effect. We were sending a message to the other teams but it also underlined something else that made Brian and Noel special: there's nowhere else like this, lads, there's nobody doing things the way we're doing things.

But Brian would never let us play up to any idea of eejitry. He was a serious man and we were serious about what we were doing. If Noel knew everything about all of us, Brian simply knew everything.

As the country has learned during his time as a pundit, he knows all there is to know about every team but when you broke it down to individual players, he knew everything about them too. He would prepare you for the game by telling you what to expect from a player. A full-back would know if the player liked to cut inside or go wide; a striker might be told to watch out for the centre-back feinting to clear the ball and turning inside and, invariably, this is what would happen.

The format was that the top team in each group would reach the final and the group runners-up would be in a play-off for third place. A minor thigh strain had kept me out of playing any part in the qualification games, so I went to Iceland expecting to begin games on the bench.

Brian's aim was that we'd win the competition but when we lost 3-2 to France in the opening game, that didn't look achievable. We beat Switzerland 1-0, which meant we needed a draw against Israel in our final game to finish second. I came on against Switzerland and didn't do much, but I did more than enough against Israel in our 1-1 draw to earn my chance to start in the play-off.

The most memorable thing about the group stages was a disruption during that game by flag-burning anti-Israel demonstrators waving Palestinian flags and chanting stuff none of us could understand. If the intention was to bring the wider world's attention to the cause, it was an odd choice of event, given the game wasn't televised and barely forty people were watching.

On 31 July 1997, one year to the day since the party in our house to wave me off to Millwall, we played Spain in the third-place play-off and I was named in the starting line-up. Before this, I had always been a sub and hadn't scored. There were plenty of nerves and, obviously, my inner critic questioning my selection.

Noel O'Reilly chose the perfect words to focus my mind during the warm-up.

'Imagine you're playing for Belvo,' he said. 'I've seen you run amok loads of times in Fairview Park, just do the same out there today. You're good enough. I know you are. You mightn't realise it, but I do. You've never shown it yet for Ireland, but today's the day.'

Scoring in that third-place play-off became a fact that followed me around and for a while it was something that people would slag me about. But not now and not at the time. Six minutes in, I put us one-nil up. Twenty-two years later, I can still recall how I felt but I can't explain it. It was elation and relief, pride and excitement, and a massive two fingers to every Millwall fan who had booed me at The Den. Most of all, maybe, it was a *fuck you* to the voice in my head that said I didn't deserve it.

Brian pumped his fist and screamed 'Well done' at me as I jogged back to the halfway line to restart the game. I don't know why this memory is still so clear.

Eleven minutes later, we were 2-1 down and that's how it finished. France beat Portugal in the final, thanks to a goal from Louis Saha.

That night, Brian and Noel brought us to The Dubliner pub in Reykjavik. Brian had befriended the owner on a previous trip and he gave us the run of the pub's upper room. Paul Buttner, one of the travelling journalists, was the barman for the evening. We were given a three-pint limit each, but I knew who the non-drinkers in the squad were and they sorted me out for extras. Noel had his guitar, so a singsong broke out. The French team's coaching staff came in at one point and didn't know what to make of us, marvelling at the togetherness and the morale that Brian had created. The extra few pints above the three-pint limit made all the difference. Before long, I was belting out a rendition of 'Black is the Colour' on my own, one of my favourite Christy Moore songs. An unforgettable day.

Sixteen years later, I was a panellist alongside John Giles on RTÉ for Arsenal's Champions League qualifier against Fenerbahçe when the caption appeared: 'Scored in UEFA European U-18 Third-Place Play-off'. It went viral and amused many people.

When I see that caption now, I think back to the way I felt when it happened. The emotion was entirely positive. I wanted more of this feeling, and I wanted more of whatever Brian and Noel were selling.

Playing in Iceland was fun and exciting, enjoyable and new. Everything that Millwall wasn't.

By the time Docherty had left, the fans had turned on the team and a lot of the team had turned on the club. Some lads found it hard to forget about the tens of thousands the club had failed to pay them. The players were rightly sick of being hammered by the crowd every week, and the crowd, justifiably, thought we were all shite.

However, whether it was the few weeks in Dublin getting blind drunk, or scoring what would become the most famous goal in the history of the UEFA European U-18 third-place play-offs, I returned to pre-season training a different player. The club was a different place, too.

I was a lot more confident in myself and determined to silence my numerous critics. Despite having little self-belief, a big part of me was driven by the need to prove people wrong. I had used it to get out of lines with Mr Casey in school, and I would use it at Millwall. I wasn't short of ammunition to take with me into this battle, but now I had a manager who rated me, which made a big difference.

Billy Bonds had been coach of QPR's youth team the previous season when I'd scored the hat-trick against them in a 3-2 win. It was a stroke of good fortune for me that he succeeded Docherty. Most lads hope to have a clean slate when a new boss arrives, but I was already ahead of the pack because of that hat-trick.

Nine days after scoring my first goal for Ireland, I started the opening league game in the team, and scored our third in a 3-0 win. I had finally given the crowd at The Den something to cheer about, and given myself the first indication I might actually belong there.

I followed this up with a goal away at Preston, which was better than any I'd ever scored before or since. I got the ball on the halfway line, ran for goal and walloped it into the top corner from 25 yards – exactly like I'd imagined doing in the field behind my house when I was ten.

Then I scored another at The Den the following week, my third goal in four league games. Instead of getting booed as I walked onto the pitch, I was being applauded for what I was doing. The walk from the main reception to the car park after the games was actually enjoyable. Instead of aggressive questioning about why things were so shit – and being told I was absolute shit – we were being praised and encouraged by fans we met along the way. Instead of being called a 'no-good IRA cunt' by angry coked-up fans, some were now asking me to sign their match programmes. A first-team player, signing autographs and

scoring goals. It was nice to be asked to sign things, but I knew the
support was conditional. One bad game and I'd be a 'cunt' again.

Billy offered me a three-year deal on more than double my wage.
Negotiations were conducted differently this time. Since Billy was one
of the most intimidating men you could meet in professional football,
there was no need for Rhino to do his thing. I was brought into his
office and told the offer. It wasn't so much 'Take it or leave it' as just
'Take it'. I was ready to agree.

'Here's a phone, son. Ring your old man or the PFA if you want
advice, but we don't deal with agents and we ain't gonna increase the
offer anyway. It's a fair deal, just sign it.'

It was £800 a week, rising to £950 a week by the third year and a
lump sum of £10,000 each year. After all those false starts, this was
what the big time really looked like. A few months earlier, I was on my
way out, but now, thanks to a phone call from my mum, I had made it.

With a new contract, I was a real professional embarking on a new
season. I was also surely moving on. My dad now came to watch his son
play professional football in England, the very thing I'd always wanted.
The thought of the tears in his eyes when he saw me playing my second
match remained when plenty of other memories disappeared. I wasn't
sure what that was about, but with a huge contract and a professional
career which would stretch out long into the distance, those things
were bound to become less important. Soon I wouldn't concern myself
with childish things. I was a man living in a man's world.

6

The Enemy Within

'What's the problem? Can't you run?'

'No, no, I can run, no problem.'

'Is it when you kick a ball? Can you not do that?'

'Eh, no, I can kick a ball grand. That's not the problem.'

'Is it when you shoot?'

'No.'

'Then what's the problem, son?'

'Eh, it's just with, eh, girls. Erm. I can't, eh, I can't do, em, anything, y'know, with them.'

'Eh? You mean shagging? Is that all you care about?'

I was talking to Billy Bonds about my latest injury problem and wondering how I'd found myself here. It was August 1997 and we were alone in his office in the training ground. The medical team had signed off on the proposed treatment, but I needed his approval to go ahead with the recommended surgery.

I was asking one of football's toughest men for permission to miss games for surgery because I was unable to have sex. I had tried once and it hadn't gone well. If the newspapers were to list the players missing from the next game in the standard sports reporting form – Robbie Ryan (hamstring), that kind of thing – they'd be printing the word 'penis' in brackets after my name. Yes, I had a penis injury. My foreskin was too tight, something which probably should have been established when I was a kid. Either way, as I found out to my cost, it was incapable of withstanding the physical demands of intercourse. So now I was explaining to Billy Bonds why I would have to miss a couple of games to be circumcised, solely so that I would be able to have sex for at least a second time. By this stage, I was in my first proper relationship with a girl I had met in May. My injured penis, acquired on a drunken one-night stand months earlier, was holding us back.

Billy checked the fixture schedule for the season ahead. There was no suitable time so he told me to get it done straight away. Word got out, as it inevitably would, and I was known as 'Nobby' to a section of fans from then on.

By this time, I was getting used to an idea that might seem strange for a professional athlete: my body was my enemy.

From the most trivial to the most damaging, emotionally and physically, my body always appeared to be out to get me. My back was too sore, my hip hurt, my foreskin was too tight. I lived with this knowledge all the time. I lived with an awareness that my body was going to set a trap for me.

At times, it was comical, like my body was the punchline to every joke. I discovered not so long ago that the reason I'd never been able to satisfactorily give a high-five was down to a problem with my peripheral vision. This was diagnosed after I'd retired, several years after I'd spent many goal celebrations feeling stupid for failing to connect with a teammate's hand.

The sight in my left eye didn't properly develop when I was a kid, despite having to wear glasses and an eye patch to help it along. It's not something that laser eye surgery can correct, so to this day I can't read a word if I close my right eye.

Long before I became a professional footballer, my body was affecting me. Jobs I took on for a bit of spare cash, like selling Christmas trees or delivering papers, would have to be abandoned when my body couldn't take it. I would have to choose between cash and football and football always won.

I was sacked from Alonzi's chipper because I had torn my hamstring playing for Belvedere the day before. When I rang to say I couldn't make it in, I was told: 'Drop in your hat and jumper, Richie. We're running a business, not a fucking circus.' The return of the chipper's jumper and protective net hat was a ceremonial reminder that my body couldn't take on too much and, also, that people take life way too seriously.

I broke my wrist working at a dog-food factory when my arm jammed between a moving crate and the wall. I was only sixteen at the time, and not wanting to make a fuss, I carried on and said nothing until it went purple. One of the old lads told me to show it to the boss. He ran it under cold water and told me to go back and finish the final 45 minutes of my shift. I clocked off as normal at midnight, and when the X-ray in hospital confirmed the break later that night, I never went back.

My body didn't fail me in every job, but I was always conscious of it. I was always trying to find a way to manage my fitness when others didn't need to think about it at all. Naturally, this became a much bigger issue when I became a professional footballer, especially since the club I played for was Millwall. You weren't greeted with sympathy and hugs if you were injured; you were viewed with suspicion, a double agent, the enemy within.

Declaring yourself unavailable to train or play matches was interpreted as a statement of weakness.

'He don't fancy it.'

'You wouldn't want him in the facking trenches with ya, that's for sure.'

'Facking puff.'

Even if the injury was serious or long-term, getting the injury in the first place was held against you.

It didn't matter how many games you'd played for the first team, once you were out injured you didn't have any status, as you'd often be reminded. Certain coaches would take it upon themselves to pop their heads into the medical room before training each morning to mock anyone in there.

'Fackin hell, usual suspects in here, then!' would be the general opener, before the coach would decide which player to belittle in front of everyone. 'Are you gonna be constantly in here, ya cunt?'

One morning it was my turn.

'Oi, Sads! What's the matter with you, then?'

I was sitting on a physio bed with ice packs above and blow my right ankle. I was tempted to point to an area of my body that didn't have two big fucking ice packs covering it, but I resisted.

'I went over on it at the end of training yesterday and Gerry reckons it'll be a few days before I can train,' I said.

The minute I said the physio's name, I knew it was a mistake. It would look like I was ducking responsibility.

'Gerry reckons?'

I braced myself.

'Gerry reckons? What's the matter, Sads? Can't you make your own facking mind up? Do everything other people tell you to do, yeah? You're too facking soft. I keep tellin' ya. You ain't no good to no one sat in here so get your facking finger out!'

I would have loved to, but it wasn't up to me. It was as if there was another character in this drama. There was what I wanted, what my inner self told me I could and couldn't do, and then this wrecking ball I called my body which could intervene at any time.

My body had a knack of picking the worst times to let me down. I was on a hot streak in the beginning of the 1997/98 season. I'd scored those three goals in four games at the start of Billy's era, which had swiftly followed the signing of a three-year-deal and being newly circumcised.

One day Niall Quinn rang me at the request of his manager at Sunderland, Peter Reid. It wouldn't be the last approach Quinn would make on that club's behalf. He was one hell of a salesman: charming, friendly, funny and smart. I had never met him before, but he'd been a hero of mine since Italia '90. He told me to ring Reid, which I did. Reid gave me the spiel about life in the north-east and the ambitions of the club at the time. I didn't have an agent so I didn't know who to talk to. I couldn't tell anyone in the club in case word got out and it was held against me for considering the move. He finished the call by saying we should now leave it to the two chairmen to agree a deal.

Two days later, I felt pain in my groin. This injury was originally diagnosed as a hernia, but I still had the same pain and stiffness two months after having surgery. Then they realised it was osteitis pubis, an inflammation of the pubic bone. They knew what it was now, but they weren't much clearer on how to treat it.

I was told to rest and hope it went away in time. In the end, I was out for eleven months.

I never spoke to Reid again. The week after that call, I bumped into then Wimbledon chairman Sam Hamman in the tunnel before our League Cup tie at The Den. Because of my groin injury, I couldn't play.

'You're the next one,' he said. 'We'll be back for you.'

It was the last time I spoke to him too.

It is unbelievably boring being injured, but that's the point. The adrenaline you feed on is taken from you. The natural cycle of a week is gone. There is no tension, no nerves and the only familiar feeling is crushing disappointment. You clock in and clock off and, to make it worse, everyone else at the club thinks you're skiving.

With the pubic bone inflammation, I continually told myself that I was a week or two away from returning, which meant the disappointment of no progress on a regular basis.

Hopes were raised, hopes were dashed. For eleven long months. All the while I would try to avoid those inevitable conversations.

'When are you back then?'

'Don't know.'

'How can you not know?'

'It's still not right.'

'Puff.'

If you were injured, you lived a different life from the other players. You reported for treatment at 9.15 every morning. Show up at 9.16 or later and you'd be heavily fined. Fit players just had to be ready to train by 10.30. I spent more time in the physio room than I spent anywhere else in the club and became closer to Gerry the physio than anyone.

The pubic bone inflammation meant I wasn't part of Brian Kerr's squad for that summer's U-18 European Championships in Cyprus, which I was still young enough to play in. I watched from my sitting room as Ireland won the tournament.

In moments like that, I addressed myself as if I were a Millwall coach. *You fucking useless fucker. Look what you could be doing if you weren't so weak.*

In those moments, I had fully absorbed the Millwall code.

I spent that summer – like many others – in Gerry's company, when all the fit players were away on their holidays. We spent far too many afternoons and Sunday mornings together as well.

At that time, I was renting a place on my own for six months. Gerry had been renting it before me, having moved down from Scotland the previous year, so he gave me a lot of help moving in. He and his wife Deirdre lived nearby and would often have me over for dinner. These were pretty much the only nights I didn't eat pizza or chipper food. Before long, I was babysitting their two kids.

Gerry knew when to push me hard and when to go easy. He'd know when morale was sapping in the physio room and he'd suggest an afternoon's drinking if we got our work done early. There were some days he'd just pull me aside because he knew I needed to offload on someone.

I remember one of the Leeds United youth players telling me he'd been given a week off one January to go on a sun holiday with his girlfriend. He'd been injured and his coaches felt the break would rejuvenate him. It was different at Millwall, where you'd always be made feel as if something much deeper was wrong, like there was a fundamental flaw in your character.

You're not tough enough.

You're too weak.

You're unreliable.

You're flaky.

I believed this. I bought into this culture way too much, often playing through injuries when I shouldn't have. I was afraid to speak up when I should have, fearful of the bollocking I'd get if I said I wasn't up to taking part. It was easier to mask that fear as having the bravery to play through pain.

There was no reason to stay off booze when I didn't have a game, so I launched into that. It was important to do something to keep the spirits up, especially when another challenge came my way.

One morning, I noticed a lump under my right nipple. The club doctor told me to keep an eye on it which, obviously, I didn't. A few months later, she asked for an update. Just as obviously, I had none, having ignored it ever since. But when she felt it, she immediately sent me to the hospital for further tests. It was noticeably bigger. They kept me in overnight and removed the lump under general anaesthetic.

They asked about any history of breast cancer in my family. Apparently, men can get it too, which I never knew. I was discharged and told to take it easy over the weekend.

'Come back in five days for the biopsy results,' they said. 'And don't come alone.'

I could see the sense in their advice to take it handy, but, on the other hand, six of my mates were due over from Dublin for a long weekend. They were arriving the following day and staying at mine. What kind of host would I be if I didn't join in with whatever plans they had?

I told McGrath about the lump and asked him not to say it to the others. I didn't fancy spending the weekend being asked about it.

Talking wouldn't influence the outcome of the biopsy, so why bring the mood down? I drank solidly for the weekend and showed up drunk for physio treatment on the Monday morning. It was better than sharing my worries that I might have cancer.

One of the lads had accidentally shattered my car windscreen by jumping on it over the weekend, which added an extra layer of difficulty to the journey. Like Jim Carrey in *Ace Ventura*, I set off for the training ground with my head stuck out the driver's side window for the entire journey.

I guessed Gerry wouldn't fine me for showing up drunk since I was awaiting the biopsy results, and I was right. I avoided sanctions and was sent home early.

On the Tuesday morning, I went to the hospital appointment on my own despite my parents offering to come over for support. I got the all-clear.

Back to the serious business of trying to play football again. Back to the serious business of wondering what would go wrong next.

———

Before a pre-season friendly against Spurs at our training ground in 1998, I was adamant I'd be fine despite the pain in my right knee. I didn't tell anyone my knee was sore until I couldn't kick a ball in the pre-match warm-up. I got hammered for that one, particularly as I worsened the injury by giving it a go. A proper professional would have known not to risk it, they said. You've got to learn to understand your own body, they said. I should have spoken up sooner, like a good pro, but the prospect of playing against David Ginola had excited me.

But there was another problem. How would I know when a good pro played and when he pulled out? I never knew how to read the signs properly. If I listened to my body, I wouldn't get out of bed in the morning.

I was injured so often throughout my career that I became obsessed with how differently I'd do things once I returned. *If* I returned. I'd begin every pre-season training with a list of what I would change. I'd eat better, train longer, sleep more, drink less. I'd be a proper professional this time.

In May 1998 Rhino succeeded Billy Bonds as one of the joint first-team managers, along with another former player, Alan McCleary. Both men believed in the code of Millwall. If someone had told Rhino he was Mr Millwall, he wouldn't have disagreed. In my early days, he used to mark me in training in order to toughen me up. He would give me a kicking, throw me to the ground, pull my shirt to stop me from getting ahead of him. It was all done, he said, because he thought I had something. I needed to toughen up, he said, and this was his way of helping. In his softer moments, Rhino would tell me he liked me. Despite it all, I really liked him too.

Ray Harford was brought in as first-team coach and I loved everything about him. We got on so well the lads would slag me about being his son. I hung on his every word. Anecdotes about his past successes didn't bother me like they had with Docherty. I couldn't get enough of his insights and memories of working with Kenny Dalglish and Alan Shearer at Blackburn Rovers. He kept telling me it was a matter of time before I'd play in the Premier League.

Unfortunately, one extra session when Ray was at the club sabotaged my preparations for the '99/'00 season. I decided to attempt an overhead kick and smashed the two bones in my left forearm when I hit the ground. One of the lads heard the break from the halfway line. I didn't even make contact with the ball, never mind score a goal. I just lay there in shock with what looked like a second elbow in my left arm.

McCleary was standing behind the goal and was the first to react. As sore as it was, I wanted answers.

'How long does a broken arm keep you out?' I asked him. 'When will I be back?'

Only the previous day, McCleary had told me how important the coming season would be for my career. He told me the crowd used to hammer his former teammate Teddy Sheringham when he had first played for Millwall. He won them over and now that I had too, he was expecting big things. This was my time.

I was carried by stretcher to the physio room. Ray was one of the stretcher-bearers and halfway back across the pitches, he needed a rest, so they put me down while Ray took a break. I lay there in savage pain, waiting for Ray to catch his breath, saying nothing, being the dutiful and quiet son again, when all I wanted to do was roar, 'Get me somewhere fast, I'm in fucking agony'. But I didn't. I never did.

Eventually, I was taken to Blackheath Hospital, but we had to leave as Millwall owed the hospital money and they wouldn't admit me. From there I was taken to a doctor's surgery around the corner to sit and wait until I could be seen. When we got there, Gerry forgot to hold the door open, letting it swing back and smack me right on the broken arm.

When I was eventually admitted to the hospital, they kept me in for five nights, which seemed excessive. I was allowed out for an hour to do a photo-call in The Den for that season's squad picture on the Monday. It took a fair bit of time to manoeuvre my arm behind my back so it wouldn't be noticeable in the photo, but I somehow managed it.

At some clubs they might go out of their way to be supportive at times like this, but not Millwall. All I got were reminders that Rhino had suffered a similar injury during a game on a Saturday and went on the piss for the weekend before reporting to hospital on the Monday. Even if they were exaggerating (which they probably weren't), they were also making a serious point: I should have dealt with this better. I should have been able for the pain.

I was told I might never be able to straighten the arm again because of the severity of the break. The kid who had wanted to prove Mr Casey wrong was motivated again. Tell me I can't do something and I won't stop trying to do it. That was why I wore a Glasgow Rangers jersey around Dublin in the early nineties. It's not that I didn't care about religion or the history of the Glasgow clubs, nor was I oblivious to the cultural symbolism attached to the rivalry. I just wasn't prepared to be told I had to choose Celtic because of where I was from. Fuck you lot. I'm going to be Irish, a Catholic and a Rangers supporter.

To prove the doctor wrong, I would sit next to the radiator at home and wedge my arm behind it. I'd lean at an angle that forced my arm to straighten more than it wanted to. I don't know how many hours I spent at this, but today I can straighten my arm without any bother. A rare victory for my body over the medical profession.

I was out for twelve weeks with the broken arm and missed the start of the season, which is never good. Results were bad and there was yet another change of management before I was back to full fitness. Rhino and McCleary were sacked and Mark McGhee was appointed.

If Gerry Mooney at Belvedere had pointed me in a certain direction and I wouldn't have travelled without him, the same was true of Mark McGhee. I don't think I would have improved as much as I did from that point were it not for him.

He brought me into the office and told me I had been a tall, skinny lad with potential for too long. It was time to deliver. McGhee knew exactly what buttons to press to get the best out of me. He used a bit of reverse psychology to nudge me out of the physio room when my arm was nearly better.

'I hear you're one of those that needs loads of extra time to get fit?' he said one day.

Fuck that, I'll show him.

I took to his style of management straight away. He was enthusiastic and positive. He actually coached us, so I was getting specific instructions and pointers on how to improve. Instead of threats to cancel days off if we didn't perform, like we had been getting previously, McGhee would stay back after training to coach me on certain aspects of centre-forward play that he had picked up from his own time as a striker. Hold-up play, positioning in the box, timing of runs, technical pointers on shooting. Information that was useful. My squad number changed from number twenty to number ten, which was a confidence boost in itself.

The fitness coach was assigned to work with me on an individual weights programme. This was the first of its kind at the club. Nutritionists prescribed a strict diet, along with fat-burning sessions before breakfast in the training ground gym. The plan was to be fitter and stronger than ever. It would help me reach my potential while also protecting me against getting injured again. The science behind it was sound, but the variable that was most unreliable, my body, had other ideas.

7

The House of Sin

I had no idea what was involved in hosting a housewarming. I had just bought a townhouse, a three-storey terraced home half a mile from Millwall's training ground in Bromley. It had four bedrooms and the plan from the first time I saw it was to fill those rooms with visitors from Dublin. I was delighted with it. I'd saved for the deposit and secured the mortgage myself by the age of nineteen. It needed work, but there would be plenty of time for that.

I didn't know much about home ownership, I just knew you threw a party when you bought one. I figured that, once there was enough alcohol and some decent CDs, my job was done. We were short of glasses so my mates from Dublin went to the pub to nick some. There was no place for Champagne or charcuterie boards at this party. We were all set with crates of Stella and the odd bag of peanuts.

Apart from my Irish mates, most people there were older than me. And since most of my mates in London were Millwall players themselves, a lot of the squad were at the house that night. Once the pubs closed, the house all of a sudden became packed. There were plenty of people there I had never met before, but that didn't matter to me in the slightest. A party is nothing without guests, so the more the merrier.

I walked up the stairs and saw a couple of lads outside the toilet.

'Alright, lads, everything OK?'

'Yeah, Sads, great party, mate.'

'Cheers. How long have you been waiting to get in there?'

'We can wait all night, mate.'

'Why's that?'

'Seb is in there with a girl. She told us it's our turn next. She's up for it.'

I nodded as if this was nothing I hadn't experienced before, even if it was nothing like anything I'd experienced before.

Was this an English thing? A football thing? Or was the party now out of control?

I thought it might be a combination of all three. Certainly, I felt the difference between Ireland and England may well have been as vast as the difference between the real world and the football world. Especially as I had no experience of the real world.

As the night went on, the stories kept coming about what various men and this woman were doing together. It was like keeping track of contestants' behaviour over a series of *Love Island*, except it was all playing out in one night, in my home. Every hour or so, a new name would be mentioned.

'She's in a room with Lefty now.'

'I think Alec was involved in some way.'

'I just shagged Jeff in your bedroom, Sads. Hope you don't mind.'

From a distance of twenty years and with a new perspective, I'm not going to wag my finger at the people involved, or even at my younger self. England was a very different place from Ireland. If sex was something people were ashamed of in Ireland – and we've seen how well that worked out – in England men and women were more comfortable in saying what they wanted. The woman at my housewarming party was entirely happy and comfortable with how the night unfolded.

I wasn't brought up with any education in this area, nor were any of my Irish mates. Sex was rarely discussed, and when it was, the idea that a woman could enjoy sex or speak about it comfortably would have been used against her. Women taking agency in this area wasn't presented as a positive. In most cases, it would be cited as a reason to keep your distance. As far as we were led to believe in Ireland in the '90s, a woman who enjoyed sex had baggage, whereas arguably, she may have had less baggage than the rest of us put together.

In the classes I have taught on sexual health in the last few years, one of my primary tasks is to remove shame from the equation at the outset. I grew up in a world that said guilt and regret should follow almost any sexual encounter. If we are going to have honest conversations about what sex and consent involve, we'll have to embrace the idea that men and women both enjoy sex. The shame we bring to these conversations is useful to nobody.

But during that housewarming party, I genuinely didn't have a clue what I was meant to think.

Everyone left the house having had a good time, but it did feel like throwing a party while your parents were away and realising pretty quickly you weren't the one in charge. If this had happened in a house in Dublin, I'm sure I would have considered it extreme, but in my new environment, nothing seemed off limits. The abnormal, especially when it came to sex, was entirely normal.

It was in this world that I would learn about sex and, more important, relationships, which wasn't always healthy. Sex was transactional, approached by women and men with the same disconnection. The culture was one of instant gratification. You didn't work on relationships, building trust over time before being intimate. Within hours of meeting one another, sex was on the cards. And women, just as much as men, were the ones proposing it. Safe sex or monogamy didn't seem important to many people either. I have no trouble understanding now why I became so cynical and untrusting about relationships, or why I became adamant I would never be so foolish as to ever get married.

———

After that night, my house became known as 'The House of Sin'. But it was also a home from home for anyone over from Dublin. Robbie Ryan, Millwall's left-back, moved in with me. Robbie was two years older than me and grew up in Ballybrack. He loved telling non-Irish people he was from Dalkey and that Bono was his neighbour. We roomed together for away matches and went on holidays together in the summer. We were inseparable back then, and my family and mates from Dublin all loved him.

Like me, Robbie was full of self-doubt. But while I kept my insecurities as hidden as possible, he told anyone who would listen about his own. He could never see what others saw in him, and convinced himself that various managers, the fans or the chairmen didn't rate him. I could see how self-defeating it was to be so self-critical, but the ability to observe the pointlessness of it in others didn't stop me doing the same thing.

We turned the house into an exile's cliché. A huge tricolour hung on the sitting-room wall, the soundtrack was usually Irish music of some kind and a framed Proclamation of the Republic was pinned up at one stage. On Saturday nights, it was a party house. There would be Belgian, Australian and British teammates belting out 'Ooh ah, up the Ra' without any knowledge of what they were actually singing. It wasn't that any of us supported the IRA, but the songs were Irish and catchy, so that was enough.

I was living a life that seemed impossible to my friends. I had money, free time and a great job that came with lots of perks.

If one of my mates from Dublin couldn't come over because he was broke, I would pay for his flight on the condition he didn't tell any of the other lads. I never had to pull out of something because I couldn't afford it. I had no expensive habits, I didn't gamble and nobody ever went bankrupt buying their clothes in JD Sports. My biggest outlay was on DVDs.

My mate Johnny was a regular visitor. During one trip, he jumped naked out of the upstairs window to pay for our pizza. He landed on the lawn, did a couple of awkward tumbles and then breezily jumped to his feet to pay for the food. He just shook your man's hand afterwards and walked back into the house.

I wasn't in Kansas any more, and I tended to connect with people who were finding their way too. While my friends from Dublin were always over, soon there were others who would become just as important, and eventually nobody became more important to me than Hicksy.

Mark Hicks arrived at Millwall a couple of years after me and he was younger, funnier and more talented. Those factors could have been massive hurdles to our friendship but once we got to know each other, they didn't matter at all. For the next ten years, a day didn't go by when I didn't talk to Hicksy. The person I drunkenly shared my secrets with? Hicksy. The person I asked to accompany me when my career was on the line? Hicksy? The person I asked to fly to America with me when I was making a comeback? Hicksy.

Hicksy was different and he knew it. He was from Belfast and had made news as a kid when he turned down an approach from the Irish Football Association to play for Northern Ireland. He was from the Falls Road and, to him, there wasn't even a choice.

That didn't matter to the clubs who wanted him. He could have gone to Leeds or Celtic. Unlike me, he had options, but he chose Millwall. I was always grateful that he did.

At Millwall, there was something about his manner that encouraged coaches to go hard on him. Maybe it was because he always gave the impression he didn't give a shit, but he was always picking up fines. He was fined for eating a sandwich once. Another time, he was fined two weeks' wages for going bowling the night before a reserve game. He was regularly called a pisshead, solely because he was Irish. Yet when he was recovering from an operation, a member of the coaching staff visited him in hospital and brought him eight cans of lager, just to tide him over.

I wanted him on my side and he always was.

———

I was a professional footballer and people were relying on me. Millwall supporters demand a lot from the players, but a lot of the time I could forget about that. A lot of the time I was a teenager, doing what a teenager does.

I did a questionnaire for a Millwall fanzine when I was nineteen. They asked what song I would like to walk onto the pitch to. I went for 'Teddy Bear's Head' by the Wolfe Tones, a rebel song about getting the English out of Ireland by force. 'What's your lifetime ambition?' they asked. My answer? 'To shag Toni Braxton.' This was pre-Twitter, thankfully, so I wasn't shamed all over the internet and branded a misogynistic, nationalist thug for life. Back then teenagers could get away with being teenagers who said dumb things.

I was also a teenager with nobody supervising me. All my friends in Dublin lived with their parents while I owned my own home. Three mates from home – Ed, Ste and Sketts – moved in with me and found work in a local travel agency. There were no grown-ups in our world and I certainly wasn't one. I was Tom Hanks in *Big* – suddenly catapulted into an adult body but with interests that were still primarily juvenile. Everyone would share in my good fortune, especially if the good fortune involved the lads filling condoms with water and hanging them on the bushes outside the house, where I'd see them when I came home from training.

In the outside world, people would ask me questions about football and expect a profound answer. There was nobody waiting to hear what

I had to say about who would win the Premier League when I was with
the lads and that was what I wanted. Nobody was hanging on my every
word. If they asked me a question, it was so they could take the piss out
of my answer. I was the butt of all their jokes and that's where I wanted
to be. Don't get serious, don't look to me for answers. Fuck that, let's
get the lads over and throw darts at each other's bare chests. That will
pass the time.

In most senses, my social life was ordinary. Looking back, what's
extraordinary is not how wild we were, but how well behaved we were.
I had few responsibilities and, most of the time, I did little that would
cause alarm. I would spend afternoons watching episodes of *Friends*
and arguing with Robbie over who would cook the dinner.

There were other benefits, of course. I had arrived at Millwall as
a virgin, incapable of approaching girls. I never quite learned how
to approach girls, but that didn't matter if you were a professional
footballer. I was in a different world from my mates back home. We all
grew up believing lads were the ones who made the first move, but in
London girls would approach *us* every time we went out.

The Millwall lads would call me 'Paddy-at-the-bar' when we went
out. I wasn't one for dancing or jumping on tables or doing anything
that attracted attention. I'd just sit on a barstool and the conversation
would take place around me. While others might be trying it on with
girls, I would happily spend the night chatting to whoever happened to
sit next to me. The opportunities for casual hook-ups were so common
that if you didn't make a conscious decision to go home alone, you
probably wouldn't.

This didn't concern me then; the opposite, in fact. I was having fun
and nights out were an extension of the juvenile world I was living in.

Later, when I grew cynical about relationships, believing they were
always doomed, I wondered how much of these ideas were formed
during those years.

Behaviour that might be considered alarming was tolerated and joked about. To some lads in the dressing room, sleeping with someone other than your partner was talked about as matter-of-factly as where you might go on a Friday night. There was no fuss, no sense of obligation. The only people you owed anything to were your teammates. That was what we were told to believe and, because it suited many of us in this situation, we believed it.

I remember mentioning to one of the academy staff that one Irish lad was having problems settling. He immediately came up with a solution: 'Not being funny, but why don't you all chip in and get him a brass?' I was young, naïve and stupid, but I still didn't think that getting the young and bewildered player a prostitute was the best idea.

The dressing room was a strange place. There were teenagers mixing with men in their thirties. By the time you're twenty-seven, you're expected to have a maturity – at least on the football pitch – that you wouldn't expect from someone of that age in any other walk of life. Within the dressing room everything is accelerated, but outside it you can easily remain the adolescent who first walked in.

There were other elements which made it a little different, too. It wasn't unusual for two or three lads to be knowingly sleeping with the same woman. If she spent one night with me, she might spend another with a teammate. Sometimes there might be more than two consenting adults involved, which I had never even heard of in Dublin.

My life was fun and this all seemed harmless. Nightclub bouncers would usher us past queues, straight into VIP areas. When I left Dublin, I had never even seen a VIP area, let alone been in one. I would take the favours when they were handed out, but I would never go up to bouncers and tell them I was a Millwall player, even when mates would ask me to.

I didn't venture into London much so I went to the same pubs, the same clubs, with the same mates all the time. And then I slept with the same girls.

If you'd asked me if being a professional footballer had changed me, I'd have argued that it hadn't. The world around me had altered and the way the world responded to me had altered too, which was the most important change of all. I was still the same bloke, but everyone treated me differently. Of course, I *was* changing; I can see that now. I became more guarded around people, less trusting of their motives. And when it came to relationships with women, I kept them all at arm's length. I wasn't particularly sure why I was doing it, but I knew I was. Empty, emotionless one-night stands were on offer and they suited me because nobody would ever want to get close.

I had always tried to fit in. I was hyper-sensitive about not making a fuss, so I wouldn't make any demands. But if the world wanted to treat me differently, I was going to go along with that too. It was what I'd always done and I wasn't going to change now, when going along with things was so much fun.

It quickly became routine to me. It was only when friends from Dublin came over and pointed out how different it was that I'd take notice, but only briefly.

But even then there were times when my own behaviour shocked me. These moments couldn't be laughed off so readily. I would get a glimpse of another person and wonder if that was really me. Inevitably, this would happen when there was drink involved.

I was beginning to discover I blacked out very easily. Nobody could tell because I'd be talking away as normal. I could be having a chat about anything, about the big issues of the day or the latest episode of *Friends* and you'd think I was making sense, but the next day I wouldn't remember a word of it.

I could wake up in bed beside a girl with no memory of anything that had happened. In that drunken haze of the morning after, we would often try to piece it together and laugh about how little I recalled.

One night I was talking to a girl in a bar. She was very friendly so we were chatting away and, as I was ordering a drink, I asked her if she wanted one too.

'Sorry, I didn't introduce myself, Richie's my name.'

I leaned over to shake her hand. She didn't take it.

'You're fucking joking me,' she said.

'What do you mean?'

'We met last week.'

'Ah, I'm sorry. Here listen, my memory goes when I'm drinking. This happens all the time. Really sorry.'

'You don't remember?'

'No,' I said, still quite breezy about the whole thing.

'We went back to your house.'

'Ah, right . . .' I said, but still nothing registered. Lots of people came back to my house, nothing unusual in that.

'We had sex.'

My breeziness disappeared. My heart raced. I had never seen her before. I had no memory of any of this. Fuck. Fuck. Fuck.

She looked at me with contempt and walked away without saying another word. My mates confirmed the girl was telling the truth. They remembered meeting her and said she was lovely. My mates found it all hilarious. 'Jesus, Sads, what are you like?'

It was becoming a running joke that I forgot everything.

But in the minutes between her telling me we'd had sex and me joining in the joke with the lads, I had a moment of realisation that scared me. It wasn't profound and it wasn't anything that was going to make me reconsider my attitude to drink or sex, but I didn't like it. That was all I knew.

I didn't like myself if this was the sort of thing that happened when I was in blackout. I felt like a complete prick, even though I also felt that anything that happened was out of my control. Again, I was passive, a spectator trying to piece together the events in my own life. But that didn't really matter. You are what you do, defined by how you act. To the girl I'd slept with the week before, *I* was the person who had done this. *I* was the prick.

After a while, though, nearly everything could be laughed off.

One Sunday morning before training, the manager asked one of the senior pros what his plans were for that day.

'Think I'm off to the missus's parents' house for a barbecue,' he said.

'I wouldn't if I were you, mate,' the manager said in a fit of laughter. 'Check out page seven in the *News of the World*.'

A woman had given an interview claiming she had slept with a different footballer from each of the top four divisions. Our teammate was representing the second division.

We knew all the pitfalls and we laughed them all off. A wife could catch her husband cheating on her – a serious event in the real world but a source of great amusement in our dressing room at the time.

I didn't want that kind of marriage, but at that time I didn't want any kind of marriage and the more I learned of life – life viewed through this prism – the more certain I was that I never would. Relationships were all doomed anyway, so marriage was pointless.

I was lucky that my friends from home were always around to keep me grounded, even if their methods of keeping me there were sometimes unwelcome. They were the one constant through every up and down I'd had since I was twelve. You're never sure who's really your mate when you become a professional footballer, but in a world of hangers-on, spoofers and spivs, the closest I came to being myself was when I was with them.

I was deep in conversation with my mate Burkey in a kebab shop one Saturday night. We were having one of those philosophical chats you have over a kebab when next thing he leaned back, swung and punched me in the face.

'What the fuck!? What was that for?'

'That's just to make sure you keep your feet on the ground,' he explained, as if I was the fool for not understanding what was happening.

'Are you serious? You couldn't have just—'

BANG! He hit me again, mid-sentence. Same fist, same side of the face, but a little harder. There was more behind this one.

'Are you for fucking real? What was that for?'

'You need to toughen up. You keep getting injured. That's so you won't get injured again.'

Despite the occasional punch in the face, the lifestyle was easy to love. I'd train during the day, go home and spend an afternoon playing snooker. Even the serious stuff was what others did for fun – play a game of football. I had no children and was single the majority of the time, if that really mattered. My only responsibility was to turn up for training on time and keep myself fit.

———

When real life did intervene, my method of dealing with it was simple: stay quiet as long as you can and hope the problem would be taken care of.

'Don't you know why I'm here?' she asked.

I had no idea, as she had never called to me on a Sunday morning before, but I knew there must be a reason for the unannounced visit. Thankfully, I wasn't hungover as we had a game on Tuesday.

'No,' I said. 'Come on in. What's up?'

'You've no idea? Really?'

We had been hanging out in the same group for a few months. Her mates and my mates regularly ended up at the same parties, which were usually in my house on Saturday nights.

'No, go on,' I said, but something was starting to register. I remembered being in my bedroom with her the previous month but I couldn't remember the specifics. I knew my memory wasn't a reliable source for my weekend behaviour. If I wanted to know my exact movements on a night out, I had to rely on the accounts of whoever happened to be in my company.

Then it came.

'I'm pregnant.'

'Jesus. Really?'

I'm not sure what I said after that. She didn't want to stay long as she had a friend sitting outside in the car. She told me she wasn't sure what reception she would get so she wanted the moral support. I was a little insulted that she thought I would react badly, but I understood. These aren't situations anyone prepares you for.

We agreed that she would call back on Wednesday night to discuss it properly. My old Belvedere manager Gerry and his wife were staying with me for the weekend and were due to return any minute. I was keen to avoid any questions from them so I was happy to postpone the conversation.

I didn't really know what to do. Who could I tell? How could I explain it? Even though I was used to it by now, I was embarrassed that I couldn't recall my own behaviour on a night out. Jesus, I was going to be a father and I didn't even know the woman's surname.

I had no trouble concealing my emotions when Gerry and his wife returned. That bit was easy, as not showing my feelings was my specialist subject. I didn't mention it to them or anyone else and stored it away in the part of my mind I'd wilfully ignore. I'd had years of practice at that.

The following evening, the phone rang. It was the friend who had waited outside.

'She's in hospital, they think she's having a miscarriage.'

'Jesus. Eh, thanks for letting me know. Is there anything I can do?'

'Not really.'

A couple of hours later, she rang again to confirm it.

She called over as planned a couple of nights later. I was on crutches, having badly injured my ankle in the game on Tuesday. We spoke about it all for about three hours, with neither of us really knowing what to say. We didn't try to romanticise our relationship or catastrophise the miscarriage. We were both a little in shock, realising that our drunken antics could have made us parents, and both relieved that we were looking back on a miscarriage rather than ahead to parenthood. We both said that if the miscarriage hadn't happened we would have fumbled our way into being parents and done our best. We wondered what kind of job we would have done bringing up a child together. But, like a lot of young people who find themselves in a situation like this, we both saw it as a bullet we had successfully dodged.

It's easy to be hard on myself looking back, but I tried to handle this as best I could. By this stage, there was an element of chaos taking hold in my life. It was an unplanned pregnancy that time, but there was always something. All week I would be a good pro. On Saturday nights, though, anything could happen. And it was always when I drank.

8

Ooh-Aah,
Richard-Sad-lee-aah

I had won the Millwall crowd over through doggedness and perseverance. They even had a song just for me by the end. My teammate Neil Harris brought it to my attention after one of the games.

'What about that song!?' he said to me in the dressing room afterwards. 'Ooh-Aah, Richard-Sad-lee-aah!? Quality!'

'What are you on about?' I said. I hadn't heard a thing.

Because of the boos and jeers aimed at me in my earliest days in the first team, I figured no good would come from me listening to the Millwall fans. I had developed a tactic of my own to drown them out. Why listen to a noise that will do nothing but drag you down? I did my best to focus on myself and what I was doing. Anything was better than listening to what was being said.

When I was jumping to head a ball I didn't hear a thing. When I was trying to outrun a full-back into the corner for the ball, I didn't hear a thing. When I was bearing down on the goalkeeper with the ball at my feet, the noise from the stand was too far away and I didn't hear it.

But it was different in the quieter moments, when I wasn't in the middle of the action. Like standing near the touchline waiting for a throw-in to be taken, or if I had to run off the pitch to retrieve the ball from the crowd. Then I could hear all the abuse aimed at me.

To get through those moments, I came up with a system. I would assign a number to every letter in a word I saw written in the stadium during a match. Pitches are surrounded by advertising hoardings so there were plenty of signs and slogans to choose from. If the original word had, say, nine letters, I would assign the numbers 1–9 to each letter. I would then re-arrange the numbers while retaining the correct spelling. Millwall, for example, could be '1-2-8-7-5-6-4-3' as the 'L' was assigned numbers '3' '4' '7' and '8' and so could move fluidly around. You're not really meant to understand this and, writing it now, it's a wonder that the guy who filled his mind with this stuff managed to sleep with any women at all.

The purpose was to leave no room for my inner voice to bring me down, as it so often did. And there was also no room for the voices of angry fans roaring their hate. Like a watered-down version of Rainman, this was a strategy I stumbled upon that worked for me, allowing me to focus on what I could do best: scoring goals. So, by the time the fans started to praise me, I wasn't listening.

These are the kinds of mental exercises sports psychologists would promote, but back then I was doing it off the cuff. It's the same as listening to a podcast in bed to help you fall asleep, or focusing on your breath to prevent intrusive thoughts taking over. If you can focus on any one thing, you can't be thinking of anything else. And that was a strategy worth deploying in The Den on bad days.

———

Thankfully, I was injury-free when, in April 1999, I was called up as part of Brian Kerr's squad for the U-20 World Cup Finals in Nigeria.

Millwall weren't keen on me going. We had qualified for the final of the Auto Windscreens Shield, which was to be played at Wembley, and they wanted to be sure I could play in that. If we got to the quarter-finals or beyond in Nigeria, I'd definitely miss it. But I was determined to go so there was nothing they could do.

Rhino sent me on my way with a message which emphasised how proud everyone at the club was about my international recognition.

'Don't fucking come back injured.'

Injury was the least of our concerns. Nigeria wasn't a safe place, but it was also a pretty boring place because of that.

From the moment we landed, safety and boredom went hand in hand. Despite everything being agreed beforehand, the armed police said they would not escort us to our hotel from the airport upon arrival. The roads wouldn't be safe this time of the evening, they said, which left us wondering what the hell could be more dangerous than a group of heavily armed police.

There were always prostitutes hanging about in the hotel lobby. They would randomly ring our rooms asking if we wanted company. I remember chatting to one woman for about forty minutes one evening to relieve the boredom. Not one person on our trip did anything with any of them, though. Among the many reasons for abstaining was the information we had been given by the medical staff about the prevalence of HIV and AIDS in the country.

I had the chance to bring this up with one of the local missionary priests.

'How come you don't just give out a load of condoms to everyone?'

'Our experience tells us that just increases the spread of diseases,' he said.

I just shrugged it off at the time, not realising that approach led directly to people dying.

Dealing with the boredom of the downtime was one of the many challenges. There was no English-speaking TV worth watching and, for security reasons, we weren't allowed leave the hotel grounds. We had an armed guard at the end of our corridor and we pestered him to let us carry his gun around, just to relieve the boredom. In exchange for numerous Mars and Snickers bars, he eventually caved in.

We had armed escorts in front of and behind our team bus everywhere we went. A few kids came too close to our training pitch one night and we watched, shocked, as two policemen made them lie face-down on the ground and then beat them senseless. The local shops had to shut in the early evening because they had no electricity to stay open after dusk. The wooden huts on the main streets were surrounded by open sewers, which dogs would walk through as they played with the local children. We were in a different world.

On non-matchdays we passed the time with a golf putter, a golf ball and an empty bottle of Ribena in the hotel corridor. It was boring, but there was something about the boredom that made the whole thing seem more important. We were sitting around doing nothing for a reason. We were bored while representing our country.

On the pitch it was a different story. We knew exactly what we were doing. Brian and Noel had everything covered. Brian was already a two-time European champion and we had come to Nigeria to win the World Cup. This was a different level to everything I was used to at Millwall. We lost to Mexico, but came through our group after beating the Saudis and Australia and played the hosts, Nigeria, in the second round. Win this and we'd be into the quarter-finals; lose and I'd be heading home to play at Wembley four days later.

I was up front with Robbie Keane. He was still at Wolves, but he had already been capped at senior level and knew he'd be transferring to a bigger club soon. Duff was on one wing, and Stephen McPhail was in midfield. McPhail glided through games in training. One-touch or two-touch, no matter how little space. It was like he was three seconds ahead of the rest of us. Robbie seemed untouched by nerves. I don't know if he just hid it better than the rest of us, but he was an eighteen-year-old for whom huge things were expected, yet never once did he give the impression it weighed him down. I never came close to being as carefree as he seemed to be and I could never even fake it.

Duff was freakishly good. After training I would watch him
practising on his own. It was like he had a ball trapped in a magnetic
field around his feet as he did tricks and drills. He'd kick it up in the air
and kill it dead every time, or burst for five yards in any direction with
the ball under total control.

During this trip, I started to understand the advice I'd received at
Belvedere from Vincent Butler when I first joined Millwall. He'd said
not to set my standards by what I saw from the first-team players there.
There was a reason they were only in the second division. Aim higher,
he'd said. It was only when I was training with these lads that I realised
what he meant.

I scored in our 1-1 draw against Nigeria, adding to the goal I got
against Australia, but we lost on penalties and were knocked out. The
Nigerian fans invaded the pitch afterwards and the police started to
shoot their guns into the air to disperse the crowd. We huddled in the
centre-circle, mainly in tears, but also aware that we were fucked if any
of the crowd started trouble. These were the same fans who had lobbed
stones and bags of their own piss at the Nigerian players' team bus
after they lost their opening game to Mali. We linked arms and stood
where we were, as Noel roared 'Hold' like Mel Gibson in *Braveheart*.
Thankfully, the gunfire was enough to disperse and settle the crowd,
so we made it safely back to the dressing room without any casualties.

I couldn't have cared less about Wembley or Millwall at that moment.
That's not something I would have said to anyone else at the time, but
for me, nothing could have come close to getting a medal with Ireland.
I didn't care that nobody back at the club was taking the Youth World
Cup seriously. It was the biggest thing I'd ever been involved in.

———

Within two hours of the final whistle, Millwall's chief scout was on the
phone to make sure I was heading straight back to London. He wanted

me to play because it would reflect well on him – another one of his youth signings in the first team for a game of this importance – so he told me to tell Rhino I was full of energy and raring to go as soon as I got back. I was neither, of course, but this was a chance to play at Wembley. I did as I was told and bullshitted Rhino.

I landed back on the Friday, joined up with the squad on Saturday and played the ninety minutes the following day in the stadium where I'd dreamed about playing my entire life.

Of the 55,000 crowd in attendance, over 47,000 were Millwall fans, including Granny Aggie and my family. It was a great way to move on from the disappointment of Nigeria, but I played shit and Wigan beat us 1-0 with an injury-time goal that should have been ruled out for a handball.

Emotionally, though, it was one of the most hectic weeks of my career. For the second time in four days, I was lying on the pitch after the final whistle in tears that we'd lost.

With Ireland, my aim after that was to get into the under-21s and keep climbing the ladder, step by step. Back then under-21 fixtures corresponded with the senior team's fixtures, and the build-up always involved a training game against each other. I remember sprinting to close down Denis Irwin before the Macedonia game away in October 1999. He had the ball at his feet. I figured I was either quick enough to take the ball from him or strong enough to muscle him out of my way. That's how I saw the scene unfolding in my head, but it's not exactly how things went. When I got close enough, he rolled the ball through my legs and ran right past me, much to the amusement of Mick McCarthy and both sets of players.

In late 2000 I got the call-up. Well, sort of. I was invited by Mick to train with the senior squad for their friendly with Finland, along with Michael Reddy of Sunderland. The plan was to gain some experience at that level. I knew I wasn't good enough to be in the full squad, so I was delighted. We would just train with the squad without the possibility of being involved in the game. Obviously, I was also concerned that I'd be completely out of my depth, but this wasn't the time to let my insecurities run the show. Everything was arranged and I was all set to travel, but once again my body had other ideas. I damaged my shoulder and couldn't travel.

We won the league that season and were promoted to the first division. I managed to stay injury-free for the first five months of the '01/'02 season. I had scored sixteen goals by the first week of January. I was constantly being asked about an international call-up and rumours of interest from other clubs. A minor groin strain kept me out of our game with Birmingham City. I bumped into Millwall's chief scout in the corridors beforehand.

'It's a shame you're not playing, son,' he said. 'Half of football is here tonight to watch you.'

By this stage, Mark McGhee, who was manager at the time, would often mention Clinton Morrison's selection in the Republic of Ireland squad, just to get a rise out of me.

'Hard to believe that he's there and you're not, eh?' he'd say and just walk off.

Clinton was with Crystal Palace at the time, Millwall's south London rivals. We played in the same position, albeit very differently, and McGhee knew the occasional comment would act as extra motivation for me. After we beat Palace 3-1 in September 2001, he called me into his office to focus my mind. Both myself and Clinton had scored in the game, but it was one of my best ever performances. I was told to focus everything I had on getting an international call-up. If Clinton could do it, I could. We were different kinds of players, but I started to believe it was achievable.

———

After we beat Portsmouth 1-0 at The Den in December 2001, I called home and was told Granny O had died. I had been named man of the match, which was becoming a regular occurrence, and my parents didn't want to tell me before the game in case it affected my performance. I started to cry as soon as Mum told me when I called her from the players' lounge after the game, which probably made their decision to ignore my calls before the game understandable. It wasn't the ideal place to get upset, so I got out of there straight away. I blanked autograph hunters outside as I left, probably the only time I ever did that in my entire career. I walked past with my head down, holding the phone to my ear to pretend I was chatting to someone.

On the morning of her funeral, one of the Irish Sunday papers ran a story that Manchester United were keeping a close eye on me and my teammate Steven Reid. People wanted to talk to me about that at the funeral. 'Sorry about your grandmother, Richard. So what's this about you and United?'

I didn't know anything concrete, but Millwall's chief scout had told me they had been in contact enquiring about me. That's all he said. Enquiring about what exactly? I didn't want to appear too keen or too interested, so I didn't ask for any further details. I didn't have an agent at the time, so I didn't have anyone in my corner to do some fishing.

I was getting used to being linked to other clubs, while never being fully comfortable with the prospect of leaving. I felt a move was inevitable but, as usual, I wasn't sure I was ready. I wasn't one of those lads with invincible self-belief at the best of times. Even if this, in career terms, *was* the best of times, there was always a voice in my head telling me I would be found out soon enough, that this good form would end and nobody would want me.

———

Mick McCarthy showed up for the return fixture against Palace at The Den on Stephen's Day. We won 3-0 and I scored twice. Clinton had to be pulled away by teammates after the final whistle when he reacted to our defenders slagging him about the prospect of losing his Ireland place to me. My family were at the game because they were staying with me for Christmas. As I walked off the pitch, I made eye contact with Catherine as the entire stadium sang my name. It was the perfect moment, on the best of days. My life had never been better.

I felt, by this time, like I belonged at Millwall. Nobody was questioning my character. Nobody was wondering whether I was too nice or too soft. The crowd were behind me, scouts were watching me, and the media were asking me about my international hopes. Probably on the back of that performance against Palace in front of Mick, I was called up for Ireland's next game in Dublin against Russia.

I was fitter and stronger than I'd ever been, and I went into every game expecting to score. This was how it was always meant to be. It was how I'd imagined it in the field behind my house when I was a kid. If I could have scripted my ideal life, this is exactly what it would have looked like.

A television crew came over from Dublin to interview me, Robbie Ryan and Steven Reid about our hopes for the remainder of the season. We were only a few points outside the play-off positions and the World Cup was on the horizon.

'What are the priorities, Richie? Millwall or Ireland?'

I wasn't going to fall into the trap of saying one mattered less than the other. I wanted it all.

'I want to finish top scorer here, get into the play-offs with Millwall. And yeah, making a run for the Ireland World Cup squad would be great too. Suppose that's not too much to ask for, is it?' I was smiling at the time, but I was serious about what I was saying. Nothing was beyond me. If only my body could sign up to that deal.

9

Eighteen Minutes of Fame

Steve Staunton's jumper was covered in kebab and beer. He was heading for his hotel room, but he wasn't going there voluntarily. It was impressive, in some ways, that he was going at all, but that might have had something to do with the man leading him there, his international manager Mick McCarthy.

It was my first full day in an Ireland senior squad and I was watching Ireland's most capped player, with some objections from the man himself, drunkenly stagger back to his bed after a twenty-four-hour drinking session.

My international call-up had come at a time when everything seemed promising. As soon as I landed in Dublin on the Saturday before the game against Russia the following Wednesday, I saw Clinton Morrison. In every interview we did at the time, we were being asked about each other. Journalists would ask me if I had a view on the fact that he was born in England, trying to walk me into a shitstorm about national identity. I saw it coming every time and easily swerved around it.

I had flown over with Steven Reid and, along with Clinton, we made the short journey to the Airport Hotel, where the team was based. Clinton was loud, but also sound. Having been built up to think we had a rivalry, this was a disappointment. It would have helped if he had been a dick.

When I got there, I was like the new kid at school, trying my best to give the impression that I belonged. I was sharing a room with Colin Healy, the other debutant on the squad.

I had some concerns when it became clear the squad were heading for a night out as one. I wasn't sure if I wanted my first training session with Ireland to follow on from a night on the piss, but I also knew it would be a bad idea to stay away.

By about 11pm that Saturday night, I had overcome any concerns I had about being hungover during my first training session with the senior team.

We would all head to Lillie's Bordello as the night got longer and longer. It was the squad's first get-together since qualifying for the World Cup in Iran two months earlier and, it turned out, it was time to celebrate. The night went on late for most of us, but we managed to make it back to the Airport Hotel. Well, most of us did.

Training on Sunday morning went as energetically as it could, given that most of the squad were either hungover or half drunk. It wasn't exactly how I'd imagined international football would be, but it was a lot of fun. I felt more comfortable with the players after a night on the piss with them. Rather than respectfully tip-toeing round them like any young player should, I was laughing with them all about what we'd got up to.

Roy Keane didn't train with us that morning because United were playing Charlton that afternoon. The plan was for him to join the squad in the evening, just in time to attend the FAI awards. I remember Gary Breen making a quip after training that there was no way Roy would miss a friendly. That's not his style. Everyone laughed.

That evening, we were told to meet in the lobby of the Airport Hotel to get the coach to the FAI awards dinner. As I stood outside my bedroom, ready to head for the bus, I spotted Mick frogmarching

Stan up the corridor to his room. Mick looked a million dollars in his tuxedo. Stan, the professional footballer next to him, was a mess. He was all over the shop.

Having partied with us on Saturday night, apparently Stan and Niall Quinn didn't want to stop. They'd fancied another drink and, like many in those situations, they'd come up with an ingenious way of getting one. They'd headed for Heuston Station and the early train to Waterford where they figured they'd be served. Then they made a day of it.

At some stage in the proceedings, they clearly felt they should head back to the hotel to get ready for the awards. After all, Stan was one of the nominees for player of the year and his attendance was required. Once Mick saw him, he felt his attendance was very much not required.

When Stan realised Mick wouldn't let him go to the awards, he was livid. Mick knew it was inevitable that the TV cameras would highlight the state he was in. Perhaps too drunk to realise he didn't have right on his side, Stan stormed out of the hotel after we had left for the awards.

I've no idea if Mick ever found out, but Stan showed up for training the following morning. Everyone laughed it off and moved on. Only a few months later, he was one of the senior players defending Mick in Saipan, calling out Roy for being unprofessional. He was quite convincing as well.

Keane got the main award that evening. On stage he said that if the preparations were all in order, we should go into the tournament thinking we could do well.

His presence at training on Monday changed everything. I've never seen someone have such an impact on those around him. He was so small in stature, but his presence was enormous. There was very little joking around, and he was taking everything as seriously as you would during a match.

Stan was stretching next to me during the warm-down afterwards. 'Seven million pound, man, eh?'

Aston Villa were reportedly considering a £7 million bid for myself and Tim Cahill, but our chairman told the media that that would be the cost for me alone.

'Ah, I think that's just Theo's way of playing hardball,' I said.

Stan, a Villa player at the time, said his manager Graham Taylor had asked him to gauge my interest in the move. I said I'd be very interested, but that I wouldn't be saying anything of the sort in public.

We had a players' meeting that night to discuss how World Cup qualification bonuses would be divided, and to decide on issues of sponsorship and personal appearances. Roy, Robbie and Shay Given would be the most sought-after by sponsors, so there was a need to come up with a system that would spread the duties around. Quinn did most of the talking. Keane didn't say much, which surprised me. I didn't say a word but this was a thrilling world to be observing.

At the same time, I felt I had no place there, and that none of this was relevant to me, but I never imagined players meeting like this for these reasons. I had never considered the commercial side of qualifying for big tournaments, but there I was, eavesdropping on all the discussions.

The official World Cup squad photograph was taken that day. After we did the individual pictures, we were called together for the group shot. I wondered whether I should stand aside rather than put Mick in the awkward position of having to ask me. When Mick saw me ask the photographer for guidance, he settled things immediately.

'As long as he's in my squad, he's gonna be in your photo, and that's that,' he said.

That might seem small, but it was big to me at the time. I could see why people often described Mick as a players' manager and why they stood behind him after Saipan.

In the years after I retired, I felt embarrassed any time I saw that photo. Like a visual representation of imposter syndrome, I was trying to pass myself off as a member of a group I didn't belong to.

You fucking fraud.

It took me years before I could look at that photo in any other way. Today, when I see it, I'm just reminded of a day I really enjoyed.

———

Mick named the team the afternoon of the game. I was a sub, as I expected, along with Clinton. Healy was starting in midfield, as was Reidy. I remember the four of us sitting in our room afterwards like giddy schoolkids.

I texted Jamie to tell him the news. I had told the family and my mates that I would be contacting him so I wouldn't get a flood of calls and texts. I tried to sleep for the afternoon but it was ridiculous to think I could. I tried to be breezy about the game to keep my nerves from taking over, but the enormity of it all made that virtually impossible. How do you play down the prospect of fulfilling your childhood dream?

Quinn sat next to me on the bus to Lansdowne Road, and like Noel O'Reilly before the U-18 play-off five years earlier, he said exactly what I needed to hear in that moment. He made it all sound so familiar.

'You've been playing centre-forward since you were a kid. You've years of practice. You know exactly what's involved. You wouldn't be here otherwise. You're going to get on, and when you do, just play your normal game. Honestly, Sads, you'll be great.'

From anyone else those words might have sounded mundane or uninspiring, but from Niall Quinn, one of my childhood idols, I lapped them up. Richie Dunne sat behind me recounting his memories of his own debut. These were the little things that made a big difference.

I had never seen the inside of the Lansdowne Road dressing room. It was surprisingly small and ordinary, but that's what dressing rooms are. It's the people in them that make them special. I wondered who might have sat in the same seat as me over the years. I couldn't wait to get onto the pitch, but I didn't want to be the first to go out. I did my best to convince everyone around me I was completely unfazed by it all.

Within a few minutes of being on the pitch for the warm-up, I noticed my uncle Dan on the side-lines so I went over to say a quick hello. It underlined the size of the occasion, because he rarely leaves the farm in Cork. During the anthem, I saw my mate Beano in the front row behind the dugout. We gave each other a nod. I spent some time looking for other family members who I knew were in the stadium.

Every time I went for a warm-up during the game, Quinn would deliberately push me against Mick. 'Let him know you're here, Sads.' I'd apologise, but after the third time, Mick started to look at me like I was some sort of gobshite. Quinn, obviously, thought the whole thing was hilarious.

Then, with about twenty minutes to go, the call came while I was out warming up. I got the nod from Ian Evans, Mick's assistant, to return to the dugout and get ready to go on. I replaced Robbie and ran onto that pitch in the 72nd minute to a surprisingly loud cheer. I had just become an Ireland international.

The first thing I did in the game was run from the halfway line with the ball at my feet, straight into the Russian defenders. I was like the enthusiastic Labrador from my Millwall debut, unfamiliar with the surroundings and not really sure of my role in the team. I didn't do much else in the game, other than knock referee Dermot Gallagher to the ground accidentally, and I think I lost every header I tried to win. The player marking me was Viktor Onopko, who at the time was just a few games short of winning his hundredth Russian cap.

I loved every second of it. Quinn was brought on towards the end. He ran straight over to me and urged me to get forward and score a goal. We won 2-0. Reidy scored his first international goal, Healy won man of the match, and myself and Clinton finished the game up front together, alongside Quinn. A great night all round.

I met Jamie in the players' bar afterwards for a pint and later gave away my boots to my cousin John in the hotel around the corner. All the family were there, thrilled with how everything had gone. I didn't do much for the eighteen minutes I was playing, but that didn't seem to matter. I was an Irish international now.

———

On my way out of the ground at the end of the night, Quinn shouted that he'd see me next month. I knew I was going to be in the squad to play Denmark six weeks later. Mick had already told Mark McGhee that he was going to select me in each of the friendlies before the World Cup to give me every chance. There were three more to come after this one.

This was the build-up to the World Cup. It was serious now, as that discussion at the meeting about dividing up bonuses and sponsorship duties had underlined.

After that meeting, we were asked to fill in a sheet with our family's World Cup travel plans along with details of how many tickets they might want for each match. Quinn handed me mine after dinner.

'There's hardly any point in me filling that in. Doesn't really apply to me, does it?'

I didn't want to draw any attention to myself, or for anyone in the room to think I doubted myself, so I said it quietly, but I wasn't confident enough to think I would be picked to go.

I knew there was nothing I could do to dislodge David Connolly, Robbie, Duffer or Quinn up front. At best, Clinton and I might fight over the remaining striker position. But I didn't think I needed to worry myself with specific numbers of family who would be travelling to the World Cup.

'Don't be fuckin' stupid, you,' Quinn said. 'You're going if I can't and my back could go any day. You better believe you need to fill it in.'

It wasn't his place to say how Mick might react if he had to pull out, but in that moment, he was convincing in his delivery. It was time to gauge the interest of the family, so the day before the Russia match, I rang Dad to ask how many tickets he'd be looking for, on the off-chance everything went my way and I made the final squad.

The significance of the call didn't escape me. I was calling my old man to ask him how many tickets he wanted to watch Ireland at a World Cup. My dream when I visited him in rehab had been for him to take me to a World Cup. In 1994 we had watched it on holiday in France. Now, eight years later, I was calling him to ask him to watch me play at the biggest football tournament in the world, not silently hoping he'd come and see me play for Broadford Rovers U-11s. I was calling to ask him how many tickets he'd want if I was selected to be in Ireland's squad for the World fucking Cup.

After outlining the various caveats, I asked him if he and Mum would like to go to Japan and South Korea and I offered to pay. I didn't ask him for a firm commitment that night or a decision on which games he'd want to see, or for any other details about his plans. I was just letting him know the situation, and that if everything worked out as I hoped, I'd sort him out and he could come to watch me play in the World Cup Finals. I waited for an order. Two tickets for one match, maybe bring the whole family out for another. Instead, a bomb exploded.

'To be honest, Richie, I'll leave it if you don't mind,' he said.

I wanted to roar. A lifetime of rage and hurt and disappointment rose up inside me.

Dad, this is the fucking World Cup!

I could be playing in the World Cup!

I want you to watch me if I do.

I NEED you to watch me if I do.

Why can't you see that?

What have I done to you? Why can't you see how much I need your approval? Why can't you see how much I need you? Why can't you understand how badly I want you there?

'Ah, no bother,' I said.

My world was collapsing but of course I didn't make a sound.

'Just thought I'd let you know, Dad, no big deal either way.'

The rest of the call continued in this way. A polite and understanding conversation taking place several time zones away from the turmoil inside me, from the twenty years of hurt and confusion, all of which now seemed totally worthless.

'The chances of you getting some game time are fairly remote, isn't that right? It's an awfully long way to go, too,' he said.

I was full of understanding. I started to scold myself for ever thinking it was viable.

'Ah, OK. Yeah, that's fair enough. I suppose it is a bit of a trek. And, yeah, I'm unlikely to be involved,' I said. I stopped short of saying 'Sorry for bothering you', as if I'd cold-called him on a Tuesday evening to sell him some double-glazing.

But I found myself beating myself up for even raising it.

'If you don't mind, maybe we'll leave it to another time, maybe in the future. Please God there'll be plenty of other opportunities,' he said.

'Please God,' I said.

We chatted for another couple of minutes about how I was enjoying things with the squad and then we said goodbye.

I had made that call in my hotel room and I didn't leave it. I stayed where I was, reflecting on what I'd just heard. My old man would pass on the chance to watch me play in the World Cup Finals.

Maybe it was time to accept that football couldn't do what I'd always imagined it could do. No matter how far up the ladder I went, my dad would never be impressed. There was nothing more I could do, so maybe it was time to admit it would never happen. Maybe it was time to acknowledge the flaw in my thinking all along. Why did I believe he would care if I kept scoring goals or winning matches? It was either time to look for other ways of getting him to be proud of me or to accept it would never materialise the way I'd hoped.

Despite all that, I slept surprisingly well the night before the game. Or maybe it was because of all that.

I believe something changed that night. Football was not going to bring myself and my dad together. That night, the night before my Ireland debut, a part of me finally understood something I had been struggling my whole life to accept. So I slept well. There was no longer the need to strive for perfection. There was no longer the desire to fix everything through what I did on a football field.

The following evening, I played for my country for eighteen minutes.

And I never played for Ireland again.

10

Running to Stand Still

Three weeks after playing for Ireland, I hurt my hip. We were away at Barnsley. Ten minutes into the game, I attempted a shot with my right foot. A defender blocked the ball as I struck it and I got a piercing pain in my hip. It was sore, but nothing major. Nobody did anything wrong, there was no foul and I didn't win a free kick. It didn't enter my head to go off and get treatment. I said nothing about it at the time and carried on. I imagined it might be one of those injuries that simply went away – the kind of injury I'd rarely had. It was banal and unremarkable. But then again, the end of a professional footballer's career is banal and unremarkable to most people except the professional footballer.

I was twenty-three and things would never be the same. I was twenty-three and I was too young for this to be happening to me.

But it *was* happening to me. My body was doing this to me and I had to sit there and take it.

There have been times when I saw this hip injury as the final act of sabotage from a body that was out to get me. My body, I realise now, was never capable of supporting the career of a professional footballer and, in this final act – or what should have been the final act – that was becoming clear.

Other times, mostly while in therapy, I have wondered whether this was one of the rare times when my mind and body were working in tandem. I hadn't outgrown my wish for Dad to really notice and be proud of me, all the while assuming football was the only way to achieve it. But after the conversation before the Russia game, I was slowly realising football wasn't going to make this happen. Maybe this was my body's unconscious decision to bail out. It's not the kind of question that can ever be answered, but I know I'd have dismissed it as waffle if it had been put to me at the time. Whatever was happening, it was the start of a decline that wouldn't end with my retirement eighteen months later. That's when the real decline would only begin.

———

The evening of the Barnsley match, after the bus journey to London, I knew I was in trouble. When I woke up the following morning, I couldn't move.

I couldn't train for the next two days, so I was given some injections to help me start the game the following Tuesday night, but I limped off after twelve minutes.

The following week a surgeon told me I needed an operation. Millwall were fourth in the league, on course to make the play-offs for promotion to the Premier League, I had recently been capped and I had already been called up for the next international. The World Cup was three months away. This was neither the time nor the place. My plan was better: plough on through the pain.

Naturally I couldn't do it on my own. I tried painkillers and injections and resting. Nothing worked. I've no idea what was in the injections, but it didn't matter to me.

I sat out training as often as I could. If I trained too much, I'd make things worse. If I did too little, I wouldn't be picked. If I wasn't going to be picked, there was no point in delaying the operation. There were holes in my plan, for sure – namely having a hip that required surgery – but I was desperate to keep playing, desperate to help Millwall reach the Premier League and desperate to make the World Cup squad.

I rested for a fortnight and then declared myself fit. I started one game, came on as a substitute the following week and was named as a sub for the game at home against Wolves after that. I had a noticeable limp as I warmed up along the touchline, and during half-time, when substitutes stay out on the pitch to get a feel for the ball, I didn't touch it once. We won the game, but I wasn't brought on. It was obvious to everyone after that night that I couldn't continue.

Putting the operation off was no longer an option. The most basic groin and hip stretches were causing me pain. If I wanted to play again, I needed an operation, exactly as the surgeon had advised a month earlier.

I had the surgery at the end of April 2002. I knew by now that I was going to miss the World Cup. Millwall's push for promotion would continue without me. I woke up after the operation, still groggy from the medication. The surgeon was doing the rounds and popped in to see me.

'How did it go, doc?'

He started to explain the physiology of my hip and the details of the procedure he had just performed. He had misunderstood my question. I only wanted to know how soon I'd be back fit.

'Twelve weeks,' he said. 'Best case.'

'Oh, right. Actually, while I have you, what's the worst case?'

'The worst case is you'll never play again.'

His words detonated in the room.

Nobody had even hinted at this prior to surgery. I had seen it as just another interruption to my career, not its end.

'Fuck off! What are the chances of that?'

I expected a small number. One per cent. Five per cent, tops.

'About twenty-five per cent.'

I didn't hear a word after that. The full impact of it really didn't hit me while I was still groggy from the anaesthetic. Then I laughed it off, saying 75 was a bigger number than 25, and I didn't bring it up again. Nobody else was there when the surgeon gave me those odds, so I was able to decide for myself who else should know. That was an easy decision: nobody. Nobody should know. If you don't talk about a problem, it doesn't really exist. Soon I was able to pretend *I* hadn't really heard it at all.

I was living alone at the time, so I asked Hicksy to move in to help me recover. I would be on crutches for twelve weeks, so I needed assistance. The original plan was that he would stay until I was back on my feet, but that's not how things turned out.

Two weeks later, Millwall were beaten in the play-off semi-finals, conceding a 90th-minute goal at home in the second leg. I watched from the stands on crutches, and when I hobbled down to the dressing room afterwards, the door was locked. Mark McGhee didn't want any intrusions – understandable given what had just happened – but I wasn't happy about being excluded. It was a glimpse of life as a non-footballer and I didn't like it. Even though we were told to wait outside, I felt I belonged inside that dressing room. I banged on the door until someone opened it. I went inside and it was horrible. Even Dion Dublin was in tears. This was strange. He had only been at the club a couple of weeks, but everyone saw his weeping as another example of what a great guy he was. I thought it was bullshit, perhaps because I was so angry at not being part of it.

The season was over but I went into the summer of 2002 feeling positive, expecting to regain full fitness and play for Ireland again. After that, everything would work out. Anything was possible. Apart from the constant pain whenever I moved, there was no real reason to think I wouldn't be among the 75 per cent.

I went to Faliraki in Greece with my mates from Dublin and watched Ireland's World Cup group games there. Instead of being in Japan and South Korea, I was drunk by the pool with a tricolour wig on my head the whole time. I figured it was the next best thing. I was back in the House of Sin for the Spain game. Niall Quinn was interviewed immediately after the penalty shoot-out defeat, and he named me as one of his likely replacements now that he was retiring. I knew I would need an experienced agent, so I got one. As a sweetener the agency gave me £50,000 up front to demonstrate their long-term commitment to me and my career. Other companies were offering me the same. They said it was an advance on what they would earn from negotiating my next contract so it was all above board. I just needed to get fit.

But every twinge would bring up the doubts. When I came off crutches, I wasn't pain-free as the surgeon said I would be. I was bouncing uncomfortably on a little trampoline when I should have been running. I was aqua-jogging in the local pool when I should have been shooting. The further behind I fell in my schedule, the more desperate I was to make up the time, so I rushed back as soon as I had a few days without pain. I joined the squad for full training four days before our first game of the season and declared myself fit.

I ignored my body telling me it wasn't ready. It had let me down so often, why listen to it now? The quicker I returned, the quicker I could forget the surgeon's calculations. I needed a run in the team to get a transfer or another Ireland call-up. More important, there was a real fear of losing the one thing I had always relied on: football. I didn't recognise the feelings of dependence then, but I recognised the fear. I had nothing but fear.

As far as most people were concerned, I was recovering well because I was in contention for the start of the season. I came on as a sub in our opening game, but it didn't go well. My hip flared up massively, and it felt as bad as it had before the operation. Now I was terrified; 25 per cent began to look like a very big number. One in four. Three to one.

I was honest with Gerry afterwards about the extent of my pain, but I told everyone else I wasn't worried, that it was a minor setback. The surgeon had told us we would know four months after the operation what my chances of a full recovery were. By then, he said, I would be as good as I was going to be. It was now four months since the operation and I was nowhere.

Later that evening, Niall Quinn rang me.

'How would you feel about playing against Blackburn next week in the Premier League?'

Sunderland were due to begin their season the following Saturday and their manager Peter Reid wanted to sign me.

I called over to Gerry's house to talk it through.

'Quinn just rang, Sunderland have come in for me,' I said.

'I know, son. I've spoken to the gaffer. They've agreed on seven million, eh?'

I didn't know that detail, but it didn't matter to me. Only one thing mattered at the time.

'What are the chances of me passing a medical?'

'Sorry, Sads, you've got absolutely no chance.'

Right then, for the first time, the dream seemed to be over. Reality was closing in and I was scared.

———

I couldn't stop myself from imagining what my life would be like without football, having to live day to day without the focus of an upcoming match. I would have no teammates because there would be no team. I wouldn't be fit because there would be no reason to look after myself. I wouldn't have an income because I had no skills or experience that would get me a job. I ate, drank and slept in accordance with my training schedule, so without it I would be nothing.

In some ways, it was comical to think I even had a chance. I couldn't bend over to rinse my mouth in the morning without shooting pains in my hip. Sitting in traffic, going to the cinema, standing too long or having sex were all done with great difficulty.

In October 2002 I was back in the surgeon's practice, but this time it was different. I knew the 25 per cent figure was now much higher. I wasn't on my own this time either. I was flanked by Gerry, Mark McGhee and Theo Paphitis. Managers rarely attend medical appointments with players, and chairmen never do. We weren't here for an injury update, we were here for the last rites.

I was given two choices. Option A was to retire. Without hearing option B, I rejected option A. I was only twenty-three. Option B was another operation. The doctor outlined the downsides of more surgery. The only guarantee was long-term pain without any assurance of short-term success. I would never be able to do a full pre-season training or play three games in quick succession. He said this operation would leave me more exposed to bone friction in my hip on a constant basis. At best, I would extend my career into my late twenties. It was a miserable prognosis. A guarantee of pain, uncertainty throughout my career and even more misery when I retired. Nobody in their right mind would have taken it.

I said yes straight away.

The doctor looked baffled. He wondered if I wanted to talk about it with anyone. Why would I want to do that?

The other option was an abyss, so I told nobody.

I was back on crutches for another twelve weeks after the second operation. Back to getting other people to drive me around; back to mind-numbing gentle stretching in the gym on my own; back to playing down my worries to others, even though I could think of nothing else.

Given what the surgeon said, I thought I would always feel pain of some kind so I just needed to be ready for that. This made it even harder to know when to push on or when to hold back. I couldn't wait until I was pain-free because there was no pain-free anymore.

Every movement, on or off the pitch, was a potential career-ender. The thing I was striving for – to train with the squad – could be the thing that finished me, but I hadn't left Ireland to sit in a gym on an exercise bike. I needed to be out there, even though the consequences of it going wrong could be catastrophic. House-hunting was a positive distraction. I sold the House of Sin and bought a place that had a snooker room and a backyard swimming pool. Best of all, it was a suitable home for a dog.

Brian Kerr succeeded Mick as Ireland manager at the beginning of 2003 and called me to say I was on his radar once again. He wasn't guaranteeing anything – football doesn't work like that – but he laid out the possibilities if I got fit, and those possibilities were worth pursuing.

Four months after the operation, I declared myself fit. I had missed every target but now I was training with the first team again – albeit in constant pain – so that was good enough for me.

It seems strange now that I could be so screwed but still working my way towards a return to the first team. Football is full of desperate people who are happy to believe you when you say you're on the mend. When I said I wasn't far from a comeback, everyone went with it.

At the beginning of March 2003, I came on as a sub at The Den and got a standing ovation. I had now recovered. This was a happy ending and that was what the Millwall supporters wanted to believe. I knew the truth.

I played at The Den again the following Tuesday, against Burnley, and scored what would turn out to be my final goal in professional football. My agent attended the match with some Italian associates of his. I met him briefly afterwards, and he asked me if I would consider a move to Italy if he could arrange it. Sure, I said, why not?

I was open to anything, except being open and honest with anyone about how I was feeling. My hip now accounted for about 70 per cent of all my conversations, and it was the topic I was least interested in talking about.

Ten days later I was selected to start at Selhurst Park. I knew I was in trouble that morning. I limped my way through an early-morning dog-walk but I thought I'd be fine. I got a shooting pain in my hip when I tried to pick up my new puppy, Frank. Bending over to clean up after him was agony, but because nobody from the club saw these struggles, I thought I would get away with it.

I said nothing to Gerry or McGhee before the game, pinning all my faith on the power of pre-match stretches. I couldn't sprint in the warm-up beforehand, but I thought that would improve once the game was under way. It was too sore to shoot properly, but I figured the adrenaline of the game would get me through.

I kept all this to myself, not because I had finally absorbed the Millwall code, but because of the terror that admitting any of this would bring. I was scared. I knew this was the end; I knew I couldn't keep going and the only chance I had of it not happening now was if I pretended it wasn't happening at all.

Republic of Ireland coaches Chris Hughton and Noel O'Reilly had come to watch me, but I didn't make it to half-time. The dressing rooms in Selhurst Park are in the corner of the pitch so I made my way towards them as soon as I was substituted. My head wasn't a great place to be during that walk along the touchline. Some Wimbledon fans were jeering at me. My career was effectively over and they were making wanker gestures at me as I walked past them, holding back tears. When the team came in at the interval, I was already showered.

Was this it? Was I about to become an ex-footballer? I couldn't imagine anything worse. That wasn't totally accurate. I knew there were worse things, but now I was going to be without the thing that had allowed me to escape those things.

I was in a relationship at the time with a girl I knew from Dublin. We'd been mates for years and I'd always wanted more, but I'd never told her because I thought she wasn't into me. Now we were seeing each other and, apart from my reluctance to talk about anything that was going on with me, everything was going well.

Her parents were over from Dublin that weekend so I played everything down and went out for a meal with them as planned after the Wimbledon match.

'You came off today, did you?' asked her father. They weren't football fans so they weren't at the game. 'Your hip sore again?'

It's fucked.

I'm fucked.

My career is fucked.

Everything is fucked. I don't want to talk about it.

All the time, in every situation, terror was bubbling under my cheery surface. A terror I felt could destroy me. It was something I could never acknowledge.

Why won't everyone just shut the fuck up asking me about my fucking hip?

'Ah yeah, nothing major to be honest. I'm actually well ahead of schedule with everything anyway. I'll be grand.'

'Will you be out long, d'you think? How bad is it?'

They were questions I'd been hearing for too long by then. Well-meaning, polite, obvious questions, but now they were getting too close.

'Wouldn't imagine so. The physios are great so it shouldn't be too long. Maybe I just rushed it a bit. Any craic with you? Did ye have a nice day in London?'

I wasn't ready to give up yet. Or, to put it another way, I was still too afraid to accept reality. By then I had told my family and my girlfriend that this could potentially be a career-ending injury, but I had always followed it up by saying I'd be fine. I also started talking openly to Hicksy about the possibility of retiring. Hicks had that Belfast thing of keeping quiet about everything, so I completely trusted him. We only really got into things when we were drunk, but I always relied on him to reassure me I would be OK.

Hicksy had quit football when he was twenty-one and was working night shifts on the Tube. We spoke about owning a bar on a beach abroad, which meant we'd have a lifetime of free drink. Not bad at all. We bounced around other possibilities, but it always came back to that. Fantasy stuff, but neither of us was ready to consider a nine-to-five existence.

We spoke about my injury the way a couple might talk about something they were facing together. Where will we live? What will we do?

Drinking was a big help, as I saw it. It was a break from the monotony of resting my hip and lying about the pain. Usually I would make it to the physio room for 9.15 but the control I once thought I had had slipped away. One morning I was woken up by a phone call from McGhee. It was past 10.30.

'Sads, it's the gaffer. Is everything OK?'

'Jesus, sorry, yeah, I'm grand,' I answered as breezily as possible. I was far from grand.

'Nobody has been able to get in touch with you,' he said, sounding genuinely concerned.

'I just slept in, that's all. On my way.'

The smell of booze confirmed their suspicions, but I got away with it, playing on the sympathies of everyone because of my situation. The same thing happened the following week but they weren't as understanding. The players' committee, responsible for cracking down on any disciplinary issues within the squad, fined me £500. Rather than seeing it as a sign that I was losing my way, I just complained about the injustice. How can you fuckers fine me now, knowing what I'm going through?

It was time to tell my agent what was going on, but I regretted it almost immediately. He repeated our conversation to Theo as soon as I put the phone down. Theo told Mark McGhee, and then McGhee gave me a dressing-down about my attitude. This was not the time to be negative, he said. He meant well.

It was a message I wanted to hear. Talking about how you felt, how scared you were and how everything was falling apart was just negativity. I knew that. I'd built a life on that premise. I had a solution: I'd go back to telling nobody how I felt.

———

I went back to the surgeon and had another scan on my hip. He was surprised I had made it back playing and said pain management was now the focus. I could do that. I was used to that.

During the summer of 2003, I spent every morning and afternoon in the training ground gym. Every evening I went to Gerry's house for further treatment to relieve the pain from whatever work I got through that day with him.

This wasn't normal, this wasn't progress.

By then, it had been eighteen months since I'd been pain-free. It was sore to sit or stand or walk or jog. I'd know what kind of day was ahead of me by how painful it was to get out of bed each morning.

Earlier that year, Ray Harford had been diagnosed with cancer. We didn't know how serious it was initially, but he gradually pulled back from training sessions. After a while, he was staying away from the training ground. He'd make occasional visits but wouldn't change into his training gear. He'd just sit on the bench outside the treatment room and watch the lads training, keeping a hat on his head to conceal his hair loss. In our last ever conversation that summer, he encouraged me about my comeback and said I'd play in the Premier League as soon as I made a full recovery. He put his hands against the cheeks of my face and said to keep going. He died later that summer.

A week after Ray's funeral that August, I knew I was done. I jumped to catch a ball in the pool in my backyard. Nobody was tackling me or rushing me. It was the most innocuous movement in the most relaxed setting. Some mates were there, laughing and joking on what was a beautiful sunny day.

I got out of the pool gingerly and walked into the snooker room on my own. I placed both of my hands on the table and stared at the floor. Out of habit, I started to gently swing my leg from left to right to help loosen my hip but there was little point in that now. I stopped myself crying because the lads were outside. I knew it wasn't the time or place to start telling anyone what was going on, but I knew it was time to stop trying to achieve the impossible.

I wasn't prepared to let it all come to an end in my backyard pool, so I chased another couple of highs. The plan was to lie to everyone, say I was OK and see how long I could last.

I declared myself fit to train and hobbled through a few sessions. I played down the pain and did as little in training as possible. I was in agony, so like my earliest days in the first team, I started hiding again. I was named in the matchday squad for a game at The Den. There was an absurd scene beforehand in the medical room. I was asking Gerry and McGhee whether playing in the game would impact my career-ending insurance if I retired any time soon. For some reason, I was worried coming back too many times might risk my cover for the original injury. We chatted it through as if it was a reasonable discussion to have. When I was brought on in the second half, I got yet another standing ovation, with everyone convinced that, this time, I'd beaten it.

My mum was at the game and I didn't even tell her. Mum, whom I told about everything, couldn't hear about this. I knew I would cry if I told her and if I cried there really would be something wrong. When it came to this, she was just someone else I was running from. I'm sure she knew, though. She has always been one of those mums who knows far more than she lets on. She just went to the game in the supportive way she always had.

The following Tuesday, I came on as a sub away at Stoke but I had entered a surreal stage. A professional footballer is assumed to be a fit human being, but I was a mess. No matter how many times I walked up and down the aisle of the bus on the way up the motorway, I couldn't shake off the pain and stiffness. Tying the laces of my boots was difficult. Even when I wasn't moving, my hip was throbbing. I was in constant pain.

Instead of doing the pre-match warm-up with the rest of the squad, I hung around the halfway line on my own and did some light stretches. I avoided kicking a football as much as I could, but for very different reasons than in my early days at The Den. It was just too painful.

I did nothing in the game, but I remember telling myself to appreciate the view. A football pitch is an amazing place to be when things are going the way you want. This wasn't one of those days. When the final whistle blew, I knew this was it.

A week later, on Wednesday 3 September, I walked into the medical room and asked Gerry if he had a minute for a chat in his office. I was in a bad way physically but, despite being hungover, my head was weirdly clear. The club doctor joined us. Without telling anyone, I went into training that morning knowing I was going to retire. I didn't tell family, friends, teammates, my girlfriend or my agent. I didn't even tell Hicksy. I just wanted to rip the plaster off and be done with it. I didn't want to cause a fuss or upset anyone. I didn't want to talk about it or be talked out of it.

Gerry said he'd happily support me again if I wanted to keep going. The doctor said the same. After an hour in the room together, with both of them patiently waiting for me to be the one to say it, I said what I probably should have said many months before.

'I'm gonna stop wasting everyone's time and call it a day.'

That was it. I walked out, finally in tears. I didn't make eye contact with anyone and went straight to my car. I called back an hour later to have the conversation with McGhee and his new assistant, Archie Knox. McGhee gave me a pep talk but I didn't really hear much of it. I thought so much of him and part of me felt I had let him down. I had let everyone down, every manager who had helped me on my way and anyone who had encouraged me.

'What are you gonna do now, Sads?' asked Archie.

'I'm gonna go to the pub for a few days to feel sorry for myself,' I said.

'You deserve it, son.'

When I went home, I told my girlfriend and Hicksy I had just retired. I said it as breezily as if I had just bought a coffee. They were shocked, and probably a bit put out that I hadn't spoken to either of them first. But talking about it wasn't part of my plan.

I couldn't face speaking about it now with anyone either, so I sent a group text. Everyone – family, friends, teammates – got the same message. It ended, 'Don't ring me about it because I can't be arsed talking about it. I'll speak to you whenever.'

I was sitting on a park bench when I sent that text, with Frank at my feet. He was the perfect company. He was the only one that wouldn't ask me how I was feeling.

Nearly everyone texted me back straight away. Nearly all of them said the same thing. A couple didn't. One, my friend Beano, took an unusual approach. 'Delighted. That's the best news I've heard all day. You were shite anyway.' He thought someone had got hold of my phone and assumed the message was a hoax.

The other one came from my dad. Everyone else – Beano aside – had responded with sympathy and concern, as if someone had died. Dad said something different.

'Congratulations on everything you've achieved in your career. I'm sure you'll make a huge success of whatever you decide to do next. You should be very proud of yourself. Love Dad xx.'

Once again, I was floored, but this felt different.

I thought I knew him, I thought I had him pegged but when I needed him most, he had given me the words that meant more than anyone's.

I thought of the man who'd had tears in his eyes when he came over to watch me play for Millwall for the first time. I thought of the man I had idolised and feared growing up. I thought about the man who, a year earlier, had told me he wouldn't go to watch me play at the World Cup, a man I'd hated at that moment. And – not for the last time – I wondered if I knew my dad like I thought I knew him.

11

Wrecking Ball

There are ways of retiring which provide some protection for the player. I didn't take any of them. There are ways of negotiating retirement with your club that don't leave you bitter and resentful. I ignored those options.

I was a good lad, intent on pleasing others, even as my life lay in ruins. I allowed other people to dictate what happened. Some people are altered and shaped by crisis. I just retreated. It was never very good to begin with, but soon it would get much worse.

Ideally in these situations, a player would tell the club he's thinking of retiring and negotiate a percentage of the club's insurance payment. The club doesn't get paid unless he retires, and until he does, they have to pay his full salary, even if he is no longer capable of playing football. I was earning £3,200 a week with nearly two years left on my contract, which should have provided plenty of leverage, a negotiating point for a player's agent to use, but I wasn't interested in leverage. I was interested in the whole problem going away.

I thought my life was over so I saw no point in doing anything that didn't fit in with my fatalism. I asked nobody for advice or guidance, and, without even telling my agent, I surrendered all my negotiating power by showing up at the club and simply announcing I had quit football.

After that, I attended a meeting with the club CEO and Theo Paphitis on my own, believing they'd be feeling compassionate and would throw me some scraps. This was Theo Paphitis from *Dragons' Den*. This was feeding time for him.

The legal minimum payment a club must make is six months' wages. That is all I was given. Millwall got a pay-out of £1,000,000 and kept it all. Theo mentioned the transfer fee they would have got if I'd stayed fit. He was smoking a cigar throughout the meeting and blowing the smoke straight across the table into my face. As a power play, it was effective, even if it slightly undermined one message they were trying to convey: that they cared about my welfare.

The main thrust of Theo's message was that they were the real losers in all of this. My retirement was costing them millions, whereas I had my health and the rest of my life ahead of me. He was on my side, he told me, as smoke caught in my throat. To prove it, he played a voicemail from my agent. It was harmless, although at one point he said something like, 'As you know, we have a stake in Sads.' Theo wanted me to see that the agent saw me as a commodity. Millwall were different. They cared.

The club said they'd give me a benefit match. There would be a golf day and a benefit dinner, too. In the small print of the settlement they said they would *host* a benefit match – which is an entirely different thing. It would be up to me – and me alone – to attract opposition to play at The Den, which could involve a fee.

There was no need to drive a wedge between me and my agent because, as it was, he was threatening to take me to court unless I repaid him the £50,000 he'd advanced me on future earnings. He claimed that, by retiring, I had denied him the right to earn back the money he had given me when I signed up with him. I was wary of asking another agent for advice because that would have been a further breach of the agreement I had signed with my agent.

I was clueless and heartbroken and mostly hungover. Whatever was happening to me, as usual, I felt I deserved.

I handled my own media too, stumbling through a series of interviews which I felt should have taken place with sirens flashing in the background: they were at the scene of an accident, not talking to someone looking forward to the next stage of his life.

Sky Sports News sent a camera to my house to do a piece with me in my backyard. I wore a Dublin GAA jersey because it was the only clean bit of clothing I had in the house. My mates Kitt and McGrath were standing behind the camera baring their arses to make me laugh. When I'd announced my retirement, they'd immediately booked flights to London. I hadn't asked them to come over but it didn't surprise me that they did. We had that kind of friendship, and we still do.

I arranged to do a phone interview with an Irish newspaper but forgot all about it. By the time the reporter called, I was already drunk, which was a risk you took if you called me any time after noon. I handled it well enough, though I went on some tirade about medical science being able to change men into women but being helpless to fix my hip. You couldn't buy that kind of publicity.

My act seemed to fool people. One paper wrote at the time that 'the poise and grace with which he has reconciled himself to the end of his soccer life suggests that Sadlier is, as Housman had it, a "Smart lad, to slip betimes away/From fields where glory does not stay". I wasn't sure about the poetry, but people were buying my front.

I was happy to keep telling this version of my story. I went on *The Dunphy Show* with Keith O'Neill, who had also recently retired. It was my first experience of a live chat show, and my first time meeting Eamon Dunphy. I kept the uglier sides of my story to myself and spoke about the excitement of taking on a new job. It was a polished act.

My dad was in the audience that night. Eamon talked to him during the programme and he said he was amazed I had kept fighting with my injury for as long as I had. He was proud of me, he said, and he had no doubt I would make a success of whatever I did. Once again, when I needed him, he was there.

There was sympathy for me out there and help was available if I wanted it. But the problem was me. I didn't want anything. I didn't feel I deserved it. This was my failing.

My phone was ringing all the time, but I just wanted it to stop. Robbie Keane called to offer to play in any testimonial I arranged. Brian Kerr left the kind of voicemail you'd like your kids to hear one day, but I deleted it as soon as I heard it. The last thing I wanted was someone telling me how well things might have gone if I had recovered from the injury.

I needed to numb the pain and drink wasn't enough. Nobody was going to randomly drug test me now, so I happily added drugs to my retirement plan.

Three weeks after I retired, I was in a mate's apartment in London when I took cocaine for the first time. It was no big deal, everyone else was doing it.

Just as there was no hard decision when I started to drink as a teenager, there was no dilemma for me now. The only reason I hadn't previously taken drugs was because I could have been banned from playing. I knew footballers who took them anyway but I wasn't one of them. Now I wasn't a footballer, so fuck it. My life was over and nobody would care what happened to me now, so why shouldn't I? I didn't have to get up in the morning. I didn't have a job or a boss or any responsibility. My time was my own. Drinking came second to football during my career – most of the time – but now it was the undisputed number one. And now there was a bonus: the more coke I took the longer I could keep drinking.

———

When I did get a job, it didn't change how I felt. Within a month of retirement, Fintan Drury, the owner of the Irish-based sports agency

Drury Sports Management, approached me and asked me to begin working with his agency.

I initially met with Fintan's business partner Eamon McLoughlin to discuss the role. Eamon had some meetings scheduled with the Ireland squad, so we arranged to meet in their team hotel on the morning of their friendly with Canada in November 2003. I didn't want to meet any of the players. I was too embarrassed to explain that I was now working as an agent. When Brian Kerr saw me, he told me I'd have played in this game if I was still a footballer. He thought he was being helpful. I left Ireland's game against Canada at half-time, unable to get Brian's words out of my head. I told Eamon my hip was too sore to stay.

I took the job because I needed something to do. I was lucky to get a job with such a respected agency, but I quickly came to dislike it. While it allowed me to think I was creating a life outside football, it was too close to home. Supporting the development of the careers of others while still mourning the loss of my own was just too hard.

My role was to build relationships with their younger clients based in the UK. I was also ringing former teammates to see if they needed a new agent, something I was never comfortable doing.

Brian Kerr was one of Fintan's clients so I would drive him around England to watch games when he came over. I was now the Ireland manager's chauffeur.

My first big gig involved being in the room for Liam Miller's contract negotiations with Celtic. I was one of a three-person delegation, but I was there to say nothing. Martin O'Neill and Celtic CEO Peter Lawwell were at the other side of the table. O'Neill opened the meeting by saying that Celtic had been interested in me before I was injured, which was the last thing I wanted to hear.

Liam was transferred to Manchester United shortly afterwards. When the deal was announced I got a call from another agent congratulating me. Maybe I would have felt differently if I had known Liam for years. Maybe if I had negotiated the transfer myself, I would have felt pride.

And maybe if I wasn't in such a mess myself, I would have been able to acknowledge that it was a great day for Liam and for the company. I felt nothing.

One day I found myself sitting in Alan Lee's house in Cardiff. Following one of my cold calls, Fintan and I were there to persuade him to join the agency. Alan was a centre-forward, like I had once been. There had been a time when we had been considered rivals for a place in the Ireland squad, but Alan didn't have to worry about me any more.

I sat in the kitchen as Fintan delivered the pitch. I had nothing to say. I sat in silence, thinking that the darkest thoughts I had were better than this.

Why are you here?

You're just Fintan's gimp, why are you doing this?

This is no life.

Is this it?

———

A football club's Christmas party is a red-letter day in most players' calendars. Millwall's was always taken seriously. Everyone attended and it was scheduled to take place at a time when we could get a couple of days off training.

From the moment I retired, I had this in my head as a hurdle I would have to clear. Later, when I stopped drinking, I would feel the same about weddings and Christmas, but then I had help. I was going to do this on my own.

For a couple of months, I knew I would have choices to make. Would I go? How would I manage it if I went? When would I go? How long would I stay? And, most important, how would I survive the questions I'd be asked?

I had tried to steer clear of the other Millwall players since I'd retired. I was living with Hicksy and my girlfriend and there was some overlap with certain players. I lived a mile from the training ground and I couldn't avoid them, but the Christmas party was something else, the Christmas party was a time for players.

It was traditionally a time for others too, although not in the standard Christmas sense. A lot of Christmas parties can become a bit loose, but Millwall's could be debauched, featuring a cast of characters that could make the rest of the year look tame.

The Christmas party followed a certain format. The afternoon was for the dressing room only. It was understood that, even though I was no longer part of the dressing room, I was welcome to attend the magical hours between two and seven when it was just for Millwall . . . and whatever lap dancers they'd invited along.

After that, anything goes. In the weeks leading up to the party, the youngest players in the squad would be sent into the nail bars, hairdressers and beauticians of Bromley to hand out invitations to the best-looking women.

Before the invited guests arrived, we – the Millwall squad and I – drank for five hours on our own and I had the same conversation twenty times.

'How are you, Sads?'

'How you getting on, Sads?'

'Alright, Sads, how you been, mate?'

I had one answer, one response, one lie that I'd roll out in return, in different variations.

'Ah, I'm grand, glad to be getting on with things.'

'Ah I'm grand, happy out.'

'Ah I'm grand, you know yourself.'

But I wasn't grand. I wasn't grand that day. I wasn't grand any day. I wasn't happy fucking out. The only thing that stopped me thinking about killing myself was the thought of drinking and drugging myself into oblivion, but on a day like this, surrounded by my old teammates, even that prospect wasn't appealing. I guess if I didn't want to be asked about my football career, I shouldn't have spent time with footballers.

During the private part of the private party, two glamour models were on the stage, dancing and performing sex acts on one another. They were well known to their audience as they featured regularly in the *Daily Sport* newspaper, and they had a man with them stopping anyone taking pictures. When the women called for volunteers to join them, the younger lads were put forward, whether they liked it or not. Much to everyone's amusement, they were too nervous to become aroused, so they were discarded by the women until others were ready to step up.

I knew then, as I know now, that I wasn't in a position to judge anyone. I just sat at the bar detached from the madness like a 35-year-old senior pro who had outgrown it all. But I hadn't outgrown it. I was only 24, not much older than the lads being encouraged and jeered, and the ones doing the laughing were all my mates. I felt I didn't belong there, but I also felt I didn't belong anywhere else. In this empty nightclub on a December afternoon, I was lost. It was bleak and grim and depressing, in line with my mood.

As the afternoon went on, it became clear that this had been a bad idea. The more drink we all consumed, the more each player became convinced I needed a pep talk. It turned out 'Alright, Sads. How you been, mate?' was only the start. They all had a little party piece lined up, a little Christmas message for me.

The drunker they got, the more intent they were on delivering this uplifting talk. A boost to remind me how good I could have been, what potential I had, what Millwall had lost. What I had lost.

One by one, they gave me this speech and one by one I saw them off. Then I headed to the bathroom and saw Tim Cahill walking towards me. I sensed this would be bad. Tim was going places, we all knew that. More important, Tim knew that. He was brilliant and he never doubted it. We loved him for his confidence. I might have loved him most of all for it because he was not like me. But not tonight.

Not now, Tim, mate. Just leave me alone, Tim. Don't tell me what I've lost.

To be fair to Tim, that wasn't his style. It was about 7pm and we were about five hours into the party. The one thing I knew about Tim was that he wouldn't keep me long.

'You know what, Sads?' he said, when he caught up with me at the bathroom door. He was going to tell me, no matter what. 'Seeing that you can't play ever again, and knowing that I still can, means that I'm absolutely fucking buzzing.'

His intention, I think, was to say that what I was going through made him appreciate his career even more. Maybe he was aiming for a broader point about the nature of destiny or fate or something philosophical like that. It came out differently.

Tim was so buzzing that he couldn't even get the words out properly because I remember thinking, *that doesn't make sense.* But I understood enough. This wasn't the place for me. This was the worst possible place for me.

'Sorry mate, I'll be back in a minute,' I said.

I was about to start crying again, so I headed for the door. I couldn't get a cab home because all the drivers in the area were Millwall fans and I didn't want them to see me in this state. It was only a mile and a half to my house anyway, so I walked. It was pitch dark and pissing down rain, so even if I passed someone on the street, I could hide the tears.

Thankfully, some English friends were back in the house. After a few lines of coke and several cans of Stella, I was good to face the world again. Later that night, I went back to the Millwall party to show everyone I still had it, I was still the Sads they loved. I was doing grand and to prove it I brought everyone back to mine afterwards.

When I woke up the next day I was still faced with the same reality, though, and it was getting harder and harder to believe things would ever improve. The thing that had put me in this mood couldn't be undone. This was going to be my life from now on.

During my descent following retirement, I kept looking for a way back. Part of me could never accept that my career was over, so I would occasionally pursue other options. I tried ointments, magnets, needles, prayers.

I went to a faith-healing nun in Kilmacud in Dublin, whom I'd heard about from a family friend. She had worked wonders with a man undergoing chemotherapy. I figured a hip injury, by comparison, would be a doddle to her. I sat for hours with magnets positioned carefully around my hip. I applied ointments to the area and took tablets that helped to rid my body of various toxins, while at the same time filling it with drink and drugs. She said she was praying for me. Of course, neither of us at the time fully appreciated the help I really needed.

I contacted an acupuncturist I had heard about in Frankfurt. I half-kidded myself that I was doing it for pain relief, but I knew the ultimate aim was a return to playing professionally. I went to see him for ten days. In every session he would insert over a hundred needles around my hip. He said he had visions regularly and these visions involved me being happy in my life again. A return to football was my only conception of such a scenario.

It was all desperate, but that's what I was. Nothing made a difference.

My girlfriend was still living with me at the time, but this version of me wasn't able for that to continue. There was always the danger she would ask me how I was feeling – those things happen in relationships – and I didn't want that. So I pushed her away. As Christmas approached, she moved back to Dublin. Maybe I would follow, maybe I wouldn't. I had no idea what I wanted other than to be on my own.

The girl I'd been mates with and fancied since I was 15, one of the soundest, most decent, caring, trustworthy people I knew, was banished.

I needed to be alone for another reason, too. I didn't want her to find me if I killed myself.

I didn't always think this way, but when I considered all my options, suicide seemed to be as good as, if not better than, a lot of them. I never once said it to anyone, not even to Hicksy, for obvious reasons, but the fact that I was contemplating it made me turn on myself even more. The Millwall way was to persevere through pain, something I had tried and failed at, but I now realised I couldn't even deal with a normal life.

You pathetic little prick.

There wasn't much that could lift these feelings.

My life had become as messy as the thoughts in my head. The prospect of suicide was becoming more and more appealing. While I could put on an act in company, I would cry when I was on my own. I was hungover most days, which meant I was miserable almost all the time. It got to the point where, three months after retiring, I contacted a solicitor to draw up a will. I was still waiting on an insurance payment of £500,000, so that would be enough to soften the blow for the family. The idea was to fill my jacket pocket with rocks and jump into the pool in the backyard, a scene I remembered from the film *Down and Out in Beverly Hills*.

I never got as far as standing on the edge of the pool, or anything as dramatic as that. I didn't wake up any morning thinking I would die that day, but it seemed like the only course of action that would ease my pain. As far as I was concerned, there wasn't another way. This felt like a rational, practical solution to my many problems.

At the time, I had no understanding of the short-term nature of feelings like this. They're distressing, intense, painful and real, and they feel like they'll last for ever, but they pass if the right support is sought at the right time. And in most cases, and thankfully in mine, they don't return.

———

I had a little previous experience of therapy. In January 2001 I started to cry on the pitch during the team warm-down after a league game against Bournemouth. I was in conversation with one of the coaches jogging round the pitch when I felt myself well up and I knew I was in trouble. If the Millwall Christmas party is the worst place to start crying, doing it in front of the whole team after a match is probably a close second.

I pretended I needed to tie my lace, buying time to hide my tears and compose myself. I got back up when I knew I was ready, jogged back to the group and said nothing. My main concern was ensuring that nobody around me knew I was struggling, but that moment also made me realise it was time to say it to somebody.

It hadn't come out of the blue. I'd been finding it hard to sleep, I'd been struggling to motivate myself to get out of bed, but there wasn't any specific reason I could think of to explain it. Nothing had happened around that time to throw me off course. I mentioned it to my mum and she knew of someone in London I could see. So I went to see a therapist.

I was living with Robbie Ryan at the time, but I didn't feel like I could even tell him that I was attending therapy. Every week, we'd have the same exchange.

'Where are you off to?' he'd ask.

'Going to see a man about a dog,' I'd say.

I always smiled knowingly as if to say it was something pretty exciting. I think he assumed I was having some sort of illicit affair. Obviously, I was happy to play along with this. Far better to be thought of as a roguish lothario than someone who needs therapy.

I had no idea how to begin a session. I didn't know what to say first or which bits to leave out. I didn't know what parts of my background were relevant to how I was feeling, even if I could have found the words to express this. I was pretty sure of one thing, though. I was confident the therapist wouldn't tell me I should be grateful to be a professional footballer and that plenty of people would swap places with me in an instant. I was sure he wouldn't dismiss me like I thought everyone else would.

Depression was ruled out in the first session after he asked me to complete a questionnaire. It's a fairly crude measure, but he seemed confident that wasn't my problem. I wasn't there for a diagnosis or a label anyway. I was there to feel better. Like every consultation I've had with doctors and physios about my injuries, I was always more concerned with putting things right than with learning about what was wrong.

But just like our collective response to Dad getting help with his drinking years earlier, I somehow felt ashamed to be in this position. Seeking help wasn't something you spoke about openly to others. I told nobody, and went to weekly or fortnightly sessions for about four months.

Therapy was perfect. It meant nobody needed to know I was struggling in any way. I was being helped with whatever was wrong, without, as I saw it at the time, the risk of ruining my reputation. It helped a lot, but I'm not sure exactly why. Maybe I just needed to talk, to hear myself say that I sometimes found my life a bit overwhelming. I might have needed to hear myself say that being a professional footballer at a place like Millwall could be difficult, that living away from family and friends was difficult. That being me, for no reason I could think of at the time, was often difficult. No label or diagnosis or medication was required. Talking through my difficulties with a trained professional was what was needed.

Facing this crisis after retirement, when I thought regularly of suicide, I felt it was time to ask for help again, so I reached out to a therapist I knew. A year before retirement, I had enrolled in a three-year sports science degree. There was a psychology module on the course which specifically mentioned the benefits of working with a therapist for elite athletes who had retired in the circumstances I had. I approached the lecturer afterwards on my own. I didn't know if, ethically, lecturers could see students for therapy, but I was pretty desperate.

'Everything OK?' she asked.

Butter wouldn't melt. Me with Anna, Catherine and Jamie (left to right), the soundest three siblings I could have wished for.

Me, Catherine and my dog Shambles during my eye-patch and glasses phase. Unfortunately, I still can't see a bloody thing with my left eye.

Me on Dad's lap, Jamie on Mum's. It's weird to think we had a life that didn't involve Anna or Catherine.

We took out the posh garden furniture just for this photo.

Broadford Rovers, where it all began for me.

Completely star struck receiving the Player of the Year award from Andy Townsend, club patron of Broadford Rovers at the time.

Brian Kerr, one of the most influential people in Irish football in the last twenty-five years.

Celebrating my opening goal against Australia in Nigeria with Robbie. One of the happiest moments of my life. (© *David Maher / SPORTSFILE*)

An emotional lap of honour after our defeat at Wembley Stadium, two days after I arrived back in London from the U-20 World Cup. (*Courtesy of Brian Tonks*)

A rare appearance on the dancefloor by me, with Granny Aggie (82) at the official club dinner that night.

Chuffed with the purchase of my first home, aged 19. Within a month it became known as The House of Sin.

Danny Tiatto and myself in what was a typical scene from our games with Manchester City back then.
(© *PA Images*)

Ireland v Russia, February 2002. Playing for Ireland was all I ever wanted to do, but it took years before I could look at this squad photo and not feel like an imposter. When I look at it now, I'm just reminded of the memorable few days I spent with them all. (Top © *Ray McManus / SPORTSFILE*; centre © *David Maher / SPORTSFILE*; bottom © *Damien Eagers / SPORTSFILE*)

I watched the 2002 World Cup in Falaraki with my best mates from Dublin. The next best thing to being there.

Myself and Hicksy: alcohol-fuelled superheroes.

Six years after retiring, saying thanks and goodbye to The Den. (*Courtesy of Brian Tonks*)

Getting my Psychotherapy MA in 2014. It turns out I was right to stay and do my Leaving Cert before going to Millwall.

The Football Men. Watching Ireland with John, Eamon and Darragh from our studio in the Aviva. (© *Sportsfile / Getty Images*)

With Murph (l) and Eoin (r). Working with Second Captains is one of the most enjoyable things I do. (*Courtesy of Second Captains*)

I don't think I'd have written this book if I hadn't interviewed Paul Stewart on *The Player's Chair* in 2017.

My career as a football coach was brief, but unforgettable. Working with the young offenders in St Patrick's Institute led me to a lot of the work I do with adolescents today. (© *Dave Connachy, The Independent Newspaper*)

Running a 5k race for the Together for Yes campaign in May 2018. With Eoin McDevitt, David O'Doherty and Mark Horgan. (© *Paul Sharp/Sharppix*)

On the *Late Late Show* in April 2019, speaking about the sexual health module I ran in St Benildus – not exactly what I would have predicted for myself years earlier. (© *RTÉ Stills Library*)

Any day you make it to the Forty Foot is a good day, but this one was special. Celebrating my fortieth birthday with Fiona and Dad in January 2019.

There's no place like home if you live with these two, Bobbi and Joey. (*Courtesy of Julie Cummins Photography*)

My wife, Fiona, the most incredible person I know. (*Courtesy of Julie Cummins Photography*)

This book is dedicated to my family, pictured here with me on my wedding day. I don't know where I'd be without their support. (Left to right) Jamie, Anna, Dad, Mum and Catherine. (*Courtesy of Julie Cummins Photography*)

'Nah, I'm fairly fucked, to be honest, with retirement and everything. I never used to be like this. Any chance of booking me in for a session?'

I spent several months in therapy in 2004, but, once again, I didn't want anybody to know. Everyone else got the fake version of me, but the therapist got the truth. I began speaking openly about what it was like to be in my shoes. I didn't have to worry who would hear what I told her because I knew she wasn't allowed to repeat it. She didn't tell me how I should feel or go on about how grateful I should be; she just let me talk or cry, whatever I needed.

We didn't go too deeply into the origins of my feelings or try to gain a greater understanding of the enormity of my loss. Her approach was a form of cognitive behavioural therapy (CBT). It was about focusing my thoughts and efforts on what I wanted to achieve. It was about looking ahead and creating the kind of life I wanted to live.

The sense of freedom I had when I walked into each session was immense. I could be terrified, anxious or shut down, but I also felt safe. I could say what I wanted in this room. Slowly, the worst feelings passed. Sometimes I would even think I might be OK. I showed up thinking I had no options, but before long we would discuss which opportunities I'd like to explore. Everything was back on the table – coaching, management, scouting, media work, college. Would I stay in London or go back to Dublin or travel the world? I had the finances and freedom to do what I liked, and the therapy sessions made that clear.

But those feelings didn't last for long beyond the sessions. I moved away from thinking about suicide but instead felt despair that this was my life. Even if I could imagine occupying my time in some way, I thought I would always be weighed down by the heartache of everything I had lost. My life wouldn't be perfect – not that it ever was – but I had come round to the realisation that it certainly wasn't worth ending.

During my final session with the therapist, I remember thinking her job satisfaction must be pretty high. She had brought me from a place where I thought my life was over to a place where I could see I had some options (as long as one of those options didn't involve not drinking or taking drugs). I wondered whether her job was for me, but I quickly talked myself out of it. I had never heard of any footballers who had become therapists. On top of that, I figured being a bloke would go against me too. Women are just better at this than men.

———

While things settled a little in my head, they stayed fairly chaotic in my house. Before one Friday night party, some mates took the big mirror off my sitting-room wall and placed it on the snooker table, using it to chop a load of cocaine into smaller amounts. By the end, we had about sixty bags. The party lasted for three days solid, and by Monday morning the place was covered in blood-soaked tissues from all our nosebleeds. I was a paranoid mess by the end, convinced everybody in the house was slagging me.

When we finally ran out of coke, I was asked for the number of a doctor mate I knew.

'Is this Tony?'

'Yeah, who's this?'

'We're mates of Richie's. Listen, what household products – Domestos or shit like that – could we snort that would give us the most high, but do the least damage? We ain't got no drugs left.'

Tony cut to the chase.

'Go to bed, lads.'

Another night I got chatting to a girl I hadn't met before. We got on well and ended up in bed together. She was a porn actress and she was kicking herself the following day that we hadn't used protection. As usual, I could barely remember what had happened the night before. She said her job requires her to keep on top of her sexual health, so our first date was to get a health screening in a clinic. We both got the all-clear and went for pizza. It was the first serious conversation I'd ever had about the importance of contraception and the need to tend to my sexual health regularly. I could now add the porn industry to professional football as my primary educators in this area.

We saw each other casually for a few months until she was sent to prison for some financial irregularities. I visited her while she was in there and picked her up on the morning of her release. She had a 7pm curfew every day, so she had to wear an electronic tag on her ankle. I probably could have done with something similar to rein me in.

———

In some ways, I still had the lifestyle of a professional footballer, but with more pizza, more lager and no football. I had more cash than I'd ever had in my life because I was living off the windfalls that were coming my way, so I could still feel like money was coming in, even if my income had dropped by 75 per cent. I cashed in my pension and settled with the insurance company for £375,000. They had been trying to link my hernia operation in 1997 to my hip injury six years later so they could pass it off as a 'wear and tear' injury to reduce my pay-out. I could have taken them to court for the rest but I didn't have the stomach for the fight.

My former agent was still threatening to sue me, so I agreed to repay him 75 per cent of the advance he'd given me. He might have backed down if I'd called his bluff, but problems I could make go away with money I made go away with money.

I was still working with Fintan Drury even though I knew from the beginning it wasn't for me. I tried to persuade myself it would improve when I felt better, although I wasn't doing a lot to make myself feel better. I thanked Fintan and Eamon for giving me the opportunity and I resigned.

In April 2004 I was appointed head of youth recruitment at Millwall Academy. In another life, I might have been suited for this role, but not at this time, not in this life.

Dennis Wise was now the first-team manager. He'd arrived at the club after being sacked by Leicester City for breaking a teammate's jaw in a hotel fight. He was perfect for Millwall.

He pushed for my appointment. My role was to oversee the scouting operations for nine- to sixteen-year-olds. As well as having to tell kids they were being released by the club, my job was to monitor the progress of the ones we hoped would make it.

One Sunday morning at a game, I had to ask one of the coaches to be a buffer between myself and everyone else on the side-line. I would pretend I was busy on the phone or taking down important notes if anyone came too close. I had been up all night and had come to the game straight from a party in my house. I was off my head on coke. The smart move might have been to stay at home, but I felt nothing was beyond me when I was high. An even better move might be to not take coke if your job in any way relates to the welfare of kids.

I was also taking my first steps into journalism. I had a column with the *Sunday Independent* for the six months after I'd left Millwall, ghost-written by Dion Fanning. And I was starting to get regular punditry work on Setanta Sports' coverage of the Premier League. The studios were in Glasgow so I'd fly up and back on the same day. I was on with Ronnie Whelan mostly, and sometimes with Tony Cascarino. They were probably wondering why someone with my career was getting that job. I was tentative and unsure of myself. I didn't think I could be too critical of Premier League players because I had never reached that level; nor could I disagree with Ronnie or Tony because of who they were. Unsurprisingly, I was let go at the end of that season.

I had found a new pub, St Germain's, in South London that was owned and populated almost exclusively by Irish people. Every inch of the walls was decorated with Celtic or Republican memorabilia. There was no natural light in the place so it felt like another world, which also appealed to me. It became a home from home. I'd be there some mornings when it opened, and they would serve me long after it closed.

On Remembrance Day on Setanta, they were handing out poppies. I insisted I couldn't wear one. I had no strong feelings either way, but I liked St Germain's and I was pretty sure how they'd react in the pub. I didn't want to jeopardise my place in my new home. Thankfully, I talked Ronnie Whelan and the presenter around.

Another day in St Germain's I happened to be on the phone to Anna. For some reason, I found myself asking her how she felt about Dad moving out. 'Jesus,' she said, 'I was wondering if you'd even noticed. It's been two years and you haven't mentioned it once.' I realised I'd made a terrible mistake bringing this up and ended the conversation as quickly as I could. My friends in the pub needed me.

My parents' marriage was another topic I would ignore as much as I could.

———

Anna and Catherine came over to stay with me one summer to get away from things at home. My parents were going through a bad spell and escaping to London was a good idea. I thought it was a good idea too as long as they never talked about it.

After they'd gone, sometime in 1999, I got a call one evening from Mum. She told me herself and Dad were considering splitting up. There was nothing immediate planned in terms of selling the house or either of them moving out. When I sat back down on the couch, Hicksy asked me who had rung.

'It was my mum. Herself and Dad are splitting up.'

He said nothing. I said nothing. And then I shared my deepest feelings on the matter with him.

'We're going to the pub.'

Hicksy was happy with that. We didn't go to the pub to talk it through. I didn't go to tease out my feelings about it. I wasn't that kind of bloke. I didn't bring it up once, but later that night, Hicksy did.

'So your parents, eh?'

'Yep,' I said and moved the conversation on to something else.

Talking about it wasn't going to change it, so what was the point?

Despite having made the decision to split years earlier, Dad didn't actually move out until 2004. I had spent little time at home since I was seventeen. When I did go back to Dublin, I would spend the weekend on the piss. Any deterioration in my parents' marriage was something I could easily ignore. When they came to visit in London it was harder. One time, on the morning of a game, I said to Mum that in future I might invite them separately. It had been tense when they visited but I didn't ask her what was going on between them, instead I came up with a solution which allowed me to ignore it.

I figured the arrival of a second dog would improve my situation, so myself and Hicksy tracked down another Victorian bulldog, just like Frank, and named him Paddy. I'd have someone else to hang out with now that would never ask me how I was doing.

In May 2004 Millwall reached the FA Cup final, which added to my misery. I had retired eight months earlier and now I was the one who missed out, the tragic story of what might have been. If the media like one thing better than a fairytale, it's a tragedy.

I had a BBC camera crew following me on the day of the semi-final, which was against Sunderland at Old Trafford. Instead of being on the pitch (for either club), I was sitting hungover in the stands with Hicksy, explaining to the BBC what it was like to be missing out. I knew all the right things to say.

'I'm obviously gutted I'm not there myself, but I'm also delighted for my former teammates and so many Millwall supporters I know. It's an incredible achievement for the club.' I wasn't delighted for anyone; all I felt was misery for my own situation.

My BBC pass allowed me anywhere, so I headed down the tunnel and into Millwall's dressing room after the game. There were celebrations everywhere, but I was instinctively drawn to Kevin Muscat, who had ruptured his cruciate ligament during the game.

'I'm delighted for the lads, but this is the worst day of my life,' he said. He was speaking my language.

When the segment was played on *Football Focus* the following week, they called me brave. After Sky Sports News ran my interview the day after I finished months earlier, Jim White had called me brave too. Brave? For what exactly? For failing to recover and walking away? For drinking and drugging my way to oblivion as often as I could? I could see no bravery and when they called me brave it made me angrier.

After the semi-final, some of the players approached me about leading the team out on the day of the cup final against Manchester United. Wise was the player-manager so there was an opening for someone to walk alongside Sir Alex Ferguson in a suit. My plan was to drink my way through the weekend in Cardiff. There was no room in that plan for a global television audience looking at me trying to walk out at the Millennium Stadium, so I told them to drop the idea.

I hung on by my fingernails for the final year of my sports science course. I blagged a few deadline extensions and missed a lot of lectures, but I did enough to get the degree in the summer of 2005. Then I got a call that set me on a new course for the next eighteen months. The degree wouldn't be needed now. The job in Millwall Academy could go too. It might be time to lay off the coke for a bit and lose some weight. By now I wasn't in the best of physical condition and always felt self-conscious taking my T-shirt off in the backyard pool.

The call was from Kevin Kyle, a Scottish international striker playing for Sunderland. His hip was in a bad way and he was looking for advice, or maybe just someone to talk to. There are times when professional football feels like a fellowship and this was one of them. He was just ringing to see if he could learn from what I had been through and I was happy to help him out. He was struggling too and the outlook was bleak. It got to the point where he was looking for a steer on how best to retire. I told him he'd be fine as long as he did the opposite of everything I did.

Then, like a bolt out of the blue, he told me about Dr Marc Philippon, a surgeon based in America who had developed a new procedure to repair the very hip injury I had suffered. Sunderland had sent Kyle to Colorado as a last resort to see if his career could be saved. It turns out it was exactly the right place. He made a throwaway suggestion that it might be worth exploring for myself, but even before he said it my mind was already made up.

I contacted Dr Philippon and set about trying to prove the medical world wrong. The plan was to travel to America and come back with a perfect hip. This could change everything. Soon the possibilities would be endless and the misery I was going through would be temporary.

12

The Comeback

'Let's aim for that weekend then. We're at home on Good Friday and away on Easter Monday. We'll look to get you involved for those, eh?'

It was early February 2006 and Mick McCarthy was talking to me about playing football.

I had once been too unfit to pass a medical when Sunderland wanted to sign me for £7 million in 2002, but now the plan was that I would become a Premier League player, nearly three years after I'd retired from football.

The Good Friday game was the Tyne–Wear derby at home against Newcastle. The game on Easter Monday was away at Old Trafford. And the plan was for me to be in both squads.

I kept calm as Mick was talking. I might have cocked my head to one side to suggest I was listening intently and considering his idea. Maybe I did a bit of chin-stroking to add to the impression that I might have something to contribute, perhaps a slightly different plan or an alternative schedule.

We ended the conversation and I walked away breezily, but my mind was out of control. My career was being resurrected and, more important, it felt as if I was being saved.

—

After my initial contact with Dr Philippon, I sent every document I had on what happened to my hip to the Steadman-Hawkins Clinic in Colorado where he was based. I put every other plan on hold, which was easy because I had no plans – at least, none that didn't involve drink and drugs.

This wasn't going to be cheap, but I knew it would be worth it. The clinic insisted I stay a minimum of ten days after the operation for rehab and they needed someone to travel with me. I knew just the man.

In September 2005 myself and Hicksy travelled to Colorado. We were four days early and we planned some R&R in the Rocky Mountains ahead of the operation. I had no club to pay my way so the trip was going to cost me close to £30,000. With that outlay, I thought the least I could do was stay sober for a week.

I had a series of tests on the Tuesday morning, but we found out it was White Trash Wednesday in the local bar the following night. Our minds were blown by the potential of such an event. Who were we to turn our noses up at a celebration of American culture like this? It would almost be disrespectful not to attend. Good job we had brought some going-out clothes, even if the operation was taking place thirty-six hours later.

The procedure involved taking some tissue from my IT band in my thigh and relocating it to my hip socket to replace the lost cartilage. Despite my disregard for all the advice to take it easy beforehand, the procedure was a success, but the rehab was different. Instead of being on crutches for twelve weeks, I had to cycle on an exercise bike within half an hour of waking up after the operation. I was still fairly groggy from the anaesthetic and other drugs, so I asked Hicksy to stand next to the bike in case I fell off. The faster I got moving, the faster I'd heal. I wouldn't be allowed out of the hospital until I was able to complete a thirty-minute ride.

For twelve days in Colorado, I had to sleep with my right leg in a portable machine that would continually bend my knee to keep my hip moving. When I needed to use the bathroom, Hicksy would arrive with a bedpan because I couldn't move.

I had physical therapy twice a day in the clinic. I was following all their medical advice . . . up to a point. On our last night in Denver, we went to a Carl Cox gig. It would be too risky to ask total strangers for drugs, so I stuck to drink for the night. It had been twelve days since the surgery and now I was standing in the middle of a dance floor with my crutches raised to the roof. We ended the night by playing bowling in our hotel room with bottles of Gatorade. In hindsight, it's not much of a mystery why I didn't fully recover.

———

A couple of months after the surgery, Kevin Kyle helped to arrange for the Sunderland physios to assess my progress. Later it turned out that Kevin thought I was a defender and didn't realise I was a striker who would be in competition with him. When I got to Sunderland, Kenny Cunningham and Steven Elliott took it in turns to exaggerate my scoring feats at Millwall, just to piss him off further. I did my bit too, making up elaborate stories of imaginary glory days.

The physios said it would be easiest to do the assessment next time they were in London. So before Sunderland played Arsenal at Highbury in November 2005, they examined my hip in the dressing room while the players were out doing their pre-match warm-up. All was heading in the right direction, they said. Just keep going.

I saw Mick McCarthy and apologised for the intrusion. Mick was aware of what his physios were doing and, given the positive prognosis, he invited me to continue my rehab in Sunderland. I had other options – Bolton, Cardiff and Stoke had all invited me to train with them – because news of my comeback was spreading. But having worked with

Kevin Kyle's injury, Sunderland's physios were the only ones in the UK with experience of rehabbing the operation I'd just had, so it was the best option.

I knew there were some legal and logistical things to sort out. I couldn't play for Millwall again. They would have to return the compensation they'd received if I signed a contract with them, so that was out. They'd never paid a million quid for a player, let alone one as fragile as I was. I could play for anyone else, just not them.

I wasn't entirely sure how I'd get around the fact that I'd received a pay-out myself; I just assumed that whichever club signed me would resolve it directly with the insurers. In the grand scheme of things, £375,000 isn't a huge amount.

Working with Mick was an attraction too, so in late December 2005 I finally arrived at a Premier League club. I would be playing football again. Everything would work out if my hip held together, so I put my dogs Frank and Paddy in kennels, rented a flat in Durham and threw myself into full training.

My hip was flying through every stage of the prescribed rehab programme and I was feeling great. A few minor muscle strains kept slowing me down, but I'd been told to expect that.

One morning I was too keen to join in some shooting drills before I had properly warmed up and pulled a muscle in my thigh. Mick was twenty yards away and saw me on the ground in pain. He came over and saw how disappointed I was.

'Rome wasn't built in a day, Sads. You'll be alright.'

And a few weeks later, I was. The hip was fine, so it shouldn't have bothered me as much as it did, but I was agonisingly close to playing and I was getting impatient. I was bounding comfortably over hurdles and twisting and turning around cones at pace. I was shooting, jumping, turning and landing without pain. I was about to return to professional football after an absence of three years.

Mick had bigger concerns than resurrecting my career. It was clear Sunderland were going to be relegated, possibly with the lowest points total ever achieved in a Premier League season.

There was a dark mood around the club, but not from me. I didn't care about any of that. Six months earlier I couldn't lift myself out of my car without groaning like an old man. Sunderland, as far as I was concerned, was the best place in the world.

Mick was sacked in early March and his replacement, Kevin Ball, was one of those coaches who liked to join in training sessions with the players.

One day, he tackled me a little too enthusiastically and I ended up requiring surgery on my right ankle as a result. I was well acquainted with UK hospitals by this stage, but this was the first time I'd had to pick up the bill myself. I was back on the treatment table, out of pocket again, and the manager who'd brought me to the club was no longer there.

There would be no glorious comeback for me over the Easter weekend, as I had discussed with Mick, and Sunderland's relegation was confirmed when they only drew at Old Trafford.

But things were changing at the club and soon it became known that an Irish group, the Drumaville consortium, with Niall Quinn at the head, was going to take over. Quinn, after looking for some alternatives, appointed himself as manager.

My ankle had recovered to the point where I could do most of the training for a few days in succession. In those few days, contract negotiations finally began. I asked Quinn to deal directly with Fintan Drury, my former boss, whom I'd recently taken on as my own agent.

Some parts were easier to agree than others. My starting wage was to be more than double what I'd finished on at Millwall and would rise steadily over the course of the proposed three-year deal. Sunderland would meet all the insurance repayment costs, but there was a bit of a gulf on some of the peripheral clauses. Fintan, for example, was looking for a bonus of £1 million for me if Sunderland were promoted back to the Premier League.

Quinn rang me to ask me to talk Fintan down in some of his demands. It's a classic tactic often used by clubs – get between the player and his agent and you'll save money. I said I'd do my bit, without meaning a word of it, but we both agreed that I'd have to fully recover from the ankle injury before signing anything. Maybe get through a game or two and that would be enough.

I was in the local library when I took that call. Quinn has often retold this story in interviews, saying how refreshing it was to see a modern player spending his free time in the library. I think he liked the idea of a footballer having a keen interest in literature. Years later, I put Quinn straight and told him I was only there to rent the latest box set of *The West Wing*.

Quinn may have felt he was dealing with a serious, bookish pro, but the reality was different. Despite my determination to get back to fitness, I wasn't entirely ready to abandon the lifestyle I had embraced since retirement, and it nearly put an end to my comeback.

I would still have a drink at the right time, and a drug at the right time. In acknowledgement of my healthier life, I only took half an ecstasy pill while out with some mates one weekend. Some might describe that as reckless but at the time I thought it showed there were almost no limits to the sacrifices I was prepared to make. Then I showed up at training on the Monday morning to the news that we all had to provide urine samples. Everyone was to be screened because research had linked muscular injuries to undiagnosed STIs.

I wasn't under contract, so technically they couldn't force me to give a sample against my will, but refusing would be a fairly obvious admission of something. If it was a blood test, I could have come up with something about fearing needles, but this was a urine test so I couldn't really come up with an excuse not to have a piss.

I knew an ecstasy pill was detectable for one to three days after it's taken. If you take them regularly, they're still detectable after three to five days. My test was to come on day two. I didn't trust anyone enough to ask them to sneakily provide a sample on my behalf. Pulling a sickie and going home on the morning of a test wouldn't work either.

If the test came back positive, I knew what I would do.

I would play the retirement card. I would say I'd been in a really low place and had made some bad decisions. Hell, maybe this was what needed to happen for me to get the help I needed. People don't know how to react when you play the mental health card, so that was pretty much my best option.

I was sure of one thing, though. There was no way I was going to make the same mistake as that former teammate of mine at Millwall. Until you know you've failed a test, say nothing.

I had a couple of hours to play with, so I got as much liquid into my body as possible. There was a fridge full of water and flavoured sports drinks next to the physio area and I practically emptied it.

I left it as late as I could to provide my sample, by which time the doctor had a tray full of little bottles of urine. Everyone else's looked a deep yellow due to dehydration from doing so much training. This was pre-season, in the height of summer. My sample was as clear as tap water. The doctor made some comment about it being different from all the others. 'Healthy living, Doc, you know yourself.'

All the tests then came back clear so I had no need to play any cards. My comeback was still on track.

For the final pre-season friendly in 2006 against Carlisle United, the physio cleared me to be involved in matchday activities, as long as I didn't play. I was to be an unused sub. I felt like I was making my professional debut again. My ankle was far from perfect, but I was training fully at last. I did the warm-up on the pitch with the squad before the game and ran up and down the line during the match as if I was preparing myself to go on.

I absorbed every second of it. The bus journey. The pre-match meal. The walk around the grounds of the hotel before the game. The way players behave to help ease the tension on matchdays. Admittedly there would be little cause for too much anxiety in a pre-season game at Carlisle, but the club had just been taken over by people with money and that brings its own pressure. They can afford replacements if you aren't producing. And in football, there's rarely a time when laughter isn't helpful.

Sunderland won that pre-season game 3-0, the travelling fans were there in numbers, and in the dressing room afterwards Quinn did his thing. He spoke about the uniqueness of the club and the place it has in the lives of the supporters. He talked up their past and raved about the future.

'This is where the journey starts, lads, and we're all in it together,' he said, his voice rising with the emotion of the whole thing.

We were the rabble and we were being roused. The dressing room responded, shouting and whooping. Hell, we were all in this together. Whatever Quinn was selling, we were buying.

I wasn't actually a member of the team yet, but I couldn't have been happier anywhere else. I was in a dressing room with footballers again, inches away from being a footballer again. It was a matter of time before I'd be in contention to be selected for a game, and once that happened the contract would be sorted.

The truth was more complicated. My hip was in constant pain and I blocked it out. The ankle problem was a distraction. It was far enough away from my hip that it was a useful diversion but the reality of how I felt was different to everything I was saying.

I was too fearful of raising concerns about my long-term fitness so I ploughed on, silently wishing all the pain would go away.

I didn't drink or socialise with the Sunderland players as I had at Millwall. I was also determined – apart from the odd ecstasy pill – to get back so I wasn't prepared to risk it all by drinking all the time.

A week after the pre-season game, I went over on my ankle again and was back in surgery. As much of a disappointment as it was, I could still keep some perspective. This was a routine ankle operation, albeit another one, and the moment I was back to full fitness I'd be signing a deal.

Sunderland lost their first five games of the season, so it was time for Niall Quinn, the chairman, to get tough with Niall Quinn, the manager. There were rumours about a new appointment and soon the club was electrified by the presence of a man who could electrify most situations. Roy Keane was named as the new manager.

I was out injured again and now I needed to impress the hardest-to-impress man in football.

The mood in the training ground changed overnight. As a manager, Quinn was all you'd expect: approachable, affable and warm. These things didn't spring to mind when most people thought of Roy Keane.

When news of Keane's appointment came through, players were speaking both nervously and excitedly about the prospect. Some worried they'd never be able to reach the standards Keane would demand, others wondered jokingly if it would be appropriate to ask him for an autograph. All the world knew about at the time was Roy Keane the player. Roy Keane the manager was a completely unknown quantity.

When he arrived, he kept repeating the same phrase.

'Raise the bar,' he said, over and over. Every time I hear that I think of Keane's opening pitch to the Sunderland players.

We had all been asked to gather in an upstairs room adjacent to the canteen for the first meeting. I sat down the back. I wanted to hear what he had to say but I didn't want to be seen.

I was on the verge of signing a deal but I hadn't yet. I didn't have full player status, so I fell in line with the hierarchy of any dressing room. I wasn't going to be the one up the front asking questions just to impress, or going out of my way to greet him or shake his hand. And like every player in the room that morning, I had no idea whether he was interested in having me at the club at all.

His presence filled the space. Everything could be done better, he said, and he expected everyone to buy into his approach. Raise the bar in every aspect of your behaviour, on and off the field. Be as good as you could be at all times. Raise the bar. Raise the bar.

He also said to ignore his reputation and be sure to come to his office if anyone needed anything. His door, he said, would always be open. Keane's door was open, but everybody was terrified to walk through it.

It wasn't just Keane's reputation that held people back. From one day to the next, you'd have no idea how he was going to be or how he would respond to any situation. I had grown up in a world like this, a world where I was finely attuned to the underlying mood, so I knew how to stay out of the way, I knew how unpredictable it could be.

One day, it would be all about being ultra-professional; the next day, he'd be bollocking lads for behaving themselves rather than misbehaving on a mid-season squad getaway. When the lads came home early after a night out, he was unimpressed.

'You won't win anything with that attitude,' he said.

During a game when Sunderland were 3-0 down at half-time, he just folded his arms and sat in silence in the dressing room until it was time to go out for the second half.

He lost it with the physio one day because he walked past the medical room and heard a few of us laughing as we sat getting treatment. Nobody should enjoy being injured, he said.

The players didn't know what to make of him, which was possibly his intention, but you can't impress your manager if he keeps changing his mind about what he wants from you.

I was ready to raise the bar in every way imaginable, but my ankle never got close to being 100 per cent. I recovered well enough to make it back into full training, but I was now getting a bit desperate. There was only so long I could stay at the place if I was going to remain in the physio room all the time, so I rushed myself back that November, sooner than advised. By this stage, I had been at the club for eleven months, working under four different managers and two different owners.

On my second day training with the squad, my hip went again. As bad as it ever was. The game was over. Again.

The deception was finished. I had spent tens of thousands of pounds on this desperate attempt to escape the real world, but I had to accept it wasn't going to work.

It was a Wednesday afternoon when I faced it. I couldn't dodge this bullet anymore. It was over. I went up to Keane's office to tell him my hip was too bad to continue.

I was grateful he didn't kick me out the moment he arrived at the club, and I wanted to tell him that. He urged me not to make any rash decisions and to take a couple of days to consider my future.

'Come back to me on Friday and we'll talk then. Go out on the piss in the meantime,' he said, 'if you think that would help.' I took his advice.

I went to Leeds to meet my sister Anna and some of her mates. I knew it was over this time so I didn't waste my time and energy trying to plot a different approach. I knew there was no point in going back to America for more surgery. Acupuncturists and faith-healing nuns were no use to me now. I had to accept that I didn't have a body capable of playing football professionally. This time I was done.

I called back to Keane's office that Friday afternoon, hungover after the couple of days' drinking, with the intention of thanking him briefly and getting out of there. There was no reason to drag it out any longer. In my fraught state, I knew there was a risk I'd cry and I didn't think either of us would appreciate that.

He thwarted my attempt at a quick exit and told me to sit down. I explained what the situation was and that I was done. It was time to move back to Dublin and get a real job. He let me talk. We compared hip injuries. He didn't seem put out when I nearly cried.

He praised me for the work I had put in to get that far and enquired what my options were. I mentioned the possibility of media work, and he advised me to speak my mind, always. There were enough spoofers out there, he reckoned.

'Don't be another one who says nothing. If you do get work in that area,' he said, 'tell it like it is.'

At that time, in that office, I felt I couldn't have had a better man to talk to. I walked out of the room with more of an insight into why former teammates spoke so highly of his influence on them.

If you'd asked me as I left how far I thought Keane was going to go in management, I'd have told you he could become one of the greats. At that moment I would have followed him anywhere, done anything for him, believed anything he told me. I couldn't see how he could fail.

After I left his office, I went to the physios and thanked them, Dave Binningsley in particular, for all they had done for me.

There would be no club statements this time, no onslaught of well-wishing letters and emails from fans. I could leave without saying goodbye because few people really knew I'd been there in the first place. Nobody would regret my departure. This was banal and uneventful.

I rang Mick to thank him a few days later. He had since taken over as manager at Wolves and they were about to play Sunderland. It would be the first public encounter between Keane and McCarthy since Saipan.

I knew there was nothing left for me back in London. Hicksy had moved to Belfast, which made the house less appealing to me. He had been a constant in my life since my first couple of years in London. For nearly seven years, I had always known Hicksy would be there. We didn't exactly talk about things, but I knew he'd be around when I didn't want to talk about things.

There were other factors, too, which I wasn't prepared to acknowledge. London was where I'd lived as a footballer and now I knew I wasn't a footballer anymore. The two years after I'd left Millwall had frightened me and I'd decided that it was the city I was living in rather than anything to do with me. Later, I would hear this described as a 'geographical', a persuasive idea that says all you need is a change of scene – you just blame your surroundings, rather than look at your own behaviour. I would eventually understand the truth that, wherever I went, I would take me with me.

I put my house on the market and headed home to Dublin. I hadn't lived there in over a decade, but it seemed like a safe haven. London was chaos. Stability was what I needed and where better to find that than at home? I was sure I would find it there. Not for the first time, and not for the last time, I was wrong.

13

Homecoming

Ten years after I left Dublin for London in tears as an innocent seventeen-year-old, I returned on the ferry from Holyhead to Dublin. I was less innocent but more unsure of myself. The seventeen-year-old me had some certainty. He knew what he wanted to be. The twenty-seven-year-old me had no idea who he was or what he was going to do with his life.

Ten years earlier, I had the ambition to be a footballer and now that was gone, replaced only with a sense that life was complicated and that mine was full of uncertainty.

I returned to Dublin in December 2006 with an idea that my problems wouldn't be so great here. My family were close by, the wildness of London would be curtailed. Dublin was different. Dublin was a sanctuary.

I was happy to be out of London and away from what my life there had become. I had cleaned up my act at Sunderland, but I definitely didn't want things to go back to how they had been. Surrounded by family, friends and normality, things would be different in Dublin. I'd take fewer drugs and do a lot less drinking. I wasn't going to live like a monk – no chance – but I was determined to rein things in.

I had a degree in sports science and two Victorian bulldogs to show for my decade in England. I put the remainder of my retirement windfall towards buying a house in Firhouse. The pot was worryingly close to empty after that, but house prices had been rising continuously for years at that stage, and you can't really lose on bricks and mortar, can you? Finally, I was making sound financial decisions.

Shamrock Rovers and Sligo Rovers approached me about working for them, but I wasn't mad on becoming a club promotions officer in either place.

I was invited on to the board of St Patrick's Athletic, which I jumped at immediately. It was the club my dad had taken me to see all those years ago. Fintan Drury's firm were involved in a consultancy role, so my name had been put forward. The role was outlined in very vague terms, and it was to be a voluntary position. Property developer Garrett Kelleher had just bought the club and the plans were exciting. I still had no idea what my input would be, but I was happy to throw myself into it with an open mind. The role as outlined was non-specific enough for me to blag my way through.

I started to get the odd gig on RTÉ's coverage of the League of Ireland. I was self-conscious, awkward and unsure of my views on anything. I had no experience playing in the league, so I felt like an outsider next to the other pundits. The plan was to just keep spoofing until I got caught out.

The *Sunday Independent* sports editor John Greene asked if I'd write a column for three weeks. That was pushed out to six weeks. After a month it was extended to six months.

I had no schedule, no boss, no real responsibility. I just had to email the column each week by Friday evening, and that was it. I kept up to speed with what was going on in the world of football and then wrote about it, with the help of some anecdotes and memories.

I had no formal guidance or training in how to write, but I knew I had to offer something different if I was going to last. Some former players are so high-profile they can rely on clichés all the way through an entire career in the media. I knew I wouldn't last a fortnight with that approach. I assumed the people I wrote about would never see what I had written, which freed me up to say things others wouldn't.

I didn't have the confidence to submit anything to the editor without Dion Fanning checking it first.

'Don't hold back if you think this is shit,' I'd say, and then formed my opinions on what I had written based almost solely on what he said. It was like waiting to see if my dad laughed at the television first.

I was encouraged to use my contacts to get player interviews, but I had little interest in listening to footballers playing it safe and being dishonest. I had bullshitted my way through too many interviews myself.

In 2007 Sunderland left-back Clive Clarke, a player I had once roomed with for the U-21s, had a cardiac arrest at half-time during a game while on loan at Leicester City. As soon as he said he was up for speaking about it, I was in. I was keen for it to go well. In journalistic terms, it probably did. As far as I was concerned it was a disaster.

It was my first interview with anyone and I wanted to make sure Clive was OK with it. He had been critical of Keane's style of management, so I emailed him an advance copy of what I had written on the Friday night. I had known him for a few years and the last thing I wanted to do was print something that would piss him off. I texted him the following day. He gave it the thumbs-up, along with a tip for a horse running that day. I thought there was no issue, but on Sunday morning, after he had read the paper, his attitude changed.

A text arrived.

'Jaysus lad, didn't think you'd put in all that about Keane.'

'Are you for real? I sent it to you Friday and you said you were OK with it.'

'I thought it was just gonna be your normal column so I assumed it would be grand.'

He hadn't even read it.

Sky Sports News ran with his quotes about Keane for twenty-four hours. Nobody had criticised Keane's management this openly before. Keane was furious. He fined Clive £10,000.

A couple of days later, a withheld number showed up on my phone but it didn't take long to identify the caller.

'I knew you'd do this, you spiteful cunt.'

The last time I'd talked to Keane I was overcome with the generosity and empathy of the man. This felt different.

'I knew you'd come at us, you spiteful cunt.'

Shortly after I left Sunderland, I had asked Keane if he would consider bringing Sunderland to The Den in a pre-season friendly for my benefit game. I had abandoned the whole idea of a benefit game while I was attempting my comeback, for obvious reasons. Now that I had accepted there was no way back, I wanted to get it played as quickly as possible. Once Millwall gave me a date, I had to find an opposition. It had been proposed for August 2007, but Sunderland were understandably unavailable because they had a better option – a friendly against Juventus to mark ten years in the Stadium of Light. Opting to play one of the biggest names in European football is an understandable choice to make, especially when one of the alternatives is a game at The Den.

Now Keane thought the whole interview was my way of getting back at the club. He roared at me for about five minutes and then hung up.

I had to submit the recording of the interview to Aengus Fanning, the *Sunday Independent* editor. My fear was that Clive would say I had misquoted him. Ten thousand pounds is a lot of money. That would have unfairly trashed me as a journalist, so I needed to be ready to defend myself. Clive was in negotiations with the club for his own retirement settlement on the grounds of ill health, so he was relying on their goodwill. It was the worst possible timing to criticise the manager. After a couple of curt texts between us, we never spoke again.

I interviewed a few others, but I wasn't overly keen to do many more. Everyone at the paper was delighted with the Clive Clarke interview but it only emphasised to me how far I was from my previous world.

One of the only other interviews I did was with Clinton Morrison at Crystal Palace. I felt awkward at the thought of meeting him at Palace's training ground. We used to be rivals; now I was there asking him about his career and his international ambitions.

Before I met him, I saw one of my old teammates, who was now playing for Palace, walking towards me. I hid behind a bush; I didn't want to be asked how my life was going. He wasn't going to get the truth and I didn't want to lie, but mostly I just didn't want him to see me.

———

This was how my life went. I would retreat to the safety of the weekly column and then lose myself in a weekend of drink and drugs.

Cocaine, it turned out, was as widely available in Dublin as London, and I didn't have to travel far to get it. I grew up watching films depicting drug dealers as dodgy types, but in 2007 drug dealers in Dublin were lads like me. A few lines went hand in hand with having a few pints. If there were pills or MDMA knocking about, all the better. I was conscientious enough to keep it away from work, which was evidence for me that I didn't have a problem.

My parents' divorce went through that year, another unsettling episode I now had to ignore. I didn't want to know about how their relationship had broken down, but that also allowed me to ignore how it might have affected me.

Drinking sessions helped with that. I wasn't concerned if they regularly went on for two or three days or if I was out several nights a week. I wasn't in debt to anyone, it wasn't getting in the way of work, and I was the only one affected. I didn't have kids I was neglecting or a partner I was ignoring. It was just me, on my terms. Where was the harm?

Hicksy had moved back to Belfast while I was training at Sunderland but when I came back, he decided to head for Dublin too. He moved into the house in Firhouse and it soon became as lively as London had been.

Once again, I never wanted the party to end and often it didn't. To me, that was normal. I would wring every last drop out of a weekend, recover for half the week and then get back on it. And those were the good weeks.

Around this time I earned the nickname Strokeface, due to a weird reaction I often had to taking pills. My tongue would swell up, affecting my speech, and – though I assume this was exaggerated greatly at the time – apparently the left side of my face would drop a little. Given that everyone who saw me on pills was likely to be taking them too, it's hard to gauge the truth of that. Nonetheless, the name stuck.

I was asked to contribute to an educational DVD for secondary school students about the dangers of alcohol. A religious organisation was funding the production and had seen an interview I had given about retiring from football. They were impressed by my honesty when I talked about turning to drink, unaware I hadn't exactly turned away from it since.

The interview for the DVD was filmed in my house. The crew arrived and set up while I tried to conceal how I was really feeling. I was feeling bad. I'd agreed to deliver this message but I saw no contradiction then between my words and actions. I was still suffering from the excesses of the night before. I just needed to get this over with. I needed to tell the youth of Ireland to watch their drinking and then get through the rest of this hangover in peace. Hell, I might even have a drink when the interview was done.

When I saw the finished piece, I noticed that the stamp on my wrist from Coppers the night before was still visible. No better way of getting a message across. Later, I appeared on the *Afternoon Show* on RTÉ to help promote it. When asked whether I still drank, I said I enjoyed a glass of wine with my meals.

The drift that had begun during my time at Millwall, which had accelerated when I retired in 2003, was still going, this time in a different city with different characters, but with most of the same behaviours. I had swapped London for Dublin; I had swapped the life of a footballer for the life of whatever I was now – and the same things kept happening. Maybe it wasn't London, maybe it wasn't football. Maybe, just maybe, it was something else.

———

For two years, I existed like this. A little bit of punditry, a column every week which I'd usually (although not always) deliver before getting drunk. One night I was too fucked to write anymore, so I asked a mate to finish it off, which he did, and I sent it to the paper. His final paragraph was written at about 7am when he was full of coke.

I clearly didn't have much of a career plan. I was spending more money than I was earning and it was obvious I needed a proper income. My financial pot was nearly empty at this point. The crash had hit and I couldn't remortgage the house because it was plummeting in value. It turns out you can lose quite a lot on bricks and mortar.

My dad was aware of my plight and one night he offered to help me out.

'You left home at seventeen and never cost us a penny,' he said, partly to explain his offer and partly, I think, to make the conversation less excruciatingly awkward for me.

I turned down his offer. My pride wouldn't let me take it. Five years earlier, I had more than £700,000; now I was listening to my dad saying he could bail me out.

Luckily I got a job, although it wasn't really what I was expecting. In June 2008, at the age of 29, I was appointed CEO of St Pat's.

I had made an impression while on the board, and now I was being asked to run the club, a challenge I was happy to accept, even though running my own life was an unmanageable task most of the time.

The job offer from St Pat's came at the right time, however, not just in financial terms. It brought some much-needed structure to my week. Before that, there was no reason to turn down midweek pints with mates.

Part of my role was to put a professional face to the club, which was quite a challenge some days. On my first day in the job, I had to deal with a crisis. One of the players had drunkenly smashed through a window over the weekend and needed emergency surgery to save his life. A few weeks later, the manager rang to say another player hadn't made training because he had been arrested. Shortly afterwards, the media were reporting that another member of the squad had been placing bets on us losing matches.

The morning after we won a UEFA Cup game against a Swedish team that summer, the FAI rang. We had just qualified for the play-off stage and everyone was ecstatic.

'Are you sitting down, Richard?'

'Shit. What's up?'

'One of the players on the bench last night wasn't registered to play in Europe. I'm afraid this is very serious.'

Without realising it, the manager had selected a player who hadn't been included in his chosen list to submit to UEFA. The game had fallen on transfer deadline day so I had been busy trying to complete four deals throughout the day. I hadn't seen the team sheet before he gave it to the referee, but none of that would matter. I would have to take responsibility for it all. We were facing expulsion from the competition and all the negative publicity that would come with it. We would be the latest example of why the League of Ireland was a laughing stock.

If the player had been brought on, we would have been finished, but he hadn't been used so we got away with it. We were given a small fine by UEFA and told that John Delaney would ensure it wouldn't be published anywhere.

We drew Hertha Berlin in the following round and, as part of my plan to improve communication with supporters, we immediately posted the dates of the fixtures on the club website. We assumed matchdays would be Thursdays, as they usually are in that competition.

Within an hour, we had to take it down because a German television network had approached Hertha to bring their home leg forward to Tuesday. You can make a lot of money in European competitions from securing TV rights, so you have to be flexible. However, several fans had already booked their travel plans with the original date in mind. I was in a shitstorm yet again, entirely of my own making.

This happened on the first day of Electric Picnic, which I had planned to attend. Now there was a crisis that needed to be managed, so it seemed I would have to stay in Dublin and get on top of the situation. That was one way of managing the crisis, sure. But I had a better idea. I saw no reason to change my plans and I headed for Stradbally anyway. It was time to get away from the crisis by getting out of my head.

Some of the details of the weekend are a little hazy, but I do remember spending the Saturday afternoon sitting outside my tent, reading abusive emails on my BlackBerry. I'm sure I would have been a lot more upset by them if I hadn't been high on ecstasy at the time.

'You haven't a clue how to run a club.'

'You owe us a full refund for our flights.'

'I can't believe someone like you is allowed run our club.'

I didn't disagree with some of them, but I stayed to enjoy the weekend. On Sunday I couldn't remember where I had parked my car, so I had to make my way home without it.

Back at St Pat's on Monday, we went into damage limitation mode, something I was becoming familiar with from my own life. We cobbled together a compensation package for out-of-pocket fans and returned to the daily firefighting that came with the job. The following day we even got some positive media coverage for our response.

On Wednesday I got a lift back to Stradbally to pick up my car, which was the only one in the field where I'd left it.

By now I was personally aware of how easily available drugs were in Dublin. I took them most weekends. Something had to be done about this crisis and, to demonstrate how concerned I was, I made enquiries about randomly drug-testing the entire St Pat's squad. My thinking was sound: if I could get drugs easily, so could everyone on the playing staff, and that wouldn't do.

It was my job to ensure certain standards were upheld throughout the club. I wasn't ready to consider how any of this might apply to my conduct. I wasn't a professional athlete, so the rules were different. We didn't have the grounds to force anyone to provide a sample, so I was advised against it. I tried unsuccessfully to enforce a new code of conduct on the players, even sacking one of them for his poor fitness levels. My own standards were nobody else's business.

My thirtieth birthday party went ahead without me that January. I had arranged to meet mates in a pub in town, but I had to pull out at the last minute. Pat's had big ambitions during the boom, but the crash meant something different and I was handling the fallout of a club decision to slash the wage bill, which meant either offloading players or convincing staff and players to take wage cuts. The job had changed a great deal from when I had taken it on. It was no longer about pursuing trophies and improving the squad, but I was determined to see it through. My dad said it wouldn't look great to leave after six months and he was right.

Work didn't always get prioritised over drinking. I was on a rollover one Monday afternoon when I was due to attend a board meeting about the future of the club. Unlike that day on the side-line at Millwall, I had the sense to stay away. I made up some excuse about a possible diagnosis of rheumatoid arthritis. I said further tests were needed to be sure but that I was too upset to attend the meeting. The people I told, as you'd expect, were very understanding.

———

When I'd finished playing, my Millwall manager Mark McGhee had offered to name me as a sub in our next game so I could go onto the pitch in the final minutes at The Den to say goodbye. I'd declined the offer at the time, thinking that the benefit game would be sorted soon enough. Six years later, in 2009, it finally happened at a time when I didn't really care if I said goodbye to Millwall or not.

I had moved on, but not in any positive sense. I had my own ideas of how I liked to spend my weekends and they didn't involve pretending to be a footballer or taking a trip down memory lane. There might have been some money in it for me, but not much.

In the summer of 2009 I arranged a game against Gareth Southgate's Middlesbrough at The Den. By that stage, I just wanted it out of the way so I could move on. Or so I could tell myself I had moved on. I kept using the word 'closure' to describe why I was doing it, even though I don't think closure exists. If it does, I was nowhere close to achieving it. Some people plan a benefit or testimonial game the way couples might plan a wedding. Every minute of the day is choreographed: gifts for both teams, little mementos of the day, as well as speeches and words of thanks. I did none of those things. I never spoke to Gareth Southgate or any of the Middlesbrough lads. I barely spoke to the Millwall lads because, by that stage, I knew very few of them.

For tax reasons, you need to form a committee to organise these games and somehow I managed to get one of these together in the build-up to the game. We met twice and that was it. I put no effort into drumming up revenue or sponsorship for it.

It was the final pre-season game of the summer on the first day of August. My two-year old nieces, Catherine's daughter Jessica and Jamie's daughter Niamh, were the mascots. I eased into the day by having a couple of whiskeys beforehand.

The plan was that I would come on for the last ten minutes of the game. I tried to take part in the warm-ups but, even with the whiskey, I was too stiff to do anything so I milled about, edging closer to the side-line and eventually standing there chatting to people in the crowd. I was in my full Millwall kit with my boots on but, at half-time, I headed up to the executive lounge for a drink. If I was feeling anything, I was going to suppress it. I wasn't sure who I was any more, but I definitely wasn't a footballer.

To prove that point, I came on as planned and quickly found my lungs burning. The whiskey had numbed me, but it also gave me a little bit of pointless aggression.

Robert Huth was playing for Middlesbrough. As soon as I came on, he dropped the shoulder and went by me as if I was a statue. As he did, I leaned myself into him and smashed him clumsily with my own shoulder. I staggered around the place, won one or two headers and barged into a couple of other players. From the moment I came on, I was waiting for the ref to blow it up. I wanted it to be over. When the final whistle went, I applauded the fans and walked around the pitch, waving goodbye. I hadn't kicked the ball once in my farewell game, which seemed kind of appropriate.

There were fewer than four thousand people in the ground. Only one stand was open and there didn't seem to be anything special about the day. But, at the end, the crowd started to sing my name. It was the first time I'd heard it sung in six years. As they sang, I could feel the tears coming for everything I had lost. I left the pitch before it became obvious I was crying. I composed myself in the tunnel before I got back into the dressing room and stayed completely silent as I got changed.

One of the Millwall players had ruptured his cruciate ligament in the game so the mood was a little sombre. The manager was giving a rousing post-game speech about the importance of the season ahead. I had more pressing concerns. My lungs felt like they were going to collapse. Jack Daniels wasn't the ideal fuel for elite performance.

I went into the lounge where Millwall's press officer Deano Standing interviewed me. My mates from Dublin were there, as were my parents and the rest of the family. Some of them had been close to tears during the game and, as Deano talked to me, I knew I could go off again. Jess crawled to the front of the room, so I picked her up and held her for the rest of the interview, which stopped me falling to pieces.

The rest of the night passed as I wanted it to, in a haze of drink. I remember as the night went on feeling a sense of happiness that everyone was here together.

At one stage, someone from Millwall handed me a spreadsheet of the costs they had incurred. Well, it was somewhere between the back of a cigarette packet and a spreadsheet: they had scribbled down a few numbers in an illegible scrawl on a piece of paper. They handed it over to me and I scrunched it up and put it in my pocket. One for the next committee meeting.

———

When I got back to Dublin, I had to deal with reality again. It became clear it was time to walk away from the job at St Pat's. I had been very active in arranging for greater communication and cooperation among the clubs. Nobody was getting anywhere by serving their own interests at every step. I'm not sure if we made any actual progress, but I knew we'd get nowhere after I received an email from Bohemians that summer. Cristiano Ronaldo had just been signed for a world-record fee for Real Madrid and his debut was to be in Tallaght Stadium against Shamrock Rovers. The fixture fell the same week as St Pat's and Bohs were due to play in the qualification rounds of the European competitions, so Bohs felt we should get the FAI to cancel the Madrid game to ensure bigger attendances at our games. They emailed me a copy of the letter they were sending to the FAI and asked me to sign it. I thought this was petty, small-minded, amateur and misguided, pretty much in keeping with how the league was run at the time.

The constant firefighting that comes with the job had worn me down, and once relegation was avoided – our target since the opening weekend – I saw out the end of the season and then resigned.

Once again, I had no plan. I didn't think I needed one. I threw myself into my old routine almost immediately. Midweek pints lasted for days. Friday night drinks didn't finish until Sunday. Every time I went back to a house party, I was taking drugs. But most of the parties were at mine. It was simpler that way. It was a safe haven. But there were no safe havens for me, as I was finding out. Everywhere was a danger zone and the only way of escaping danger was oblivion.

14

The End of the Beginning

One afternoon in the summer of 2010, I received a text message from Anna.

'You're the furthest thing from the older brother I used to have. I used to look up to you and everything you did. It's heartbreaking to watch you destroy yourself like this. Love you loads xxx.'

I was in a vulnerable state when I got the message, as I often was at that stage. I wanted to blame the last stages of a hangover for how I felt, but I was beginning to wonder if I could.

The truth was, I knew what she said was true, but I also felt I had no option. I would often catch a glimpse of myself on a drunken night out, or hear somebody say something about me, and feel wounded.

That's not who I am.

That's not who I really am at all.

But the person I thought I was only made the odd appearance. You are what you do. And what I did was drink.

A few days before I got that text from Anna, I'd called her from the Blue Light pub in the Dublin mountains. I had been going non-stop since the previous afternoon and the fear was kicking in. I was fifteen minutes from home, but I was too fragile to consider a conversation with a taxi driver, so I needed my kid sister to take me home.

When we got to our house in Ballinteer, which was where Mum had been living since the divorce, three young lads were waiting outside. They wanted me to sign an Ireland match programme. This was before selfies were a thing, which is just as well. I hadn't slept and I was off my head so any photo of the moment wouldn't have aged well. I signed the programme, avoided eye contact as best I could and headed straight for my old bedroom as soon as I got inside.

A few days later, when things had calmed down a little and I was capable of interacting with someone other than my dogs, I contacted Anna. I knew she was right in what she said. I knew there was nothing I could say that would put her mind at ease. She knew me too well. A cleverly worded text or speech wouldn't do any good. I just thanked her for being concerned and said I'd try to get my shit together. At the time, though, I had little reason to believe I could achieve that.

After I left St Pat's, I had time on my hands. I still had the weekly newspaper column but I was idle a lot of the time. I often found myself thinking back to the feeling I'd had in the final session of therapy in 2004.

Would psychotherapy be worth considering as a job? I no longer saw myself as simply an ex-footballer, so I was no longer restricted by the limitations I thought came with that title.

Since retirement, I had been a columnist, a CEO, a pundit, an agent and head of youth recruitment at Millwall Academy. I was unsure whether a bloke would be taken seriously in the psychotherapy field. Or, more to the point, I thought nobody would take *me* seriously. Even though I knew I was more than just an ex-footballer, I was worried other people wouldn't see it that way.

Despite these doubts, I googled courses in Dublin in September 2010 and, a fortnight later, I enrolled in a two-year HDip in Dublin Business School. If nothing else, it would bring some routine and structure to my week. And on top of that, as a course requirement, I would have to return to therapy.

I thought it would be female-dominated and I was right. I told myself I didn't belong, although strangely I felt I did. I assumed my age would be used against me too. What could a thirty-one-year-old know about life anyway?

If I could get over those hurdles, I had some ideas about what would happen. I thought I was going to learn all about fixing other people, something I was keen to do. I was always more comfortable focusing on other people's issues rather than my own.

So psychotherapy, I thought, would allow me to save people by the dozen. I'd be saving them morning, noon and night and there'd be no time to think about anything else.

I'd be learning fancy phrases and clever analogies to bang out to clients who needed guidance. But – and this was going to become a theme over the next few years – everything I knew was wrong.

I'd had no concept of how much of the HDip would be spent on self-reflection. In order to be able to support and help other people, it was essential we started by looking inwards. We needed to work through our own stuff first if we wanted to help others. This was a massive task and one I wasn't sure I wanted to take on.

Within a fortnight of the course beginning, I asked one of the lecturers how you would know for sure if you had inherited alcoholism. There had been a reference in the lecture to addiction being hereditary and I wanted to know more, though I didn't say anything in front of my classmates. He said it was a combination of environmental factors, childhood traumas and genetics. I was looking for confirmation that I was in the clear, but all I got was a list of causes that related to me. I opted not to bring it up again. I suppose I could have explored it further in therapy, but I wasn't ready for something as radical as that. If you say you have a drinking problem, the obvious suggestion might be to stop, and I didn't want to hear that. Like retiring from football, I wasn't willing to discuss it for fear it might be needed. And, just as with retirement, it was all I could think about.

I organised my weekly sessions for Tuesdays at 4pm, a safe enough distance from the carnage of every weekend. Despite organising my therapy around my drinking needs, I didn't mention alcohol with my therapist for my first year of therapy. I was starting to learn what it really entailed. Therapy wasn't just about talking about problems, it was about working towards resolving them. It wasn't like sitting in a pub complaining to your mates about your life, it was about actively exploring ways to deal with life's challenges in a better way.

In another lecture, self-help groups were mentioned, and I was curious to find out more. These groups held regular meetings to support one another in recovering from addictions to everything from food and sex to drugs and drink. I knew someone who had attended meetings for recovering alcoholics and thought she was the person to speak to now. Obviously there was no way I was going to tell her I was considering it myself. Pretending to be concerned about a friend's drinking, I asked her how we would know for sure if he's an alcoholic. What are the tell-tale signs? Where's the line? How would we know if he'd gone from being someone who was just mad for pints to being an alcoholic? An *actual* alcoholic. Just how bad would things have to get before he should go to a meeting?

Again, I wanted an answer that ruled me out. I wanted a definition or a description that didn't apply to me, so I could walk away from the conversation knowing I was in the clear. It didn't go well.

There are no entry requirements, she told me, no specific type of rock bottom you've got to reach. The only requirement for attending meetings is a desire to stop drinking. There is nothing else.

This was not what I wanted to hear. I had a desire to stop drinking all the time. Often times I only got rid of that desire to stop drinking by drinking. That was something else I'd have to figure out.

She told me this on a Sunday afternoon. For the next few days, I could think of nothing else. According to the picture painted, these meetings were exactly what I needed. I wondered how much desire counts as enough desire, but I certainly knew I had *some* desire to stop. But a life without drinking, just like a life without football, didn't seem like the kind of life that would work for me.

Nearly everything I did with my mates revolved around drinking. I had never been to a gig without drinking in my life. I had never gone on a holiday and stayed sober. I was uncomfortable being around footballers once I became an ex-footballer; would giving up drinking mark the end of my friendships with my closest mates? And how the hell would I go on a date if I couldn't drink? Stopping now would mean I'd be celibate for the rest of my life.

By Thursday evening, I decided I had given the matter enough consideration. I had given the question my full attention for those four days, and now I could say conclusively that I was OK. I had been through enough in my life already. I had overcome enough difficulties. It was unnecessary to add being an alcoholic to all of that. I needn't worry about it any more, so I went for a drink.

Like the end of my time at Millwall, some clarity would occasionally sneak through the denial and the bullshit. I wasn't ready to say I was an alcoholic, but I wondered if the amount of time I spent thinking about drinking was normal.

Even when I wasn't on a session, I would be thinking about the next one. And every session would begin with the fear of what could happen when I lost control, but also a fear that this would end. The end was the thing I feared most; the end would see me hungover and frequently in tears.

I would take my first drink with part of me scared of the power I was giving up. I had a feeling it might be a bad idea. Another part of me was terrified that there might not be enough drink and that the night would eventually come to an end.

Later I would hear this explained as 'one drink is too many and a thousand is not enough'. That explained my state of mind.

I was obsessed with the nagging question that I needed to stop. I did Dry November in 2010 to convince myself I didn't have a problem. Nobody with a drink problem could stay sober for a month, I told myself.

At the end of that month without drink, I gave myself the all-clear and headed into December secure in the knowledge I had nothing to worry about.

I took a photo of my first pint of Guinness and posted it on Facebook on 1 December. I took this as proof I didn't have a problem. I had demonstrated I could stop whenever I wanted, so there was no cause for concern here.

To prove it, I drank for eighteen of the next twenty-one days, taking each Thursday night off to be fresh so I could do the column the following day.

On Christmas Eve, I went to the local for a few pints. I ended up back in a house known to everyone in the area as HQ. Party headquarters. A couple of ecstasy pills later, I was back at home with a bottle of wine and a mate in front of my fire. He had the sense to go home around 10am on Christmas morning and I eventually nodded off to sleep myself. I woke up around 5pm with a load of missed calls from the family wondering why I hadn't made Christmas dinner. As concerned as they were, they probably knew what had happened.

I called round to Mum's house and she didn't lecture me at all. She didn't say anything that made me feel worse. I assume she knew there would be little point. She had kept me a plate of food and heated it up when I arrived. I couldn't eat any of it because I had no appetite. Pills and food don't go together. After a couple of hours, I started to feel better, so I had a drink. It was Christmas Day after all.

I thought the feelings I had on days like that were normal. Other people had them so I thought we could do nothing about them. I wasn't the first person to be overcome with guilt at the kindness of a mother who tolerated their drinking and bad behaviour, so why should I have to be the one to do something about it?

But the more therapy sessions, drinking sessions and college lectures I attended, the more it felt like the walls were closing in around me. It felt like the final few months at Millwall all over again.

———

I went to Marbella for a stag do in the summer of 2011. Some lads went for the first few days, others came for the last few days, but myself and a couple of others were determined to do it properly and went for seven nights.

Those seven nights could stand for everything I was chasing in my drinking career. We landed on a Saturday night and that first night was brilliant. We went to a bar where I met a girl, and she and her friends came back to the villa we had rented. Instead of heading to the bedroom with her, I wanted to stay where the fun was. For me, that was where the drink and drugs were, so while the girl went to bed to sleep, I headed to the pool and gave one of my mates – who had told us he couldn't swim – swimming lessons.

We spent the night and early morning laughing. As the sun came up, we were all in the pool, still laughing, still feeling this was magical. And it was.

But it didn't end there; it never did. If it had, it wouldn't have been a problem. But I was beginning to realise that it never ended when it should have. Not for me anyway. Instead it went on and on, as I chased the high, which was always an attempt to get the first high, an attempt to get back home.

But I couldn't get that feeling again, no matter how hard I tried, no matter what I took. And it wasn't for the lack of trying. During the week in Marbella, the only time I didn't have a bag of MDMA in my pocket for the entire trip was when I was in the water. The only time I wasn't drinking was when I staggered up each morning, wondering if I was able to drink right now. The answer was always yes.

I stopped drinking only when it was time to sleep, which was even harder to do after local bar staff sorted us out with cocaine. The room behind the kitchen in our rented villa became known as the panic room. If the paranoia became too much, or being around people was beyond you, retreating to that room with drugs on your own was the best solution.

It was a stag party and I barely knew most of the people there, but that didn't matter. I stayed for the full seven days while various characters came and went. I formed instant and deep friendships with some of them, the way you only can when you're drunk and high.

Getting home was horrific, the flipside to that first magical night in the pool. There are plenty of people who have been in situations like this and take it as the price they pay for a week of fun. I would have loved to have been one of those people – I used to be one of those people – but it didn't really matter to me any more how other people felt. What mattered was how I felt, and I felt like shit.

I took some Valium to get me through the flight home. On the Sunday, I sat in my house in Firhouse and put on an episode of *The West Wing* that I'd seen a hundred times. In it, Toby Ziegler is asked to identify a homeless man found dead while wearing a coat Toby had donated to a shelter, and Toby becomes attached to the homeless man's story. Despite having seen it so many times, I started crying and I couldn't stop. If you'd seen me, you'd think I was in the middle of some deep and personal tragedy, that I'd lost a beloved pet or maybe even a family member, rather than simply trying to get through a Sunday night with a Chinese takeaway and my favourite TV series.

Maybe this was what they meant when they talked about rock bottom. I'd asked lots of questions about alcoholism, but nobody told me the breaking point would be an overly sentimental episode of *The West Wing*. Was this how far I'd fallen?

I continued crying on and off for days through the comedown. I went for pints later that week and came up with a plan. I couldn't stand feeling like this. I knew the way out. I knew what would help. It was time to take action.

So I convinced the lads I'd been with in Spain to book another trip to Marbella for the end of August. It was something to look forward to.

———

In August 2011 we threw a surprise sixtieth for my mum. Naturally, the end of that party didn't mean the end of my celebrations. The following evening, I was drinking with Anna in my sitting room when I started to cry. I'd managed a few hours' sleep the night before, but I had been drinking since 10am. I've no idea why it happened in that precise moment. Anna hadn't said anything that set me off. I don't think we were even in conversation at the time.

'Jesus, what's up? Are you OK?'

After sobbing for a while, I gathered myself together.

'I just really, really hate myself. And I don't know why.'

By then I couldn't remember things being any other way. No matter what I did in my life, I never outran this feeling. Joining Millwall, playing for Ireland, being on RTÉ or running St Pat's. I never saw any of them as a worthy enough achievement. Whenever praise came my way for anything I did well, there was always a voice in my head that shouted it down.

If you knew the real Richie, you wouldn't be saying this.

But now it was worse. Now there was another person too – drunk, hopeless Richie. The person who gets women pregnant in blackout was now a constant presence. The Richie whose little sister viewed him as an imposter was always around. The other Richie, the Richie who was an ally and a protector, had disappeared.

I wanted to run away from it all, but oblivion wasn't as effective as it used to be. Usually I could suppress or ignore this voice, but not any more. Just like my hip injury, it had become a source of constant pain.

A torment that I had treated since my teens by getting out of my head. But now, I couldn't get out of my head. It wasn't working.

On Sunday 21 August 2011, the week after that party for Mum, I was on my own in the beer garden outside Bruxelles. I'd gone into that weekend, like so many before it, with the intention not to drink. I spent the week obsessing about this, determined that, by willpower, I could stay away.

But then I got the urge to open a can of Guinness in the house on Friday and I told myself that, rather than waste a whole night agonising over whether I should drink or not, I might as well just crack on.

I spent the evening drinking alone. I used to swear I'd never do that, but this promise had gone the way of all the others. The next day, I arranged to meet my good friend Ed in the Orchard pub in Rathfarnham at noon to watch Arsenal v Liverpool. My interest in Arsenal had worn off years earlier, but this was a convenient excuse to get Ed out drinking. I woke the following morning in a flat along the quays, having hooked up with a girl I had been seeing casually at the time. As usual, the memories of the previous evening were very patchy.

As soon as I woke, I knew it was time to go to the pub. I had a table to myself outside Bruxelles. I had a newspaper, a pint of Guinness and a packet of cigarettes in front of me. I was drinking like a gentleman. I got chatting to a group of Scottish lads sitting next to me who were in Dublin for a stag. It had all the ingredients of the perfect day and the sun was shining.

And then something happened. There was a moment, an intervention, a second where I could see everything clearly. I couldn't understand why it happened then, but there was nothing I could do to shake it. The weekend hadn't been much different from countless other weekends, except for this feeling. This feeling, telling me I was done.

I had spent years trying to control my drinking. Since waking up in a London police cell at the age of eighteen, I had been trying, without success, to manage the chaos. Don't have shots. Stay off cider. Stick to lager tops. Don't have lager. Stick to bottles. Avoid vodka. Only drink Guinness. Do drugs indoors. Stick to Jack Daniels. But I never found the magic mixture that kept me safe.

None of it had worked. I felt beaten. I had felt beaten before, but this was different. This time I couldn't fight – or do what I thought was fighting – any more. It was time to surrender.

The debate in my head stopped. The curiosity about definitions and causes and treatments went away. I stopped caring where the line was, because I knew it was behind me. It had been crossed many years earlier. Intellectualising and rationalising wasn't making me drink any less, or any better, or any safer. When I started, I couldn't stop, so it was time to stop trying. Like a car that had run out of petrol, I just couldn't go on. More than anything, though, I knew it was time to ask for help.

Therapy wouldn't be enough. I texted the friend I had previously spoken to about meetings. I didn't give her details of where I was or why I was sending the text, but I said what I hadn't been able to say before that day.

'I know I'm an alcoholic and I know I'm pretty fucked. Any chance you'd take me to a meeting when you're free?'

I sent that text just after four o'clock that afternoon. I had already been in touch with mates who were on the way into town, so I decided to stay out and continue drinking. I wouldn't have much hope for someone whose intention to stop drinking starts with a plan to continue drinking for the rest of the night.

Just as when I hurt my hip in the pool years earlier, though, I knew it was over. There was no point in denying the obvious any longer, but I wanted to prolong my final day before my life as I knew it would come to an end. I knew that the hangover the following morning would be inescapable, so I thought those final few hours would hardly make any difference. My mates arrived within an hour, and after a few pints at the Exchequer Bar, we went to Coppers. It was like being back in the Britannia Stadium on that Tuesday night in Stoke, almost exactly eight years earlier. I was physically present, but my mind was elsewhere. Nobody knew what was going on. I didn't tell anyone in my company how I was feeling. I was trying to savour the view one last time.

I ended up in McDonald's on Grafton Street in the early hours of Monday morning with Daniel McDonnell from the *Irish Independent*, but I only know this because he told me the following day. As usual, I was reliant on the memories of other people to find out how my night had gone.

I woke up around midday on Monday, sure my life was finished. I was single at the time, so I knew a life of celibacy lay ahead. Holidays would be out, weddings would be out, funerals would be out. I would need new friends and new interests, but I'd never go anywhere to make them. Sporting events and festivals and Arthur's Day would be for other people now. And I'd need to attend meetings with other alcoholics without anyone finding out.

I'd either be one of those people who keep falling off the wagon and then go back drinking or I'd somehow become someone who never drank again, with all the misery that came with it.

I couldn't decide which would be worse, but still I felt either would be better than how I felt now. That was how bad it was. I'd put myself in a corner where the only choices left were terrible. I knew I'd fucked everything up and I would never be able to drink again. My life as a normal, fun-loving person was over. Once again, I had been defeated. Once again, I'd failed at life.

15

22 August 2011

W̲e met on St Stephen's Green. I had a thousand questions and I was sure every one of them was stupid. Where would I sit? What should I say? How would I know what to do? But there was one question that I wanted answered above all the others – how can I not be seen?

This was the most shameful moment of my life. I was going to attend a meeting for recovering alcoholics. What if I bumped into somebody from RTÉ or the *Independent*? What if somebody recognised me?

The friend I had contacted on the Sunday afternoon about going to a meeting was away, but she had told me she knew somebody who could take me. It turned out we had met before and he said we could have a chat before heading to a meeting.

We met on a beautiful Wednesday afternoon in August. He told me to have an open mind and not to judge. Everyone is different; not everyone I'd see would be somebody I'd want to spend time with. We seemed to walk round and round the Green. He was patient and kind and everything he said made sense. I was terrified.

The sun was shining and the park was packed. It was perfect weather for a beer garden. If I'd had my way, I would have been in camouflage gear. I wanted to be invisible. I didn't want anyone to see me or ask where I was going. I didn't want anyone to ask me who I was with or why I was with them. I was about to walk into a meeting and tell a room full of strangers I was an alcoholic.

I hadn't drunk since the Sunday night running into Monday morning and it was Wednesday evening. In the days leading up to this, I'd had moments of excitement about starting off on this path, but they had always been overwhelmed by fear. I had cried every day, but that was nothing new.

This wasn't how my life was meant to pan out. Retiring had been a failure, but you could argue it was bad luck. This, on the other hand, was all my doing. I was a complete fuck-up and now I was making it official.

Just like Dad, I was now facing the prospect of a life without drinking. A boring, uneventful existence. No highs or lows, just sparkling water. The man with me knew how I was feeling. He had once felt the same. He didn't patronise me by saying it, but I knew from what he was telling me. And it helped that he did.

Those feelings remained with me throughout the meeting, but I also heard things that made total sense. People spoke and, somehow, they were telling my story. I could relate to almost everything they said. They talked about the obsession to drink and how it had lifted. They talked about how the damage was done by the first drink. That was the one to avoid, not the third or fourth. By then, it was too late.

They spoke about their feelings and they spoke about running from their feelings. The best thing about being sober is that you get your feelings back, one woman said. And then she added: the worst thing about being sober is that you get your feelings back.

The room laughed. What the fuck was this? I laughed too. What the fuck? It was warm and inclusive laughter. Laughter from a room that understood. This wasn't how I imagined the end of my life would look.

After the meeting, I had another shock. The man who had brought me introduced me to someone. I told him it was my first meeting.

'Congratulations,' he said and shook my hand with a grip which suggested he meant it. 'Well done.'

He didn't look for details about my drinking or about the reasons I'd stopped. He just congratulated me. I don't know if I ever met this man again, because as soon as I left the room, I forgot his face. But I remember his words and I remember how they made me feel. Why was he congratulating me for being a drunk?

The man who was with me told me he went to ninety meetings in his first ninety days. He didn't tell me I should do the same, he just told me this had helped him when he was starting out. I liked the idea; in fact, it seemed like the kind of plan that could get me out of this hole.

That was Wednesday evening. I went back the following day. On Friday, I went twice. The meetings were a place where what I was going through made sense. And it quickly became clear that it was about a lot more than drinking. This was a place where I could be myself.

On the Saturday I mixed up the times and showed up late. I was too embarrassed to interrupt the meeting by walking in halfway through. I wanted to be unseen, not the centre of attention. I walked up to the door and paused for a moment, long enough to talk myself out of it. As I walked away from the building, I berated myself for being such a fearful little shit.

You're thirty-fucking-two and you can't open a door?

Afraid people will look at you?

Pathetic cunt.

I walked back to the door and tried again, but the same thing happened. I got as far as holding the handle but the outcome was the same. I couldn't do it. Ireland had played England in rugby that day and the city was packed. I walked back to my car through crowds of people laughing and drinking in the streets. I didn't belong in that world any more, but there I was, too afraid to walk into a meeting slightly late. I couldn't even tell anybody how I was feeling because I was still too ashamed.

I was in no man's land, but I had been six days off drink, and it was the first day I didn't cry about it. I called my friend and he told me where I could get a meeting later that evening. So I went there instead.

The meetings were nothing like I had imagined they would be. This would soon become a theme: everything I imagined, the opposite turned out to be true. I began to see that my life might not be over. I began to understand that I would only be bored if I tried to pretend I could live my old life, but just replace alcohol with sparkling water.

On the Sunday of my first week, my mates were heading back to Marbella. I was the one who had persuaded them to go back and they weren't taking my withdrawal from the trip too well. I had been getting daily calls, badgering me into going, and they weren't taking no for an answer. I wasn't prepared to tell the truth, but nothing I said sounded remotely convincing. I sent them a text saying I was off drink. They'd heard this from me before. This was different. This time, I was done.

I told them I had some money tied up in an investment and couldn't get my hands on the cash. One of them offered to give me five hundred quid's worth of drugs. He knew it wouldn't be enough for the whole week, but it would be a start. It felt like they had drawn up a schedule coordinating their efforts to entice me back. It was relentless.

'You gotten over your hangover yet?'

'Still got the fear, you prick?'

'Snapped out if it yet?'

'You know you don't have to drink if you come?'

'It could be good to relax for a few days sober in the sunshine. Maybe just take it easy.'

I'd rather they believed I was broke than tell them I was in recovery. But I would have acted the same as them if the roles had been reversed. I could see why my parents had hidden Dad's treatment from the neighbours twenty-two years earlier. I could see why we had been told as kids that he was away on business. The shame of taking steps to address a drink problem wasn't an alien concept now. I knew I'd get nowhere without the support of my own family, but keeping the truth from everyone else was my main priority.

I told Anna first by text. I'd been crying every day of that first week and couldn't face a lengthy phone call with her. She had moved to England earlier that summer. She compared my decision to stop drinking to her moving abroad, saying it would transform my life in the long run if I could just stick with it.

I told Mum that week. We were sitting in her sitting room when I told her I had been to a couple of meetings. She didn't interrupt me once. She just silently listened to everything I said. No questions, no directives, no lectures. At the end, she looked at me and said one thing.

'Do you notice I'm not one bit surprised?'

She didn't say anything else, just gave me a hug.

I told Catherine that weekend. She cried as if it was really great news, but I wasn't ready to see things that way.

When I told Jamie, he immediately asked if there was anything he could do to help. All of them were supportive and kind. From then on, none of them drank at family dinners. It always seemed they were either driving or too tired or had something important on the following day. I didn't ask them to avoid drinking around me, but they did. I knew my family and how they would react.

I also knew I should tell Dad as soon as possible. The conversation began by text.

'Hey, Dad, are you home?'

For someone who didn't drink, he was out of his house a surprising amount. He believed that sitting in front of the TV on his own was a waste of his life. I assumed that's all anyone would do if they didn't drink, but that wasn't his way.

'I am. Everything OK?'

'Is it OK if I call over to talk about something?' It was 10pm on Saturday night. I had just been to a meeting.

'Sure. I'll put the kettle on.'

When I called over, I got straight to it. I told him I had been to meetings and that I had stopped drinking. I said I had known for ages that I had a drink problem and that my life had gone to shit. I didn't want to go too strong by declaring I would never drink again, because I assumed he knew how pointless those promises could be.

He asked if I had considered going into treatment, but I said I hadn't. I knew I wouldn't be able to do that without telling RTÉ and the *Sunday Independent*. My mates would find out too. Fuck that. I said I would persevere with therapy and meetings and keep it under wraps. I knew about the benefits of going to rehab from learning about it in college. I was just hoping it wouldn't be something I needed, while also realising I didn't have a clue about what I needed. I just knew that if I didn't get help, I wouldn't stop drinking.

I was too uncomfortable to speak for long about it, so I left fairly soon after I arrived. Dad and I hugged as I left. It was a hug of identification, I think. The first of its kind between us.

Attending meetings was how I was making sense of the whole thing. I listened, I spoke and I identified. Within a week, they had become my daily priority.

I realised how important they were pretty quickly as well. I had cleared a couple of hurdles by avoiding the trip to Marbella and getting through the weekend of the Dublin v Donegal All-Ireland semi-final sober. Normally that would have been the signal for a session, but I had avoided it.

The following Tuesday, I found myself thinking that maybe I was overstating the problem. Maybe I could drink in moderation like I'd always planned.

I had assumed weddings or big occasions would be the tricky hurdles to get over, but here I was on a Tuesday afternoon plotting a return to drink after eight days. This was why the meetings were essential. I heard talk that alcoholism was cunning, baffling and powerful. It was a disease which convinced you that you didn't have it, and that is what I was experiencing now. I went to meetings and the pressure would ease.

I was adamant I couldn't tell any of the lads, not even Hicksy. My sister Catherine and her daughter Jess, who was now four, had moved in with me. I had the stability of a family life without the responsibilities that go with it. The best of both worlds.

In my immediate circle, I had told the people who mattered, but I was determined nobody else could know. It was a mixture of shame and embarrassment. I didn't know if there would be room in our group for someone who was sober, which was a terrifying thought. Would I lose the friends I'd had for twenty years because I stopped drinking? I didn't want to jeopardise our friendship and I thought this would. I also worried they would try to talk me out of it.

To remind myself why I didn't go to Marbella, I had offered to pick some of the lads up at the airport the following week when they came home. The sight of them as they struggled through arrivals was the reminder I needed. This had once been enjoyable, and it still was for them, but this wasn't about judgement; this was about realising that that life was no longer for me.

Sometimes the enormity of what I was doing was overwhelming. When I had retired for the second time after my failed comeback attempt, I had accepted that there was no way back to football. But there was always a way back to drink. How could I avoid it when it was everywhere? Like the teenage me obsessing about the many ways I could die before I was twenty, I would spend hours worrying about the ways I could drink.

Meetings usually put me right. One day at a time is the best-known cliché, but I began to see how it makes sense. 'Don't drink today,' people would say. 'That's all you have to do.' When it was broken down like that, it made each day without a drink manageable.

I got a ticket for the All-Ireland final between Kerry and Dublin. By this stage, I hadn't had a drink in twenty-eight days, but I wasn't ready to accept I had to sit out an occasion like this. It was still a novelty for the lads having a designated driver in the group, so I was in demand. I drove into town with three of them drinking cans next to me in the car. Each of them took turns to grill me about my reasons for being sober on a day like this. This is how it is always going to be: endless questions from drunk people about why I wasn't drinking.

When Stephen Cluxton's free kick won the game for Dublin in the final minutes, Croke Park erupted.

There was adrenaline everywhere and I knew I was in trouble. I knew I had to get out of there. Fuck the lads. We weren't sitting next to each other, which meant I could run straight to my car and go to a meeting without any questions from them. We were due to get together in town after the game, but I texted to say I was needed at home. I went to two meetings that evening, feeling very sorry for myself. I had already been to a meeting that morning. Everyone I knew was out celebrating. Even the lads who weren't big GAA fans knew it was a session not to miss. It was like walking away from the Millwall Christmas party seven years earlier, except I couldn't take cocaine or drink to lift my mood.

I treated the psychotherapy college course as a practice run for the outside world. I told some of my classmates I was going to meetings. After a couple of months, I said it in our group therapy sessions. I spoke about it during a presentation I had to give about addiction to the whole class. A room of trainee therapists was the ideal crowd. Compassionate, understanding, supportive. I knew they wouldn't judge me or shame me or gossip.

I still went to pubs, but drinking sparkling water only highlighted my sobriety. Most of my conversations went the same way. People grilled me about my reasons for not drinking while talking about their own desire to stop. The drunker they got, the more bored I got. I knew I didn't belong there once people got drunk, but I didn't fit in anywhere else. It was either this or sit at home, and I didn't want that.

I was talking to a friend about this one day and he said it isn't difficult to be around people who are drunk, it's just boring. I struggled to accept this at the time; I suppose I wasn't ready to consider that I could be bored in the company of my best mates. But I was starting to realise that if things ever got difficult, I could always leave.

This helped and it was also the start of seeing life differently. A sober life wasn't a life without excitement, as long as I realised everything had changed.

My paranoia was one feeling I could have done without. I was certain that people would know I was in recovery and this drove me demented. If I missed a call from someone, I assumed they were ringing to tell me they knew I had been at a meeting. If people were breezy about me not drinking, I assumed they knew. If they were grilling me for explanations, I assumed they knew. If they didn't bring it up in conversations, I assumed it was because they knew and would find it too awkward to talk about. Whatever the response, I was sure it meant one thing.

I see it differently now. Now I have no problem with people knowing I don't drink. Why should I? The days when a conversation might lead to a discovery that I'd slept with a girl in a blackout were the days I should have felt awkward about. Not the days when I went to a meeting, talked about how I was feeling and made a conscious effort to improve my life.

Still, it was a day-to-day struggle. A few weeks in and I had to deal with something that I'd normally have handled in the pub. I'd recorded an interview for a Channel 4 programme, *The Truth about Drugs in Football*. I'd talked about an experience at Millwall where I'd spent a season taking a range of pills handed to us without question, and was then told the following season that one of them was a banned substance.

I expected a hostile reaction to this and my normal response was to deal with the feedback in the pub. Instead, I was at a meeting. In fact, I was so preoccupied with meetings that when I got a call from the *Daily Mail*, I thought it was because they were planning to run a story about me being seen at a meeting. It turned out they wanted to ask me about the programme.

As the days went by, I found life becoming easier. The things I thought would be difficult or unenjoyable never unfolded as I thought they would. I was enjoying the novelty of never losing days to being hungover.

In October I went to a wedding sober. I made sure I had an escape route planned and I didn't stay long, but that didn't matter. I went to a meeting later that night, proud I'd done something I thought I could never do.

I went to at least one meeting a day for the first 96 days. On day 97, I had a dilemma. I was offered a ticket for a Kasabian gig in the 3Arena, which would mean I wouldn't get to a meeting as planned. I wanted to go but I wasn't sure how to interpret my feelings. Were my priorities slipping? Was I starting to take my eye off the ball? Was this a tell-tale sign that I'd drink again? I rang a friend and he put me at ease.

'There's no point in getting sober if you don't enjoy your life. It's not about sitting in meetings, it's about living. Go and enjoy it. And if you're not enjoying it, remember, you can leave any time.'

Like the wedding, I got through it without drinking, secure in the knowledge I had an escape route.

As the weeks turned into months, I found that I was enjoying myself. Life without drink wasn't just bearable, it was fun.

'The best thing about not drinking is not drinking,' a friend in recovery told me. I saw what he meant. I went to gigs, I went out for dinner, I did plenty of things that I used to do, but drink was no longer at the heart of my life. When I did things with people who were also in recovery, it was easier. To my surprise, going out with people who didn't drink could be a lot of fun.

I was becoming reliable. Catherine could ask me to babysit and she knew I would be there. I didn't weep uncontrollably watching *The West Wing*. Life was getting better in all sorts of ways.

I was in the smoking area of Doheny & Nesbitt's one evening after an RTÉ show that December. I was practically chain-smoking at the time to help me get through. I made eye contact with a girl and she was giving me the impression she was keen to chat. It's an awful realisation to have when you're 32 years old, but I knew I wouldn't be able to speak to her sober. How do you flirt without drink? How do you compliment someone sober? I told my mates I was needed at home and left before she could get close.

I decided to follow the lead of some other people I knew in recovery. They stayed out of relationships in their early days to protect themselves. The emotional highs and lows that come with it all are best avoided. Some stayed single for months, some a year. Others committed to being single for a full two years. These were personal decisions they made, under pressure from nobody. They just saw that it worked for others and tried it themselves. I was ready to commit to it myself, so that's what I did. I decided to stay away from the dating world until I was two years sober.

It was easy in one way. I was abstaining from something I thought would be beyond me anyway. It's not difficult to avoid an option that doesn't exist. That's not much of a sacrifice.

The only difficulties arose because I told nobody about it. Being single was taken on by others as a problem to solve. I would regularly get calls and texts from mates or their partners with suggestions of single girls they thought I would like. The opening was always the same. 'Seriously, Richie, she's perfect for you. I wouldn't be ringing you otherwise. She's down to earth and sound, big into yoga and barely drinks. Not into pretentious shit at all. She doesn't give a shit about football and she's gorgeous. It's hard to believe she's single, actually.'

There wasn't much room to object to any of that, but I did every time.

'Ah, I'm up to my eyes with college and work and shit. I wouldn't be into it at the moment. Any craic with you?'

I had to learn how to be without drink and it was best to find out myself first without bringing anyone else into it. I was finally learning that I couldn't hide, and hiding was something I had always done in relationships, so I was better off without them for a while.

Anna suggested a few days in the sunshine in Nice. The trip coincided with my first anniversary sober, which I celebrated by attending a local meeting where a load of strangers gave me hugs and encouragement for getting that far. It was different from anything else I'd been praised for doing in my life, but this seemed to trump them all. By a distance, it had been my most difficult achievement, and there was also the knowledge that, on this anniversary, it was just another day. This wasn't Dry November. I would start tomorrow with the same intention – don't drink today. It was all I had to do. That was so liberating.

My second anniversary was different. My expectations were higher. I had steered clear of any sex or dating. During that whole time, I hadn't so much as held someone's hand. I assumed I would feel different by then. I assumed I would be the perfect blend of relaxed and confident. Basically, after a two-year build-up, I assumed I'd be hot shit. It didn't pan out that way.

I was still nervous of going near anyone or, maybe more to the point, letting anyone near me. They'd ask why I wasn't drinking. I couldn't be honest, but I didn't want to lie. If I told the truth and we broke up, my secret would be out. I wasn't up for all the socialising that would come with it either. There are only so many times you'll get away with saying you're not in the mood to go out. And on top of all that, I was still baffled about how I'd have sex. I considered pushing it out to three years at the time, because I knew I was nowhere.

Then, a few months later, I took the plunge. I went on my first sober date. I had moved to Enniskerry village in Wicklow for some peace, having sold the house in Firhouse at a loss of €300,000. One of my dogs, Paddy, had been put down by the vet after a series of illnesses, so it was just me and Frank. My social life consisted of little more than regular cups of tea with my next-door neighbour Mary, a widow in her eighties.

Every day I walked in the local woods, so when I was arranging this date, I suggested we go there. The girl was lovely, but I was a nervous wreck.

'It's so nice here,' she said, 'so peaceful.'

We had just reached the edge of the woods. I figured I'd bowl her over with some local trivia. 'Yeah, apparently Larry Murphy did some of his crimes up around here. Not sure exactly where, though.'

'Who's Larry Murphy?' she asked.

As I told her, I began to wonder if this was the ideal subject to bring up with a girl you've never met as she's about to walk alone with you into a wooded area.

'You're so lucky you get to come here every day,' she said, generously moving things on from my stories of violent sex offenders.

'Yeah, I know, best thing of all is that in about fifty yards you won't get a phone signal. I love being totally uncontactable.'

On reflection, I could have put a bit of distance between those two nuggets of information.

Unsurprisingly, there was no second date, but that didn't matter to me. Once again, I had done something which I had previously considered beyond me. I was learning to live again, albeit at a slower pace than I would have liked, but it was progress. I was back in the game.

I went on dates, began relationships. None of them lasted long, but that didn't matter. I was reliable, dependable and sober. The old me wouldn't have liked the new me, but the old me didn't even like the old me so that didn't really matter. And then, on 20 November 2013, I did something I once genuinely thought I'd never be able to do. Exactly 821 days after that last drink in Coppers, I finally had sex in sobriety.

———

The week of my second birthday in sobriety, RTÉ's caption about me scoring in a European U-18 third-place play-off appeared. I was sitting next to John Giles, covering a Champions League game between Arsenal and Fenerbahçe.

This wasn't actually the only time RTÉ used that caption to illustrate my impeccable sporting credentials. It first appeared on a Monday Night Soccer programme years earlier during a discussion about the youth tournaments. It was an odd choice even then, but at least it was relevant to that segment of the show. It was obviously still on file somewhere, so the graphics coordinator on this Champions League programme figured it would be appropriate to use it too. He couldn't possibly have known how much joy he would bring to so many people.

Where previously I would have found it difficult to be the butt of so many one-liners and internet memes, I laughed this one off. I was achieving things in my personal life that dwarfed anything I had done on a football field. This was the stuff that mattered to me now. I was able to recall how I felt when I scored that goal, the first time I scored for my country, and was grateful that I was able to have done it at all. I was two years clean and sober and I was feeling pretty good.

I was still struggling to find new ways to hang out with some of my own mates now that I was sober. I still wasn't comfortable enough to tell them I was in recovery. Some backed away, unsure how to take this new version of me, while others did their best to readjust. I wasn't drinking or taking drugs, but I hadn't got sober so I could hang out with anyone while they were off their head. Dog-walks, gym sessions, phone calls and the odd cup of coffee was all there was. No festivals or rollovers or house parties. It was the kind of social life I would have previously dismissed, but this was my new reality. No hangovers, no blackouts, no regrets and no carnage.

16

The Football Men

'Come to me first, Darragh.'

The Barcelona–Manchester City game was coming to an end and, in the RTÉ studio, we were dividing up the analysis.

As a game was about to finish, we would decide who was going to speak over which pieces of match footage and who would start the chat with some of their own thoughts – just a brief but general synopsis of the match. If you wanted somebody to put a game into a broader cultural context, there was nobody like Eamon Dunphy.

So when Eamon asked Darragh to come to him straight away to summarise the game, I just gathered my own thoughts, as usual, and prepared myself.

Barcelona had beaten Pep Guardiola's City 4-0 and there was a lot to say. Eamon seemed to have something in mind.

When Darragh came to him, Eamon spoke for almost four minutes. He discussed the flaws in Pep Guardiola's management style and why they mattered. He listed off a number of things he felt it was important to do in football, things which he said Guardiola's side were not doing. He spoke about the cult that surrounded Guardiola, he mentioned hubris and vanity. It was all there.

Eamon went on for some time, longer than I had expected, but after we went off-air, I learned why.

'I wasn't going to get a chance to call the guy who writes my *Star* column before the newspaper's deadline, so I had to dictate it to him on-air. I told him to be ready.'

I picked up a copy of *The Star* the next morning and it was almost word-for-word what he had said in that uninterrupted opening monologue. That was showbusiness, baby!

I was in awe of Eamon's talent when I first started working with him, but soon became aware that the neck which accompanied it was the more dominant feature.

When he left RTÉ in 2018, he let it be known that he was concerned about the direction the station was taking and was going to concentrate on his podcast. But I was happy he was leaving, whatever the story. My relationship with the three senior panellists had not been easy at times, but there were always ways of communicating with John Giles and Liam Brady.

With Eamon, it was different. Our working relationship, if you could even call it that, had been in decline for years. Towards the end of our time working together, I would look for some neutral non-contentious topic to break the ice between us early on. I didn't want to be his mate, but I knew the situation could get nasty if we didn't keep a lid on it. I couldn't bring myself to ask him about football in case that gave the impression I valued his opinions, so I would seize on any non-football chat he came out with. By the time he left, I'd had three years of avoiding conflict.

Things had begun fairly well between the two of us. I first met him when I was a guest on *The Dunphy Show* just after I'd retired. He couldn't have been nicer to me and my family afterwards. In my early years as a pundit, RTÉ would only offer me one-year contracts, so in 2013 when TV3 offered me a two-year contract, I wasn't sure what to do. Eamon offered to speak to RTÉ on my behalf. I remember specific advice he gave me in those days.

He was always encouraging and helpful to people when they were starting out. It was usually appreciated because he knew his way around. But he had a warning too, which he delivered with a bit of authority.

'Things are going OK for you at the moment, Richie,' he said. 'The big test is how you cope when the whole country thinks you're a cunt.'

He spoke from experience there, and on many other matters. I wanted to take it all in. Eamon, John and, later, Liam were the people the country turned to for their football education.

Back on that day in 1989 when we visited Dad in the treatment centre, it was Giles and Dunphy doing the analysis on the Malta game, with Bill O'Herlihy presenting. Watching Ireland games came hand in hand with listening to them afterwards. When I first started to do the big games with the three senior pundits, it didn't feel like I was being selected to be one of a three-person panel. It was more like being given temporary use of someone else's chair: John's to the left, Liam's in the middle, Eamon's to the right.

The panel all had war stories, Eamon in particular, and it was hard initially not to be in awe of that. Stepping on to the set with them was daunting at first. How could it not be?

After I'd worked on their League of Ireland coverage for over a year, in 2008 the producers of RTÉ's one-hour Premier League highlights show, *Premier League Sunday*, asked me to appear on a recording of a show that would never go to air. It was being filmed midweek, purely to test new software on the production side of things. Peter Collins was the presenter and I would be the only pundit. The editor of the show said I should use it as an audition, as they were looking to add to their list of regular pundits.

It wasn't the big break I hoped it might be. I wasn't confident enough to assert my opinions about anything. I was too unsure of myself and just went along with other people's suggestions about which pieces of footage to analyse and what to say about them. During the recording, I was waffly, hesitant, almost apologetic for being there. The possibility that I might work on the show for real wasn't mentioned again.

Television is a tough place for the insecure. I was trying to make a career in that business at a time when my life was out of control. I was still drinking heavily when it began, but when I got sober, it was another arena where everything changed or, to put it another way, where my view of everything changed.

I didn't believe then that I was at the level of the senior panellists, but I knew I was better than that audition had demonstrated. Losing matches is one thing, but playing terribly is another. I knew I didn't do myself justice and my aim was to put that right. I didn't give myself a target or a deadline for anything specific, I just aimed to do it better from then on and to speak my mind.

Eighteen months later, in 2010, they called me again. I was asked to work on a live broadcast of the show for real the following weekend. I'd be giving my views on the Premier League now, but crucially, I'd be working with a different set of pundits – Trevor Steven, Ronnie Whelan, Ray Houghton, Kenny Cunningham, John Giles, Eamon Dunphy, Liam Brady – every one of them with playing careers that made mine look pathetic.

My third appearance on that show was my first time working with Eamon. The pundits watch the games of the day live in RTÉ and share their thoughts with the editing team throughout the day. Not on this day, though. The Manchester derby kicked off at 12.45, and Eamon said he'd watch the match at home. He rang at half-time to say he needed sleep, but the editor was instructed to ring John Giles for the analysis. John wouldn't be appearing that evening, but that didn't seem to be an issue. Eamon said that he and John see the game the same way, so it wouldn't be a problem if the editor called John to provide Eamon Dunphy's views on a match Dunphy wouldn't be watching because he was asleep.

Before we went on air, he said he hadn't seen any of the Chelsea–Swansea game, the other match we'd be focusing on. He'd needed the sleep, he said.

He hid the fact he couldn't talk about the Manc derby by going off on a rant about City's Stephen Ireland being 'a pup'; he would often use similar strategies over the coming years. It was the most enjoyable TV show I'd ever worked on at that point, purely because of him.

It was always more exciting working with Eamon, as you never fully knew what he might say next. His best years were well behind him by the time we started working together, but he still had a presence in the studio that no other pundit could match.

When John Giles first heard I was stepping up to do the Premier League stuff, he rang and asked me to meet him for a chat. We had never spoken to one another before.

'I hear you're going to be doing a bit of work with us,' he said.

'Yeah, I'm starting this week. Doing *Premier Soccer Saturday*,' I answered, still unsure of why he was ringing or how I should act.

'Fancy meeting in Rosie O'Grady's on Friday morning?'

It didn't suit, but I figured I had no option. I had my *Sunday Independent* column to write, but it was John Giles on the other end of the phone. 'Of course, John. Just say what time suits you and I'll be there.'

We spent over three hours together, and it only ended because I called a halt to it. I really had to go home to start the column. He passed on a lot of tips, especially on the need to make sure the 'television people' didn't dictate the agenda. 'They don't know football,' he said. He offered to come in and shadow me on my first day to help me out. I declined, fearing it would make me look like an intern, but he came in anyway. For a long time, I tried to strike a balance between being respectful and not appearing to be their subordinate, which was tricky given that I was subordinate to them in every way. I knew I wouldn't last long in the job if I just agreed with everything they said, but I was afraid I'd be finished before I started if I challenged them too soon.

John was so helpful at the beginning. In addition to meeting me to offer advice, he would often give me little pointers on how to be better.

He would tell me to deliberately begin my answers with a louder tone and to project myself a little better. He also told me to stop looking up at the ceiling. During games he would openly share his observations on what we were watching, pointing out little things in the play. Even when he knew he wasn't analysing a specific goal, for example, he would share his thoughts for no other reason than to be helpful. Don't just describe a goal, he would say, give the viewers an explanation of why it happened.

Dealing with the panel was only one part of the job. Twitter reactions influenced me strongly at the time, but the voice in my head that said I didn't belong there had a much bigger impact.

Who the fuck do you think you are, sharing a platform with John Giles?

Why should anyone care what a clown like you thinks anyway?

Never played in the Premier League and there you are passing comment on Cristiano Ronaldo.

John would ring me every week in those days to discuss my *Sunday Independent* column and to ask what I was writing about. He just loved to talk about football. Even in weeks when I would have my column already written, he would still ring to bounce around his thoughts on the issues of the day. He was generous with his time, his advice and his experience.

I began to grow a little in confidence the longer I was there.

———

Working on the highlights shows of the 2010 World Cup was the next step up from the Premiership shows. Then, I was on the panel for live games during the 2012 European Championships, but not for Ireland games. After that tournament, I was told I would be working on some Ireland games during the qualifiers for the 2014 World Cup.

Bill O'Herlihy ran the show but back then the RTÉ panel were three specific people when it came to Ireland games. Three household names, three broadcasting giants. Two of them – John and Liam – are among the best players Ireland has ever produced. And then I come along with my eighteen minutes in an international friendly.

Ryle Nugent, Head of Sport, advised me to make sure I had my 'ducks in a row' when going up against them. 'They won't hold back if you disagree with them on air so you better be able to back it up.' He was dead right.

I found it difficult to work with Liam Brady early on. He had an aura about him which I found intimidating. I would sit next to him wondering what the hell someone with my career was doing swapping opinions with a Juventus great like him. He never once said anything that suggested he thought the same, but at the time I assumed he did. Sometimes, I didn't help matters.

My first live Ireland international was the match against Kazakhstan in September 2012. Ireland scored two late goals to win 2-1 but hadn't played well. On the back of being awful in that summer's Euros I didn't think the analysis afterwards should be about the spirit of the players or their never-say-die attitude. Bill came to me first. I think he noticed I had reacted differently from Liam and John, the other panellists, who had both punched the air in delight when Ireland had scored. I was just pissed off that the result would mean the continuation of Trapattoni's era. I had already made up my mind that he needed to go, and Bill sensed I might have something to say. Bill was always switched on to things like that.

I called on John Delaney to do what was required. Liam strongly disagreed, saying it was now the players' responsibility to get Trapattoni to alter his approach. Liam had worked with Trapattoni for years and they were good friends, so me calling for him to be sacked didn't exactly bring us close together. I think whatever goodwill Liam may have had towards me evaporated that night.

My relationship with John Giles changed too when I was selected to be on the panel for the Ireland v Scotland game in June 2015. According to an unnamed source in *The Star*, 'the panel' were reportedly furious that John would not be working on the game the following Saturday. Just like the Scotland away game earlier in the campaign, Liam, Eamon and I were chosen to do this one together. 'RTÉ AXE GILES' was the headline on Monday's front page.

Weighing in behind the unnamed source, Eamon wrote a column in *The Star* slamming the decision. John himself appeared on Newstalk that Thursday saying he was at a loss to know why he wasn't working on the game. He said he'd do it for free; it didn't matter to him that he had completed his contractual list of games. He said his situation was still undecided for the following season – as it was with every other panellist at that time – which led to some accusations that RTÉ were disrespecting an idol.

I was being hounded all week for comment, but I didn't answer my phone. One caller got through, though. *The Star* had decided to begin a public campaign to get John reinstated to the panel and a reporter got on to me.

'Hi Richie, I'm just wondering if you've any thoughts on John joining the panel as a fourth member on Saturday,' he said, after introducing himself.

'Write whatever ye like, lads. I'm staying out of this one,' I answered, and I wished him well and hung up the phone. He included those quotes in his article the following day.

Everyone I met that week asked me about it, but I just kept my head down and stayed out of it. Privately, I had plenty to say. I saw it in the same light as a player going to the press to complain that he'd been dropped. Not only would that be an obvious show of disrespect to the manager, but it's a public slap in the face to the player who has been selected in his place. John suggested on Newstalk that Eamon had approached Ryle Nugent on his behalf to argue his case. I found Eamon's behaviour predictable, given how things were between us at the time, but I was surprised by John's response to the whole situation.

Ryle had told us all three years earlier that, due to their looming retirement, the panel would be in a type of transition phase, with other pundits being used regularly. I could have done without the attention for the week, but I wasn't dealing with anything new. The feeling that I was sitting in someone else's seat was never too far from my mind.

On the day itself, things were frosty enough in the studio, with no handshake or interaction between myself and Eamon. We thawed out a little during the show, but had a row on the air at the end about schoolboy football. As ever, it had nothing to do with the topic under discussion. There was no time for any post-show interaction, because as soon as the programme ended, I sprinted out of there to a nearby vacant room, where I had thirty-five minutes to write a column for the following day's *Sunday Independent*.

John left RTÉ a year later, immediately after the final of Euro 2016. He should have been given a huge send-off but things had gone pretty sour between him and RTÉ by then. He said he didn't want anything, so nothing was arranged. He had publicly called out Ryle Nugent for not renewing his deal and said he was very much still available for work elsewhere.

The phone chats about the football issues of the day had long stopped by then, but I rang John a couple of days after he left to wish him well. I wanted to thank him for all the help, particularly in the early years. He didn't need to be as supportive and generous as he was, and I was grateful for that. The call was polite and civil, but only lasted around a minute.

John and I never fell out, but things were different during that last year between us. We kept it short and sweet whenever we saw one another.

Bill O'Herlihy was great from the start. He'd pull me aside before shows and give me some words of advice or encouragement.

'Be sure to say your piece in there. You know your stuff, don't hold back. People want to hear from you as much as the other panellists. Remember that.'

I wasn't so sure, but I appreciated him saying it.

Bill would always give me little nods of encouragement off camera during live discussions, as if to say, *Well, Richie, what do you think? Get involved.* He could say it all in a look. He'd give me a little wink occasionally to settle me down, particularly if I had stood my ground in a debate. *Good man. You're doing fine.*

He did an interview on radio where he was asked about the long-term future of football punditry on RTÉ and he singled me out for praise. He gushed about the range of experience I brought to the panel. 'This guy has done almost everything: player, agent, journalist, club CEO, he's worked in the academy system in England, and now he's a pundit – the only gap on his CV is management itself.' While it mattered a great deal back then that someone like him was saying that, it certainly wasn't how I was seeing it at the time.

I'd just landed in Dublin Airport on a lovely summer's day in May 2015 when I turned on my phone and learned Bill had died. I hadn't been in contact with Bill much after he left RTÉ, but the news stunned me. Bill had a presence that always left me looking forward to seeing him again and it felt so cruel for his family that he wasn't going to have the long retirement he deserved.

On his final night in RTÉ after the World Cup final in 2014, he managed to make a night that should have been about him into a memory cherished by everyone else who was there. He always made you feel better about yourself. It was his gift as a broadcaster. It was his even greater gift as a human being.

———

The furore about John's exclusion had followed on from an on-air argument between myself and Eamon during the final stages of the Champions League in May 2015.

It was to do with Pep Guardiola, but it was really nothing to do with him. It was a turf war. I had been there too long and he seemed ready to chop me down.

After we had finished our analysis of Juventus drawing 1-1 with Real Madrid, we started to discuss Barcelona's 5-3 aggregate victory over Bayern Munich in the other semi-final the previous night. Eamon started to lay into then Bayern manager Guardiola for his inability to set up a team defensively.

I didn't contradict him, I just said that I'd want several examples of this over many years before I'd reach such a conclusion. To me, it felt like a knee-jerk reaction to two bad performances by a team missing several key players through injury, not to mention being up against one of the best striking trios there has ever been (Messi, Suarez, Neymar). Eamon interrupted and things spiralled from there. By this stage, I didn't care about being the respectful new recruit anymore. I was no longer preoccupied with how I was perceived by the other panellists. I was there to do a job.

I stood my ground and pulled Eamon up on a couple of inaccuracies, something I wouldn't have done before. He said only two teams could win La Liga due to their financial dominance – Barcelona and Real Madrid – so I pointed out that Atletico Madrid were the reigning champions. He said the winning margins that the top teams get in Spain wouldn't happen in the Premier League. I said that Man City had won their game 6-0 three days earlier.

He took great exception to Darragh mentioning on air a statistic about Guardiola's defensive record during the debate. The stat showed that Guardiola had the best defensive record in every league he'd managed in for the previous six years, a relevant point to make given the topic of the discussion and not something someone with considered opinions on the topic should be surprised about. Eamon took it as an ambush, as if Darragh had produced it to deliberately trip him up, but it was in the media pack we had all been given before the show.

He carried on the debate after the cameras were off, challenging Darragh about where the stat came from, demanding to know why he hadn't been told of it beforehand. It's not exactly an obscure detail about a manager nobody knows about. Like any football stat, there's still room to debate the merits of it, but there was no post-show handshake between us from that night.

These spats made for good TV and there were plenty of times when Liam and John or Eamon and Liam would have a row and it would have no bearing on their relationship. The dynamic between myself and Eamon was different. Our relationship had a bearing on every argument. The days of it being a thrill to be alongside him were long gone. It was all getting fairly tiresome by this stage.

Things were never the same after that. The two years that followed John Giles's retirement were unpleasant between Eamon and me. Working with him could still be enjoyable, but it was like eating a meal thinking your food will be taken away at any moment. You needed to be vigilant talking on air with him nearby. He was always ready to lob a grenade in at any time.

When Ireland played Wales in Dublin in April 2017, one of the features of the game was the physicality of some of the Irish players. I called out some of the challenges as being bookable or red card offences, but Eamon wasn't having it.

'I need to stop this,' he proclaimed, as if he was about to introduce some much-needed sense into the discussion. It descended into a row about aggression versus indiscipline, but, as ever, that wasn't what the argument was about. And just to illustrate how learned he is on the topic, he said that the use of elbows as a tactic hadn't been a part of football until the last ten years. There was no handshake and no farewell that day either.

By this stage I was deliberately saying as little as possible in pre-show production meetings if we were working together. I'd ring the programme editor beforehand to outline my views and what I wanted to say. If you shared information or opinions in front of Eamon, you ran the risk of him saying it all on air before you had the chance. It's a lesson that every new pundit working with him learns the hard way.

A large part of my prep when working with Eamon was to get myself ready for his nonsense. Don't bite on anything daft he comes out with, but say my piece every chance I get without unnecessarily provoking him. Life's too short to be arguing with Eamon Dunphy, but then again, it was probably a fundamental part of the job.

By the time the 2018 World Cup came around, it was tough to be in the same room as him. I'd always look to find common ground, but we knew we were reaching the end. Ryle Nugent had recently been replaced but there had been no announcement on any of the panellists' future. All our contracts were up at the end of the tournament, but Eamon was acting like a man who knew his fate. He'd regularly arrive late for pre-show meetings, smelling of drink.

But he was still a potent force so I would manage him as best I could off air. Sometimes I would ask about his family. During the World Cup I'd amuse him by showing him whatever new footage was doing the rounds of Diego Maradona in the vicinity of a bag of cocaine.

One Wednesday night in February 2018, we discussed media reports about Susan Boyle's financial situation. A couple of days earlier, I wouldn't have predicted we'd be speaking to one another at all.

On the previous Sunday evening, I'd been tagged in a tweet by *The Star* that Eamon's column the following day would be a no-holds barred critique of me and *The Irish Times*.

I had written about Wes Hoolahan's retirement from international football in the *Times* the previous day. Rather than repeat the line that he should have had more caps by the time he retired, I wrote about the credit we should be giving him from transforming himself from the person he'd been in his early twenties. He'd had some edges which needed to be smoothed out, something Wes himself had acknowledged in interviews several times. Even if I hadn't seen the numerous quotes from Wes over the years, I was aware of it all because I'd been working for the sports agency that represented him at the time.

I chose not to bother reading Eamon's piece, as I had long since decided his opinions weren't of any interest. But on the Monday evening, RTÉ asked me to read it. Eamon and I were due to be on the panel together for coverage of Porto v Liverpool in the Champions League two days later. Better to know what was actually written, they said, in case it gets brought up on air, which I suppose was true. 'Sadlier Made a Hool of Himself' was the headline on the top corner of the front page, and inside was a two-page spread in which Eamon attacked me personally.

'As usual,' he wrote, 'Richie Sadlier makes it all about Richie Sadlier.' He went on to call my opinions 'utterly shameful', 'disgraceful' and 'deeply unfair'. The column was damaging and demeaning to Wes, too, apparently. 'The Irish Times and Richie Sadlier should be ashamed,' he concluded.

I was livid. Then about twenty seconds later, I was no longer livid at him, I just turned on myself for taking any notice of what he had written. Why should I care what Eamon Dunphy thinks about anything? Briefly I did, though. I was fed up with being put in a position where, yet again, I'd have to remain silent for the greater good. If I said anything publicly, or even to his face privately, it could have all kicked off between us. I was beginning to resent having to be the bigger man with a 72-year-old.

Knowing we were due to be on together two nights later, I had a decision to make. What's the best way to act when I see him in the studio?

The following day, I had a column in the Health section of the *Irish Times* about teenage suicides, which had taken me weeks to write. I had moved on from the previous night's brief eruption. I realised there was nothing in what he said that should have riled me. Eamon thrives when he's in conflict with someone; it was just my turn. *The Star* did their bit to fan the flames of a row that nobody cared about. 'Pundits due for Valentine's showdown live on-air' was their headline at the top of the front page the same day.

I told RTÉ I had no issue with anything he had written and there was no reason, as far as I was concerned, to bring it up on the night. As soon as I saw him in the studio before the game on Wednesday night, I walked straight up to him and gave him a hearty handshake.

'Howaya, Eamon, good to see you. All well, yeah?'

'Oh, hiya Richie,' came his delayed reply. And the rest of the night was civil, almost enjoyable, between us. Liverpool won 5-0, so there wasn't even an opening for a negative comment about anything.

Our final show together was the World Cup semi-final between France and Belgium in 2018. My aim was to get through it all without things blowing up completely, which is tricky enough given the nature of the job. We're there to express opinions and to robustly debate them if needs be. And it's not like we'd have to go far to find topics we disagreed on. By this stage, though, I wanted to have zero interaction with him at all, which is exactly the opposite of how a pundit should be approaching the job.

A few months later, we were in the same room at the launch of an anthology of *Sunday Independent* sports writing, compiled by my former editor John Greene. We avoided each other for the night. We'd had plenty of practice by that stage.

When we both worked for RTÉ, I had to find a way of handling Eamon. When he wrote another column criticising me following the Irish supporters' protests against the FAI in March 2019, I was happy to finally be in a position where I could just ignore him.

17

Reality

After I became sober, there were fewer reasons to beat myself up. There were fewer reasons to hate myself. I could still find some if I went looking for them, but I recognised it when I did.

I also began to think about why I used to drink the way I did. And I knew I had to face the one fact in my life I'd always wanted to run away from.

This secret had been shadowing me for many years. It had slipped out very occasionally, but I had always found a way to dismiss it or lessen its significance. It was this big secret that I had released in a flood to the psychotherapist in Dún Laoghaire in 2008. Of course, at the time, I had quickly closed the floodgates and blocked them with alcohol.

When I was fourteen years old, I was sexually abused by a physio I was seeing for back pain.

It was one of my earliest experiences of physiotherapy, where bodily contact and the removal of clothes are perfectly normal. I saw him regularly over a period of six weeks. My mum would drive me to his clinic and wait nearby to collect me after each session.

He did certain things in the first session which I knew weren't right, but looking back, I guess he was just testing me to see how I'd react. I spent years wishing I had responded with more than silence and confusion. I spent years blaming myself for everything that happened after that.

I assume he realised the kind of boy he was dealing with. If I wasn't on a football field, I rarely fought back. I was a good kid. I didn't drink then. I loved football and did well in school. I got on with teachers, managers, neighbours and all my relatives. I never really fell out with anyone. I just wanted my mum to be happier than I sometimes thought she was, while always hoping that things would improve between me and Dad. I was a good kid, I really was.

I wasn't one for causing a fuss. I wasn't one for confrontation. It wouldn't have taken a psychoanalyst to have spotted that then. I certainly wouldn't have been able to handle people knowing the truth. In other words, fourteen-year-old me was the perfect target.

Things escalated further when I went back another couple of times. I wondered for years why I didn't just invent a reason that I couldn't go to see him again, but I suppose I didn't see it as an option. Looking back, maybe I was afraid I'd arouse suspicion in some way. At the time there was nothing more important than being fit to play football; how could I cancel an appointment with the man helping me to achieve it?

Six weeks after the first session was to be my last visit. What happened in that room that day is the 45 minutes of my life I would most like to erase if I could. I had no clue that something so brief could hurt for so long, and I had no understanding up until recently of how it affected me. I wish I could have buried those memories and feelings long ago, but I did my best for years to just move on. Drinking and drugging ultimately failed me as I attempted to do that. For years, I believed I had failed myself.

I wish I hadn't spent so long blaming myself entirely. I considered the entire episode to have been my fault. I could have stopped it. I could have spoken up. I could have hit him. I could have reported him. I could have warned others about him. I could have done all these things, but I didn't do any of them. I blamed myself for everything that happened, giving no thought at all to the possibility that none of it was my fault.

I was just a kid, a powerless kid abused by a powerful man. I turned on myself and continued to do so for years.

I had acted in precisely the opposite way to what I thought was expected of men, even though I was only a boy at the time. Lads defend themselves. They fight back. They don't take shit from anyone. They're tough and durable. They speak up. They're not passive or submissive and would never allow these things be done to them. I had failed at the most fundamental aspects of being male.

I said nothing to anyone about any of it. This is another huge regret, but how does a kid bring that up in conversation? And because I didn't report it after it happened, I took full responsibility for the suffering of anyone else who followed me. I was sure there was no way I was the only one. I couldn't imagine why he wouldn't at least attempt to do it with others too.

So, having not reported it, I convinced myself I was now an accomplice to his awful crimes. My silence, to my mind, was as damaging as his actions. I was equally to blame. It's hard to think positively once you believe that about yourself.

Whenever something went wrong, even if it wasn't my fault, I took responsibility in my head for it all. When others wronged me in some way, I just blamed myself for my inability to spot it earlier. No matter what anyone did, in my mind I would find a way to make it my failing.

If ever someone complimented me, the voice in my head would do its best to drown it out.

If you knew the real me, you wouldn't be saying this.

Over time, this became my instinctive response. Without thinking about why, I just took it to be true. I'm sure there are several other factors behind why a person turns on themselves, but this was certainly a primary one for me. I'm still uncomfortable receiving compliments of any kind, thanks to the hatchet job I did on myself.

For over twenty-five years I've carried guilt and shame for what that man did. His actions. His crimes.

Many times, I've driven through the area where I know he lived. There have been days, plenty of them, where I imagined confronting him. I would knock on his door, drag the sick fuck out of his house and unleash every pent-up feeling I've ever had about what happened. I'd hold nothing back. I'd leave with no regrets and walk away. Then I'd finally see a proper man when I looked in the mirror.

Other times I'd imagine knocking on his door, calmly introducing myself and reminding him of what he did. There'd be no breaking off eye contact. I wouldn't show any emotion, any weakness or brokenness. I wouldn't allow him to think for a moment that he'd hurt me in any way. I wouldn't give him that satisfaction. My head would be high, my shoulders back. Then I would wonder if this was realistic, and I knew it probably wasn't.

It's hard to describe what it's like to live with this. It's not something I can consign to the past. Some days, some weeks, it never enters my head. I can go long spells without it coming to my mind in any conscious way.

When I was drinking, I could drink for days without remembering it, or have sex completely unaffected. Other days – and I wish I knew why – the clarity and the force of the images and feelings from what happened would hit me like a bus.

There were times when I was in bed with a partner and something would trigger a memory. Midway through having sex, I'd have to stop. This would usually lead to a series of questions I couldn't answer.

'Why have you stopped? What's wrong?'

'Ah sorry, I've a bit of a migraine or something. My head is banging all of a sudden.'

'You don't get migraines. Listen, Richie, if you're not into this any more, just say so.'

'No, honestly, I think you're—'

'Look, if you don't like me, that's fine. Blokes don't just stop having sex. That's twice you've done this now. I'm not stupid, you know.'

My partners were often as unsure of themselves as I was, so stopping sex was taken as a sign I wasn't interested. Understandably – or maybe not when I look back now – they weren't happy.

They would let me know and I would just sit there and take it. Like a mute little kid, my voice would abandon me, as it so often does in times of emotional difficulty. During break-ups, for example, I would usually just stare into the distance and wait for the long list of grievances to stop. I would wait for it to be over. I wouldn't say or do anything to defend myself. I knew that, like everything else, it would pass.

And in my silence, I confirmed another grievance. They couldn't get in.

Anyone who wanted to be close to me, I would keep at arm's length. The abuse I suffered cast a shadow which stood between me and intimacy, which is another way of saying it stood between me and the women I tried to sustain relationships with.

They could never know about what had happened. They could never hear my shameful secret, the story I had told myself that these acts of abuse were my fault, my responsibility, my shame.

I craved a closeness in relationships which I could never achieve. There was a level of trust I could never reach. I told myself that was the price I would have to pay. For what? For being abused? Why should I have to pay any price at all? But I decided that the cost of surviving it was this distance from everyone; the distance was the price I would have to pay to keep my story safe.

I could never come clean because my secret would get out as soon as we broke up.

In so many relationships, I heard the same things.

'What's goes on in that head of yours, Richie?'

'You don't like talking about yourself at all, Richie, do you?'

'Is there something you're not telling me, Richie?'

'Should I be worried, Richie?'

'Talk to me, Richie. Why don't you talk to me?'

The questions are easy to answer, but I could never tell the truth. I decided it was better to be thought less of – for literally any other reason – than to be known as someone who went through this as a kid.

Although I only went for one psychotherapy session in 2008, that one session played a part in the steps I began to take to come to terms with who I was. I didn't go back, but that didn't make it a failure. Blanking the second appointment didn't undo the progress I had made during the first. Saying it to the therapist was a big step forward at the time and the fact that she was so supportive, patient and sound was a huge help. I had assumed she'd react by questioning or criticising me, but that's because that was the way I responded myself. I wasn't ready to go into it in any more, though, so instead of going back for another session, I went to the pub. Debating who'd win the Premier League with mates was safer ground.

I've never spoken to anyone outside a therapy room about what was done to me. I told snippets to my siblings on drunken nights out, but my memory of what I said is patchy. I just know there are certain things I would never have said.

From the first day it happened, I have occasionally spoken about it to others, but always in such a way that I could take back my secret. I spent twenty years trying to tell people and trying not to tell people. I had moments when I wanted to blurt it out and moments when I wished I could take it back.

During a coke-fuelled bender, I was in a cab with a friend and told him I had been abused. I don't know what prompted me to say it, but it came out. He looked at me and his words never left me.

'Don't ever say that to anyone. Seriously. NEVER say that to anyone. EVER.'

Men aren't meant to go through this, so it made sense for me to hear him say that I should never speak about it. I told him he was right; I suppose I wanted him to be right. I wouldn't have said a word to him in the first place if I hadn't been so out of it.

His words confirmed what I believed. And yet it kept seeping out.

I told my mother one summer's day as we walked around Marlay Park.

She simply listened as we circled the park. I remember being in the kitchen when we got home. We were still chatting about it, but the only detail I can recall now is me leaning against the radiator, in tears, saying six words over and over again.

'I want to fucking kill him.'

The following day we went along the same path, but this time we walked in almost total silence.

My mum didn't grill me for more details or start instructing me on what I should do. She didn't say anything that made me regret telling her. On that walk, she barely said anything at all. Nor did I. She just stayed by my side all the time, a constant presence, maybe just to let me know she had been there all along.

When the pursuit of oblivion through drink and drugs failed, when I surrendered, said I was beaten and stopped drinking, I was getting closer to dealing with it. As with most things in my life, my plan was to not deal with it, to avoid it until the last possible moment, whenever that might be.

Getting sober didn't change that initially. In truth, it hasn't become any easier to live with, but it has become something different.

In sobriety, I told people on my terms, not in a drunken state, and the world kept turning and the people I told didn't think any less of me. It is crazy to think they might have, but that's the way I had previously viewed it.

In sobriety, I guess I learned that. You go into a room and you talk about yourself, usually truthfully, and you make friends in those rooms, not in spite of the things you say, but partly because of them. I may not have talked about what happened to me when I went to meetings, but I learned to believe that it wasn't my fault – although that is an ongoing leap of faith.

In sobriety, I had to face things. The line I heard in those meetings about getting your feelings back wasn't a joke – it was both a good thing and a bad thing. When it came to the subject of abuse, I couldn't say it was good to have my feelings back. I could no longer obliterate the thought of it as I used to do with drink and drugs. If it came into my head, I had to let it sit there until it passed. This was progress of a sort, but it rarely felt that way at the time.

I have a very sore back as I write this today, as I did when I was first brought to see that physio. On and off, it's been a physical ailment I've had to get used to. I've seen countless physios from my early teens right up to the present day, but all anyone can offer is help with managing the pain. Unfortunately, I haven't yet met anyone who can make the pain go away.

On the days when my back is bad, I used to find it hard not to recall what happened. It was like my body knew my secret and wouldn't release me from a memory I wanted to forget. It's different today. I don't need a sore back to remind me of what I went through, nor do I automatically think of it when I'm in pain, but the emotional scars I've kept hidden for years have begun to heal. And talking about it was the thing that started that healing process.

18

Player's Chair

In addition to establishing myself in the *Sunday Independent* and RTÉ, I began to get a good bit of work on Newstalk radio around 2009. I had previously turned down a weekly Sunday slot because it would have got in the way of my drinking, but I was starting to get regular midweek work on *Off The Ball*. RTÉ weren't keen on me being part of Newstalk's football coverage, but I enjoyed it too much.

Every year Ryle Nugent and I used to have the same debate during my contract negotiations. I got on well with him, so I felt comfortable explaining my position. I thought they weren't paying me enough for exclusivity, so they couldn't demand it and, more to the point, they weren't enforcing it on anyone else. Giles had a weekly slot on Newstalk, Dunphy hosted his own show on Sunday mornings, while Ray Houghton and Ronnie Whelan were regularly on Sky Sports. You don't get much money working on radio, especially for twenty-minute contributions, but there was something about the *Off The Ball* lads that I really liked. They were of a similar age to me, and Eoin McDevitt had also gone to St Benildus. I enjoyed working with them more than anyone else I had met in sports media, so I fought every year with RTÉ to ensure that I could.

Not long after I became sober, the lads asked me to do a live show with John Giles in a pub in town. The discussion revolved around Ireland's prospects at the finals of the 2012 Euros. I wasn't feeling positive about our chances and said so. The crowd was booing playfully but I was rattled just being there. I no longer felt comfortable being in a pub. I kept as calm as I could on the stage next to Giles and Eoin, but I rushed out of there as soon as my segment was done.

I knew when I was leaving that pub work might be beyond me for a while. The problem was, I was booked to do a gig with BoyleSports with Kevin Kilbane and Tony Cascarino in a different pub the following night. I texted the organiser and backed out. I just apologised for the late notice and said it was unavoidable. She was livid. She had already advertised the gig as a three-header. I was too embarrassed to tell the truth and didn't want to make up a lie, so I opted to hide behind a text and say I couldn't talk about it. I knew it was the right thing for me to do, but I felt pathetic. They never contacted me again for any more work.

In 2013 the lads on *Off The Ball* left Newstalk abruptly. I wasn't aware they'd been in talks with the station about changing the plans for the show, but when agreement couldn't be reached, they resigned *en masse*. The specifics of the dispute weren't any of my business, but I knew what I wanted to do.

Newstalk called to ask me if I would still do some work for them, but I wanted to go wherever Eoin, Ken, Murph, Simon and Mark were going. My relationship was with those five lads, not the station, so I stepped away. I told Mark Horgan to count me in on any future plans and left it at that. I was starting to appreciate the value of being around certain types of people, and they were the kind of lads I wanted to be around. Later that year, they set up Second Captains to produce daily podcasts. I was delighted for them, but also for myself, as it meant I could work with them on their podcast – even though, at the time, I didn't really understand what a podcast was.

In January 2017, I stood in to present a couple of podcasts when Eoin was away. I had no prior experience of presenting and never had an urge to try it, but I loved the part where I got to interview guests. I spoke to Luke Fitzgerald, who had just retired, for one episode, and Stephen Elliott, the former Ireland and Sunderland player, in the other.

I had been working for the *Sunday Independent* for almost ten years and I'd grown a bit weary of filing a column about football every week. I decided to step away just before the 2016 Euros, but I knew I'd want to replace it with something else. *The Player's Chair* took shape after I spoke to Mark Horgan about doing more interviews. They were the lads I most wanted to work with, so I couldn't wait to get started.

Over time, I developed a style to prepare for each interview. I would learn what I could about the key moments in the guest's life and do my best to explore the impact on them of everything they'd been through. My interest is the person, not the sportsperson. I don't care who they think will win the big trophies next year. My curiosity is always about what makes them the way they are. It's an approach that can make for a very intense few days.

So I would become seven-year-old Anthony Daly, peering through the sitting-room curtains as his father's funeral procession went past his house. I would become Brian Kerr, coming to terms with no longer being Republic of Ireland manager. I would be Paul Galvin, lifting the Sam Maguire in 2009, having gone through all he had the year before. I would be Niall Quinn, trying to grapple with life after football. I would be Andrew Trimble, believing there's a God in a world like this.

I had three goes at being Mick McCarthy, but a series of unfortunate events – my inability to operate basic recording equipment – meant my attempts to interview him failed twice.

The interview with Paul Stewart would be different from all the others.

—

When the stories of abuse in British football broke in the winter of 2016, I had struggled through the Second Captains podcast. Several former footballers, prominent among them Paul Stewart, had just spoken publicly about the sexual abuse they had endured as children. We were discussing what it must have been like to have been in their shoes. What horror they must have gone through. What it must have been like for them to have carried their secrets alone for so long. We chatted about some of the long-term impacts of surviving crimes like this, and the ways in which predators manipulate their victims to stay silent. I had worked with abuse survivors in my psychotherapy practice, so I shared some of what I had learned from my time with them.

Nobody listening would have known that I was speaking almost entirely from personal experience. I wasn't lying about what I said I'd learned from working with abuse survivors. I just wasn't ready to say publicly that I was one of those survivors myself.

And that was how I found myself sobbing on the side of the road after a minor car incident in Monkstown the next day.

—

'Paul Stewart is in town next week, Richie, fancy interviewing him for your podcast?'

'I'd love to.'

It was December 2017. A year since Paul Stewart's story had broken, a year since we had spoken about it on Second Captains, and a year since I'd been overwhelmed by all of it in front of the lads in the studio. Paul was coming to Dublin to promote his new book, *Damaged*, in which he wrote about, among other things, surviving child abuse and his subsequent issues with drink and drugs. It was familiar territory.

From the age of ten, Paul had been sexually abused on an almost daily basis for three years. This wasn't going to be a chat about the goal he had scored in an FA Cup final. There would be no room for anecdotes about playing with Gazza. And, for me, it was going to be impossible to be anywhere else but right back to when I was fourteen.

Without hesitation, I agreed to interview him on *The Player's Chair*.

Paul had been through far worse than I had and yet he was willing to speak about it candidly in the hope that it would help others. Rather than be inspired by his ability to speak out, I hammered myself for being nowhere near ready to do the same. Self-criticism had long been established as my instinctive response to almost every scenario.

Throughout the interview I asked questions of him that I wanted answered of myself. Maybe I wanted to hear him say he wished he hadn't said anything. *How do people interact with you now they know? What's it like to put yourself out there in this way?* I assumed he'd be inundated with messages from other abuse survivors and I wondered about the impact all that had on him.

After the interview, I was shaken. Paul had maintained eye contact with me through most of it. So much of what he spoke about were things I could relate to myself – shame, intimacy issues, self-loathing, addiction and pain. I kept it together, though, by which I mean I didn't disclose any of my own experiences and I didn't cry. Those were two of my targets and I achieved them both.

I walked with Paul down the two flights of stairs from the office to the main front door. We hugged as we said goodbye and I wished him well.

After the podcast aired, I was contacted separately by two listeners who said they were moved by what they had heard. I knew one, but not the other. I get tons of messages when I do anything in public about mental health issues. Usually they're from people directly impacted by the issue discussed. I figured this was their way of saying they had been abused and that they needed help. I learned a long time ago that the best way to encourage someone to open up is to be open yourself. Cajoling or badgering doesn't work. Chatting openly about your own experiences is better than a lorry-load of posters saying 'It's good to talk'. I took a gamble and told both listeners that I had been abused myself, and they both confirmed I was right in my hunch about them.

I arranged to meet one of them in a café. He told me he had a drinking problem and had been battling with the prospect of going to meetings for years. I told him my story, and he shared some of his, but he said he wasn't ready to contemplate a life without drink. He wasn't comfortable going to therapy either. I had no difficulty in understanding where he was coming from, having spent years thinking exactly the same myself.

I spoke to the other man on the phone. Brief exchanges about horrible things, all done in the hope that talking might help.

'It's shite, isn't it?'

'Yeah, it's not great alright.'

'My missus doesn't even know.'

'Hard to drop that one in over dinner, eh?' I said. 'Anyone know?'

'Fuck, no.'

'I'm not mad on telling people what to do,' I said, 'but I see a therapist and he knows everything and it helps a lot. I'd be happy to give you a few names if you fancied doing the same.'

He contacted me over the next few months saying therapy was helping. None of it would have happened if Paul hadn't spoken out, which started to open me up to the prospect of doing so myself. I don't think I'd be writing any of this now if I hadn't met him then.

—

It's hard to be an abuse survivor. To be honest, I don't know why I say 'survivor' rather than 'victim', but I understand why the distinction is important to others. I don't know how significant this was in the melting pot of reasons I had when I was planning my own suicide, during that hellish year dealing with my retirement. I can't say with any certainty if this had anything to do with me being an alcoholic in later life. But I know I used drink and drugs to help quieten my mind and this was certainly a voice I was constantly trying to keep silent.

Maybe it's impossible to grasp what's involved unless it's something you've experienced yourself. I'm sure it's much easier to avoid it, or to play down the damage it does, rather than openly speak about it in any way. Maybe it's better to pretend it doesn't exist, or that it happens so rarely that it really isn't something people should discuss. I understand why some would rather stay out of conversations like this. Other comments and reactions I find less palatable.

I remember former darts player Eric Bristow's response to the child sex abuse story in English football. 'Might be a looney,' he tweeted, 'but if some football coach was touching me when I was a kid as I got older I would have went back and sorted that poof out.' He followed this up with: 'Dart players tough guys footballers wimps.'

He wasn't the only one to voice these opinions, he was just one of the most prominent. He later apologised, but his words had already done a lot of damage to a lot of people. Attitudes like that are one of the many reasons I chose to stay quiet for so long.

At the end of that Second Captains podcast on the initial story in 2016, I had said something I thought might get me in a bit of bother. I pulled Eoin up for using the word 'brave' to describe abuse survivors who speak publicly about what they'd been through. I said I felt it added to the suffering of the majority who don't speak out, because it implies that they lack the qualities and courage to do so. I was obviously referring to my own discomfort at having never reported it and for having chosen not to speak publicly about it.

I don't believe now that I lacked bravery then, nor do I think I am suddenly brave for writing this now. I did the best I could to deal with this every step of the way. For years, the thought of anyone knowing about this terrified me. I figured I'd never be able to look them in the eye again. People would gossip, laugh and question my story, all the while thinking less of me as a result. In other words, I assumed everyone would see it as a failing of mine, just as I did.

How do you talk about another man using your body as a plaything when you were a kid?

How do you talk about freezing with fear and confusion and not telling anyone?

How do you talk about playing along with the man's nice-guy act in front of your mum?

How do you talk about that on a lads' holiday?

How do you know that it's good to talk?

How do you know?

How do you fucking know?

I told my mum when I was ready. I said it in therapy when I was ready. I said it to a mate when I had enough drink and drugs inside me. On each occasion, I didn't know where I wanted the conversation to go. I didn't have a plan in mind. I guess I just wanted to say it.

This is just my story; other people have theirs. Some talk, most don't. Some report, most won't. Many along the way simply won't survive. I'm very grateful I've reached a place where I can share it openly now. And I don't only mean the part about being sexually abused.

19

From One Chair to Another

In November 2011 I was invited on to Newstalk's *Breakfast Show* to discuss the death by suicide of Wales manager Gary Speed. After giving my initial reaction to hearing the news the previous day, I was asked whether I thought enough was being done in professional football to tackle the issue of depression. This was interesting, I thought. No details were known about the circumstances of his death, yet here was the presenter assuming it was depression, as if there are no other causes of suicide that we know of. I batted the question away, saying it wasn't the time to be speculating in public about the details.

During that interview, I mentioned that I had gone to a therapist for a few months during my time at Millwall. It was the first time I had said this publicly. I was three months sober and my attitude to speaking about things like this was already changing. If ever there was a time to promote the benefits of asking for help, I thought this was it. I didn't give the reasons – 'without going into the specifics,' I said – but I said I went because I didn't feel I'd get the support I needed from either inside or outside the dressing room. It turns out details weren't necessary, because according to every article that was written about what I said, I had 'bravely' spoken out about my depression.

In early 2014 I wrote about my experience of therapy in some detail in the *Sunday Independent*. I was outgrowing the shame and embarrassment that I had once associated with seeking help and I thought my column was the ideal platform to encourage others to do likewise. I was sober three years at this point, something that never would have been possible on my own. I figured it was time to start speaking up about how beneficial talking can be.

RTÉ Radio One's *John Murray Show* interviewed me on the back of that column. When John asked me if I went to therapy because of depression, I specifically said that it wasn't depression. 'It's a bit more complex than that,' I said. 'There isn't a one-word description for what it was.' The truth is that there probably was a one-word description and that word was 'alcoholism'. The following day, a newspaper ran a two-page spread about me opening up 'bravely' about my battles with depression on John's show.

In our eagerness to promote talking, we seem to have forgotten the virtue of listening. If only mental health was a single-ticket item, like so many believe.

The therapy I was referring to in those interviews was the time I had attended in 2001 when I was twenty-one. Nothing had happened around that time to throw me off course and I had decided to do something only after I broke down in tears during a post-match warm-down.

Back then, therapy appealed to me for many reasons. Nobody knows you're there and the therapist won't repeat what you say. It's not like telling a mate something personal and then worrying if they'll let it slip when they're drunk. It's not like telling your boss and wondering if he'll then use it against you. It's absolute confidentiality with someone trained to help. It meant I could keep my worries from everyone around me, while being honest with someone who had no link to any of them. I could seek help without anyone knowing I even needed it. I couldn't describe why the therapy worked, but I knew it did.

So, when I was struggling after I retired in 2003, it wasn't that much of a leap to go again because I knew it would help. I didn't have depression when I retired from football; I was mourning the loss of something that mattered greatly to me. How I felt was the appropriate response to what had happened. I relied on drink and drugs initially to help me through it all, but it was going to therapy that set me on a journey that continues to this day.

So when in 2008 I felt I was ready to speak in some way about being abused, therapy was again the obvious choice for support.

The feelings I had in those rooms stayed with me and I was back in therapy again in 2010, as a course requirement for the HDip in Counselling and Psychotherapy I had undertaken that year.

We had to clock up forty hours minimum in therapy ourselves, but I went every week for the two years of the course. Towards the end of the second year, I felt I had sussed out the therapist enough, and I decided it was time to take the greatest risk of all. I was almost a year sober at that point, and I was ready to talk about what the physio had done to me.

By that stage, I knew about mandatory reporting. I knew therapists are legally obliged to report certain things they hear in a session. Child sex abuse is one such area. So, before I told him about the abuse, I insisted that it was on the strict understanding that I wouldn't be reporting it. And that I didn't want him to report it. I told him that if he had an issue with that, I wouldn't bring it up again. I told him I wouldn't be giving any identifying details. I mentioned that my abuser used to work as a physiotherapist but was now retired. If the therapist was OK to continue knowing all that, I'd get into it. If he wasn't, I was going to retreat to my shell and stay there. Those were my terms of engagement and I wasn't negotiating. Take it or leave it.

My therapist agreed to proceed on the basis I insisted on, so we started to talk about what had been done to me. I know people say it's good to talk, and mostly they're right, but talking about this, to be honest, was pretty fucking horrible.

Imagine saying something you've never said before. The thing you're most ashamed of, in explicit detail, to another person. You don't sugar-coat it, minimise it, change the subject or laugh it off. You say it all, feel it all, and you can't run away. You've to stay in the room and 'process' it, whatever the hell that means. And then you've to revisit it on a weekly basis for God knows how long, while keeping it from everyone else in your life at the time.

This happened, and then that happened, and then this happened.

I said this, he said that, I did this, he did that.

He did X, Y and Z, and I didn't stop him. And I've no idea why.

Why? Why? Why? Why? Why?

I've no idea why I didn't leave. Why I didn't shout. Why I didn't run. I don't know why I went back. I don't know why I let him do the things he did.

What was I thinking?

What was I doing?

What the fuck was wrong with me?

I can't explain why I didn't try to escape or tell someone immediately after. I don't understand why certain memories are crystal clear but others are blurry.

I knew one thing for sure, though. There was no way in the world I was going to the police.

'OK, Mr Sadlier, let's start from the beginning. We're going to need every detail.'

'Let's not.'

Try reporting that with so many holes in your story. So many 'I don't knows'. So many unacceptable answers to obvious questions. So many actions and inactions that don't make sense. Imagine telling that story in a court to someone whose job is to trip you up. Whose job is to find inconsistencies in order to portray you as unreliable. With no evidence or witnesses to rely on, it's your word against his about events from a quarter of a century ago.

No chance.

At the time, I couldn't even say it to the people closest to me. I had my final session with this therapist in the summer of 2012, and I'm fully convinced he took the details of what I told him to his grave when he died.

I remember a specific lecture which dealt with the issue of mandatory reporting when I undertook an MA in Psychotherapy, following on from the HDip.

The lecturer was a strong defender of the law in this area, but I had said nothing as my classmates debated the rights and wrongs of it all. I could feel myself getting more and more wound up as the debate continued, though, particularly the more I heard the phrase 'people who have gone through this'.

People who have gone through this need support.

People who have gone through this need to find justice.

People who have gone through this blah blah blah blah blah!

Maybe the room was full of people with personal experiences of this, or maybe it wasn't, I don't know, but the more I heard the phrase, the more it jarred the hell out of me. All of a sudden, I was taking a full part in the debate.

'Well, I'm one of those people who have gone through this.'

It was like jumping into the sea. I had opened my mouth and found myself talking before I was really sure if I wanted to be here.

It turned out I had plenty to say.

I told them of the strict understanding I'd had with my therapist in terms of reporting before I told him anything about the abuse. I brought this up to highlight that there are certain cases where reporting just isn't an option for some people, and that the law as it stands may be an obstacle to some people accessing help from psychotherapy. I just wanted to make a point which was relevant to the discussion.

Then I realised what I had done.

I had just said it all in front of about fifteen people. I hadn't woken up that morning with that as part of my plan for the day, but I had said it now and there was no way of taking it back. I didn't know where to look.

People reveal a lot about themselves during psychotherapy courses, and I had said a fair bit about myself up to that point, but I genuinely never thought I'd ever mention the abuse. I berated myself silently for losing my cool and dropping my guard. The damage was done, though, my dirty shameful secret was now known to them all.

As you'd expect of a room of therapists, everyone was kind and supportive. Some people had a quiet word with me afterwards, just saying they were sorry to hear what I had been through and wishing me well. Others avoided ever bringing it up with me again. After my initial shock at my own disclosure, I moved beyond it as well.

—

Twelve years after my first therapy session in London, I completed the six-foot journey and sat in a therapist's chair myself. My first sessions were as daunting as anything I'd ever done.

While my concern before my earliest Millwall games was mostly about fans roaring abuse at me, prior to my first few sessions as a therapist, my fear was that the client would be silent. What if they weren't talkative? I couldn't bear the thought of sitting opposite someone in such an intense environment, each of us looking at the other and neither of us saying anything. I knew by then my role wasn't to 'fix' them or provide them with answers, but I also knew how uncomfortable I'd be if they didn't say anything. I'd almost prefer to be in The Den with thousands of people chanting that I was shit.

Before going on RTÉ programmes in my early days, I would worry people wouldn't know who I was. Here I had the opposite concern. What if clients knew me from working on the panel? Getting animated on TV about offside decisions and disallowed goals probably wasn't the ideal way to promote your therapeutic skills. In addition, there's a school of thought that therapists should never disclose anything about their own lives to a client. It's better to be completely unknown to them. I wondered how this would work for me, since I had shared so much of my life in the *Sunday Independent* column.

As always, I had more reasons to believe I would fail than be a success. I thought any client older than me would dismiss me on the grounds of my age. I assumed women would be uncomfortable opening up to me as a man and I wondered if anyone would be able to get past the fact that I was a former footballer.

My biggest concern, though, was that I wouldn't be able to help them. I knew how hard it could be even to get as far as a therapy room, and I didn't want to be the reason someone would feel disappointed when they got there. I knew how that would have made me feel if I had been in that position. As usual, I put myself under pressure to be perfect from the very start, at the same time convincing myself I'd be a total flop.

I was keen to work as soon as I was qualified, but I didn't have the confidence to charge people or to actively promote myself. When I did any radio interviews, I would always be sure to tell the presenters beforehand not to mention my therapy work during the programme.

The presenters were fascinated by the switch from footballer to therapist, but I wasn't ready to open myself up to the opinions of others. I wanted to get to a certain point before speaking about it in public, without really knowing exactly where that point would be.

Like many other therapists, I decided to work voluntarily initially. I saw clients in low-cost counselling centres in Bray and Tallaght. Clients could pay whatever they could afford, from as little as a fiver per session. They got access to a service they couldn't otherwise avail of, and I was given a steady flow of people to work with. I was helping others in the same way I had needed to be helped myself.

There was a screening process for everyone who came to each centre and clients were then matched with suitable therapists. I soon realised that the shortage of male therapists meant I'd be in demand. Most men who came said they'd prefer to work with a man. Being a bloke wasn't the drawback I thought it would be.

Before I even met each client, I would spend much of my week thinking about them. As soon as I was given the basics of what they were going through, I couldn't get them out of my mind.

9am – Liam, 41, depression. Recently separated. No prior experience of therapy.

10am – Annie, 19, self-harming and suicidal. Specifically asked for a male therapist.

11am – Gregg, 34, sexuality and identity issues. Married. Drinks heavily.

12 noon – Jake, 81, wife of 57 years has recently died.

I would build a profile of them in my mind straight away. As soon as I met with each of them, however, the pointlessness of trying to imagine what they would be like was obvious. You learn nothing about a person by reading a one-line summary of what they've been through. People are far more complex and interesting than that.

Striking a balance between my own needs and those of my clients was an ongoing struggle. Granny Aggie died in November 2013 at the age of ninety-six and her funeral in Limerick clashed with the day I saw clients in Tallaght. These people had told me things in therapy nobody else knew. Some of them were in very distressing situations. I could identify with all of them, having been there myself. I didn't feel I had the option to cancel the sessions, so I saw them instead of going to her funeral. I realise now that I should have been standing next to my dad as he buried his mum.

Some clients didn't show for their second session and didn't come back – just as I hadn't. One man bolted from the chair about 40 seconds into the opening session and didn't return. I assume it took a great deal of effort for him to have got that far. I worked with some people for several months, others for over two years.

I was right about the hunch I'd had several years earlier. I was starting to love the work like I used to love playing football.

The two jobs could hardly have been more different. Instead of physically imposing myself on others, I was now there to support their emotional wellbeing. There was no audience of fanatical supporters urging me to do my best any more. This was just one person in a vulnerable situation, hoping I could help. My confidence as a therapist was steadily increasing, as was my public profile, because I'd been on the RTÉ panel for so long.

I'd be in television studios covering the performances of millionaire footballers while also – and often on the same day – working in the private, confidential space of my therapy room. I didn't start believing one was more important than the other, but it was sometimes hard to move seamlessly between the two worlds.

When Eamon Dunphy was kicking off about interim Ireland manager Noel King in October 2013, I found it hard to get too animated or even care. I had spent the afternoon working with a teenage trauma victim whose attacker was due for early release from prison. I had to dig deep to summon the effort to look like I was interested during the football discussion. All I could think of throughout the show was what the client had said to me earlier that day.

The more experienced I got, the more I learned to compartmentalise the lives of my clients, the way I used to do with my own. I knew it wasn't healthy to be always thinking of them between sessions, so over time I found a way of managing it all. It's essential to get that part right or it could take over your life. Before Arsenal's Champions League tie with Bayern Munich in November 2015, however, it wasn't so easy.

The day before the match, when I was due to be on the panel with Michael O'Neill and Eamon Dunphy, I got a call from the counselling centre to say a client of mine had been reported missing and was a suicide risk. She had gone missing before, so the family knew to notify the police as soon as she was uncontactable. She had called the counselling centre the previous day to say she couldn't make her session with me, but nobody had seen or heard from her in the thirty-six hours since then. I was asked if I had any information that would help their search, but I didn't. I assumed I couldn't go on air if she wasn't found; nor would I want to go on air if she had been found dead. I didn't know if the family knew I was her therapist. If they did, I was afraid I would upset them further by showing up on TV, looking unaffected by it all. And I still didn't know for sure if I could have even done that.

Ryle Nugent let me make the call myself, but thankfully she was found alive on the morning of the game. She sent me a text to say she was OK and she was admitted to a hospital, where she got the support and treatment she needed.

Arsenal were beaten and the post-match chat was about the consequences of yet another European failure by Arsene Wenger. I weighed in with my thoughts, as is my job, but there was a part of me relieved to be discussing something of comparatively little importance. What matters in the world of football can differ greatly from what matters in the world outside it.

I'm wary of saying that work like this puts everything else I do into perspective, because football is of great meaning and significance to people all over the world, myself included, but it certainly helps you disregard the stuff that isn't important.

—

As I progressed as a therapist, society also seemed to be recognising the benefits of talking about mental health issues.

In particular, men speaking publicly about their own struggles started to become more common. And when they did, the reaction was always the same – they were lauded for their bravery in speaking out. It was considered remarkable that men would talk in this way.

Any time I said anything revealing about myself in an article or interview, the response was always the same. I'd get countless emails and DMs, mainly from men, telling me they were personally struggling with the issues I had spoken about. Women would also contact me on behalf of the men in their lives, pleading with me for suggestions to get them to talk.

In pubs or at social events, people would tell me about their experiences of therapy. Strangers would open up to me about their difficulties. Lads I had never met before would come to me for advice on where to go for counselling. These kinds of chats were replacing the debates I used to have about the Premier League. People would sometimes use football just as a conversation starter before opening up about their own mental health. I was no longer viewed just as a former professional footballer, something I feared would always be the case when I'd first retired.

I worked with many people in my practice who had problematic relationships with drink and drugs. I had no trouble being empathic and fully understanding. They would say they needed a joint to relieve stress, or a line of coke to give them a lift, or a rake of pints to deal with all the pressures they were facing in their lives. Often, they didn't come to therapy to address these issues specifically. To many of them, drinking and drugging was the solution to their problem, the thing that was helping them get by. They were in therapy to help manage other difficulties, without any awareness that their relationship with drink or drugs was impacting them so much.

It is a good thing that people have become more open about their mental health – whether in the media or in therapy – but drink is often a neglected part of that conversation, particularly in Ireland. If the topic is side-lined, then we may not be as brave as we like to think we are as a society in talking about these issues. There are, of course, so many cases in which substance abuse is not an issue at all for people, but in those where it is, nothing much will change if there's a refusal to address it.

Just as I was, many of my adult male clients were ashamed they were seeing a therapist. The majority came with the intention of keeping it hidden from the people closest to them. It didn't fit with the script they had in their head about what masculinity entailed. Some were adamant they wouldn't tell anybody, but many had a change of heart along the way. I remember one man telling me the response he got when he took the plunge and decided to tell his friend the truth.

'I said it to Bob on Tuesday, don't know why I said it then, hadn't planned it or anything.'

'What was that like? How did Bob respond?' I already knew from his mood that it had gone well.

'You won't believe it. He said he went to see someone last year too. He's the last person I thought would go. We ended up chatting all night about it, saying all sorts of stuff we never knew about each other.'

These two men had been friends since their twenties, and they were both well into their fifties. We spent the remainder of the session wondering if anyone benefits from lads staying quiet.

As we go forward, I think we will become better at understanding the nuances in this area. Everyone has to take care of their mental health, everybody has mental health issues at some stage in their life. In an ideal world, we would reach a point where people wouldn't think it was brave to talk about their struggles or that it's a risk to open up. In an ideal world, it would be routine and mundane.

Maybe then we can go further in addressing the real issues for individuals and society. For many people, their relationship with alcohol and drugs is a secondary mental health issue. For others, it's not an issue in any way. For me, though, and many others, it's the primary one. I couldn't have received the help I needed until I was able to acknowledge the nature of my problem. Whatever issues people face, whether they go to therapy or not, understanding them and their situation is necessary in order to help them. It can be difficult and awkward and sometimes it's hard to know where to start, but talking about your mental health becomes a lot more useful when you talk about the right thing.

20

Doing What I Do

'T his is why I do what I do,' I said, pointing to the picture on the A4 page in front of me.

I was close to tears, but I was holding them back. I was sitting on a cushion on the floor like everyone else, avoiding eye contact with the other seven therapists in my group. It was July 2018, the final weekend of our MSc in Adolescent Psychotherapy, and we were discussing how to work with sexual abuse and trauma. We had been asked to represent our relationship to this area visually on a piece of paper using crayons and markers.

By this stage, everyone else had spoken about their drawings and what they were about. I was the last to go. I had drawn something I had completely forgotten about. Right up until the moment I drew it, I hadn't once thought of it. Out of nowhere, I had suddenly remembered that, during one training session not long after being abused, I had made an attempt to speak to one of my coaches about what happened with the physio. At that stage, I was playing in both soccer and GAA teams, inside and outside of school, and in school, I was playing in my own age group and the older one too – six different teams (a possible clue in the mystery of why my back was always sore).

I found myself on my own with one of the coaches. He knew I had been to see a physio and was asking me if it had helped. I don't recall my specific opening line, but I started to describe some of what had happened, for the very first time.

I told him that the physio had insisted I should strip naked so he could examine my back. I told him one other thing. I can't remember anything now about why I specifically chose that moment or that coach to speak about any of this. He was not the only one who had asked me about the physiotherapy. I can't remember if I wanted him to tell anyone else about it or do anything about it. Maybe I just wanted him to tell me it wasn't my fault. To be honest, I don't know what sort of response I was looking for, but I know I wasn't happy with the one I got.

Maybe he was just nervous or uncomfortable, or maybe he simply didn't know what to say and I had caught him off guard. Whatever the reason, he started to laugh a little. He found what I had said funny and wanted to share the joke. He immediately told one of the other coaches there, who also laughed. The coach he told was tying another player's boot laces at the time, so that player heard, and he laughed too. For the remainder of that training session, what little they knew about me seeing that physio amused them all. I remember having to play along as if I wasn't bothered by the laughter, but on the inside I was furious with myself for opening my mouth.

You fucking idiot.

What a clueless little cunt you are.

Twenty-five years later, I couldn't understand how I had forgotten this. The facilitator suggested that the shame of that scene was enough of a reason to bury it somewhere my memory couldn't access. That made sense. If you kept all this stuff in the front of your mind, you wouldn't survive. She wondered if the reaction I got contributed to my decision to say nothing more about it to anyone at the time. There's no way of knowing these things for sure, but it sounded plausible.

But in that final weekend of the college course, I was no longer the confused adolescent searching for the right words to say to the right people. I was now at a stage where I was ready, not only to recall it, but to talk about it. And that weekend, I sat on the floor in a room of therapists trying to make sense of it. For the first time ever, I had just said out loud that this experience is probably a huge part of why I do what I do.

'This is why you want to help adolescents, Richie. Is that what you mean?' she asked. She described the job of an adolescent therapist, suggesting that what I was aiming to provide for others was what I needed myself at that stage of my life.

'Yeah, I suppose it is,' I said. I didn't say a whole lot more, but there was no need.

I was drained at that point and I just kept staring at the drawing on the floor in front of me. It was the end of a two-year course, during which we had revisited almost every aspect of our own adolescence. Self-reflection, yet again, was an essential part of the training. And once again, it was the part of the process which I found the toughest.

Maybe I didn't need someone else to point this out for me, but the impact of what I had been through is probably the motivation for a lot of the work I do now.

—

When I started out on this road back in 2010, I wasn't sure which area I should specialise in once I had qualified as a therapist. 'Something will emerge,' they used to tell us in my early days in college. 'Give it time.' A few people on the course already had specific areas of interest – trauma, addiction, suicide – but nothing was jumping out at me at the time. There was no requirement to focus on any one area during the course, but it bothered me that I didn't have a specific passion.

In the summer of 2011 I got an email from Barnardos asking me to attend a charity football game. I was happy to go along, as I was looking for ways to spend that Friday night that didn't involve alcohol or being in the company of people drinking alcohol. At the time, there were few options like that in my life. I went along, knowing it would be a great way to help me get through the evening sober. Soon I would realise there are more effective ways of doing this, but it was the best I could come up with at the time.

I had no prior links with Barnardos, but I decided that if I was going to give a post-match speech thanking the players for raising funds for such a worthy cause, the least I could do was find out what the organisation did. I went to the game and spent the evening grilling the rep from Barnardos about their work. The more I found out about the organisation, the more I wanted to be involved.

The game was on Friday 19 August 2011. Unfortunately, football matches end and other opportunities present themselves. As soon as I got home, I was drinking a can of Guinness. Two days later I was texting a friend, asking him to bring me to a meeting of recovering alcoholics. Attending that Barnardos charity game was the last thing I did sober before getting drunk for a final time that weekend.

Barnardos offered to give me a tour of one of their places of work and to explain in more detail what they did. I was seventy-three days sober when I visited one of their centres in Dublin 15. Picking up on my enthusiasm, they asked if I would be interested in being an ambassador for their work. I said I would, but what I really wanted was to do some of that work myself as a volunteer.

The following year, I began by taking a group of eleven- and twelve-year-old boys and girls to play football every second Friday. It was a different world from the chaos I was trying to leave behind, and I loved it for that and for many other reasons. Nobody was there to become a better footballer or to win. I wasn't there to prepare them for matches or to improve their technical ability. I wasn't there to build up my coaching hours for a UEFA coaching licence. I was just there to help them enjoy themselves and to have fun.

A year after that, I volunteered in a homework group every Thursday. For a couple of years, I would help as the kids did their homework, made their lunch and played games. I'd engineer a way to get involved in the games as often as I could. The kids were like any kids, but they were growing up in poverty and dealing with all the challenges that come with that.

The busier my life became with media, college, recovery and everything else, the more I appreciated the ninety minutes I got to spend with them. Something was definitely starting to emerge.

In the summer of 2012 I was invited into St Patrick's Institute, a youth prison for 17- to 21-year-old males, by Thomas Hynes, Community Director at Bohemians football club, to do some football coaching. I went along for one hour a week with a mate, Jeff Conway, for what was initially a one-month agreement. We ended up doing it on and off for eighteen months. I wasn't there to improve their abilities either. I wasn't there to make them fitter or better in any way. It was a way of making a connection with lads who were particularly hard to reach, but at the time, I didn't give much thought to why I wanted to reach them. I was just drawn to going back every week, so I did.

The 2012 European Championships were on when we first went into the prison. After the sessions finished, I would hang around for a chat with the lads as they waited for prison staff to escort them back to their wing. This was the real highlight for me. Every week they would ask me a favour. When I would appear on the panel on RTÉ, they wanted me to use a particular hand gesture to show I was thinking of them while they were watching from their cells.

During one post-match discussion, I lost my train of thought while trying to rub my nose in the way the lads had showed me earlier that day. They told me later how hilarious they found it that they were the only ones in the country who knew what was going on. We decided to drop it after that.

I never asked what crimes they were involved in, but I was always curious to know their backgrounds. Many of them had fathers who were career criminals, in and out of prison all their lives. A lot of them had uncles and grandfathers staying across the yard in Mountjoy Prison. Many of them were in prison because they'd followed the guidance and advice of their parents. Most came from areas of high deprivation. One lad's mum was smuggling drugs into him during prison visits. They would French kiss each other to exchange the goods. Another lad was eligible for early release but he couldn't go anywhere until he turned eighteen. You can't just release a kid onto the streets without someone taking responsibility for him, but this kid literally had nobody in his life who would be able to sign his release forms.

Others had gone through the kinds of childhood traumas you don't expect people to survive. All the time, all I wanted to do was lighten their load a little, to provide some relief through football for an hour every week. I couldn't do much more for any of them, but I could at least do that. Much as I loved being there, I loved having the freedom to leave even more. The place was grim.

—

Within six months of finishing up at St Pat's, I approached my old school, St Benildus, to see if they'd be interested in me doing any classroom-based mental health support work with the students. David Gillick, another former student, had recently delivered a cooking module to the transition year students, so, inspired by that, I thought I could do something similar.

Throughout my time at Millwall, I would get letters and messages of support from some of my old teachers. The morning after I played for Ireland, I visited the school and gave them my shirt from the previous night (it hangs on a wall in the sports corridor to this day). When I retired, my old German teacher, Mr McLoughlin, sent me a letter of encouragement on behalf of the staff. So when I had the urge to work in a school, St Benildus was the obvious choice.

I put together a six-week module in mental fitness and went to work. I was now back in the same building I had been in during the times when I most needed help myself. I began by promoting the benefits of seeking support. As it's an all-male school, I did my best to challenge the perception of masculinity which discourages lads from asking for help. I was there to empower them to behave in ways I couldn't at that age. I knew I couldn't turn back time and change what I had gone through myself, but I wanted to be a visible source of support to any of the students who needed it.

Without realising it, the more I helped them, the more I was helping myself. The more I learned about their lives, the more understanding I had for what it had been like for me back then. Teenagers aren't fully formed adults. They're not equipped emotionally or physically to deal with a lot of what the world throws at them. They're at the mercy of the behaviour of the adults around them, and many, through no fault of their own, really struggle.

The more I realised this, the more compassion I started to develop for the teenage me.

In March 2016 I attended a three-day workshop in Cork about adolescent psychotherapy. We were asked to think of an experience during our adolescence where we felt we didn't get the support we needed. Close your eyes for a while, we were told, and go back to what it felt like for you back then. We were advised to think of something that wasn't too traumatic, but I had no control over what my mind recalled. I was straight back to scrambling around for support after being abused by the physio. I didn't want anyone to know what I was remembering, so I left without saying anything.

That night, I was live on RTÉ from Turners Cross for the opening game of the League of Ireland season. It was another testing experience of flitting between two worlds, but thankfully I kept it together, and stuck to debating the merits of Cork City's title-challenging credentials while on air.

On the back of that workshop, I enrolled in a two-year MSc in Adolescent Psychotherapy. I had a real hunger to learn more and to work as well as I could in this area. I was also in no doubt that I still had some work to do on myself. I couldn't shake the memories as easily any more. The things I thought of during that workshop were always in my mind. Teenage me still needed to be understood. Teenage me still needed to be forgiven.

This was an itch I had left unscratched for too long. It had been five years since I'd stopped using drink and drugs to occupy my mind, and even though I had spoken about the abuse in a few sessions with my therapist in 2012, it was time to face up to it once again.

I switched the focus of my practice to working almost entirely with adolescents and their parents. Yet again, I would learn how wrong I had been to think that being a man would hold me back. So many of the referrals to me were because parents specifically asked for a male therapist. Even when I said it would be months before I would have an opening, they were happy to wait. Working at RTÉ and being a former footballer was working in my favour, too. I needn't have worried that people would use it against me in this field. Like in most other areas, I was beginning to realise that how I used to think was completely wrong.

There are many reasons people avoid working in the field of adolescent psychotherapy. It can be tricky to negotiate the ethical and moral dilemmas that come with hearing young people speak openly and honestly about their lives. How much is it OK to know without informing the parents? How much is it OK to know without informing the Gardaí or the HSE? And how do you get on with the rest of your day knowing the troubles they're facing? It's a high-wire act a lot of the time, but I've never known job satisfaction like it on the days when things go well.

I often hear people make snide, judgemental comments about the 'kinds of people' who bring their sons or daughters to therapy. They whisper it in conversations, like they're discussing the lurid details of someone's sex life. They see it as a failure of parenting or a sign of their limitations in that area. I have seen no common thread among the parents I've worked with, other than a genuine desire to be as supportive as they can for their kid. They're the kind who know a dentist is the place to bring a teenager with a toothache. They know a mechanic is who you bring a car to when it needs attention. In Ireland we still have a long way to go before we stop shaming people who seek professional help.

Others will make comments about the 'types of teenagers' I work with, like there's a common thread there, too. They're no different from how I was. They're doing the best they can in sometimes difficult circumstances. Again, providing more supports in this area would be better than judging those who need it.

My job varies depending on the situation each adolescent is facing, but there is one analogy that I always keep in mind when I meet those in the greatest distress. It helps to keep me focused on my role.

I imagine they're in a small boat out at sea, completely lost, and completely alone. It's pitch dark and it's pouring rain. Waves are crashing all around them. They can't reach their oars, so they're just hanging on as best they can. With nobody in sight and no light on the horizon, they've little reason to believe things will improve. The scenario is as bleak as it gets.

Before I started this work, I had assumed my job was to save this kid straight away. After all, this is what I thought psychotherapy was before I began. If a daring rescue mission couldn't be completed, I thought my job was to fight back against all the elements. I'd have to calm the waves or stop the rain or replace the darkness with sunlight. It's asking a lot of myself, sure, but isn't that the job?

Now I see things differently.

Now I think the best thing I can do is jump into the boat alongside them.

I let them know that, no matter how rough things get, I'm going nowhere. No matter how long things last, I won't jump ship. I don't show any fear, because I've been here myself before. I don't blame them for making the choices that got them here. I don't shame them for not being able to save themselves. If I can, I pick up the oars and try to steady things a little. If I can't, I hang on with them to ride out the storm together. Once the conditions pass, or their perspective changes, I encourage them to do the rowing themselves. In all cases, I hope we reach a certain stage. In every scenario, I'm working towards a point where, eventually, they push me overboard.

21

Getting Comfortable

Growing up, I set myself the target of being invited to appear on *Kenny Live*, RTÉ's Saturday night chat show. It was an odd ambition, but I had my reasons. I wasn't keen on public speaking of any kind when I was young so I always assumed I would turn down this invitation if it came. I had watched Gary Kelly, Phil Babb and Jason McAteer being interviewed by Pat Kenny prior to the 1994 World Cup, so I would have seen it as a recognition of my success in football. One day, I told myself, that could be me.

In April 2019 I appeared on *The Late Late Show* to discuss consent and sex education in Ireland. This was not part of the journey I had mapped out when I was a kid. Other than the usual nerves that come with discussing such a sensitive topic on live television (not saying anything career-ending is always the target), I felt comfortable. This wasn't me talking about the dangers of alcohol while hungover. I wasn't hiding a Coppers stamp on my wrist from the night before. I wasn't afraid I'd be kicked off the show if they knew what I was really like. There was now no difference between the public me and the person who lived his life away from the media. As a result, there was no inner voice telling me I was a spoofer. There was just me, talking about the work I do and explaining why I think it's worth doing. I was, finally, comfortable just being myself.

It's also why I wasn't fazed when Rugby Players Ireland asked me to deliver workshops in this area to the senior provincial panels in late 2018. The old me would have run a mile from such a prospect. The thought of standing in a room with over forty professional rugby players in the wake of the Belfast rape trial to explore attitudes to sex, consent and alcohol would have terrified me in the past. But I wasn't there presenting myself as someone I'm not; nor was I there to lecture anyone on their behaviour. As far as I knew, not one person in those rooms needed any guidance on any aspect of this topic. I went to facilitate a discussion in the hope someone got something from it.

I kicked things off by telling them some of my own experiences. I talked about having sex in blackout. I told them the story of introducing myself to a girl who it turned out I had already slept with. I spoke about waking up in a cell in London without any idea why I was there. If you want others to talk openly, it helps if you're open yourself. I told them I was a recovering alcoholic and that I wasn't in a position to judge anyone.

It's also why I was comfortable sharing my views during the campaign to repeal the Eighth Amendment, after Anna Cosgrave asked me to get involved. I didn't care about any negative backlash. I was happy that I finally thought my opinions were as relevant as anybody else's, rather than inferior to them all. I wrote a column in *The Sun* in support of Repeal, knowing full well I would be lynched on Twitter.

The narrative being pushed by people campaigning for a No vote was that real men stand up for the rights of defenceless unborn babies. I got a fair bit of stick for fronting the 'Men For Yes' campaign, particularly when the launch photo was five blokes smiling at a camera, holding up various slogans promoting a Yes vote. Andy Lee was in the shot, so the photographer suggested we pose like boxers with our fists clenched. Not everyone was pleased with it. *'Laughing while killing babies, eh? You lot are scum.'*

A lot of the stick I got related to my gender. Why is a bloke campaigning on this? Why is a bloke – an ex-footballer – getting involved? Stay in your lane, dickhead.

Where the old me would have done anything to avoid confrontation or negative attention, I was happy to publicly explain my reasons for voting Yes and encourage others to do so. I didn't get involved in any spats on Twitter or try to convince any No voters to change their minds. I just wrote about my reasons for voting Yes and left it at that.

One of the things I remember most fondly about my involvement in that campaign was the freedom I felt to discuss my drinking and drugging in an interview for JOE. I showed up to speak to Dion Fanning, expecting to explain my views on the Eighth Amendment, and ended up speaking candidly about my past. I did the interview, thought no more about it and then I went home, walked Bobbi, my new St Bernard puppy, and got on with my day.

I had plenty of reasons for getting involved in the campaign. I had worked with several people who had been impacted by the Eighth Amendment in my practice, but I had also worked with women who had been in crises of other kinds.

A couple of years earlier, I had been approached by the CEO of a women's shelter in Dublin to provide therapy for some of the women in their care. The entire support staff was female and while that was appropriate for many of the women, given their experience with the men in their lives at that point, it wasn't a reflection of the world outside.

I was asked to reserve some time in my schedule to see women who felt comfortable working with a man. Yet again, my old ideas about the limitations of being a man in this field were proving untrue. I was becoming even less concerned by society's perceptions about what men should and shouldn't do. From then on, I decided the better approach would be just to do what I wanted with my own time.

—

Being me is a very different experience from how it used to be. My working life and my social life are unrecognisable from what they had been when I was in my mid-twenties.

If being a therapist was an unexpected turn in my career, working in sex education to promote more open discussions about sex and consent was not a role I would ever have predicted for myself.

I worked with many young men who had difficult experiences in this area, but a pattern started to emerge. They knew very little about the laws relating to sex, age and consent, and couldn't recall any opportunities throughout their time in school where they could have asked about it. They had had no meaningful sex education of any kind, and the topic of consent was never discussed. Everything they thought they knew about sex came from watching porn.

I was given virtually no direction or guidance in this area when I was younger. When my mum found out I had snogged a girl after a youth disco in first year, she gave me a book to read about sex and sexuality. I was too uncomfortable or embarrassed to bring it up with her again, though I'm sure she would have been open to further discussions. But the last person I wanted to speak to about sex when I was thirteen was my mum. My formal sex education consisted of information on how women get pregnant and that was it.

You don't need to be a parent or a psychotherapist to realise we can do more for young people in this area, but the tricky part is coming up with a way that might work. Maybe this all stems from my own trauma in this area, but on the back of some of these cases, I decided to do something.

In 2016 I made contact with Elaine Byrnes, a psychologist who has done a lot of research around consent and sexual behaviour in NUI Galway. Senator Lynn Ruane had given me her name. Lynn trains in the same gym as I do in Tallaght, and I realised a long time ago she'd be the person to contact if I wanted to get anything done. If Lynn can't help you herself, she'll know someone who can.

Elaine's own formal sex education consisted of nuns showing her class a video of a traumatic birth. That was it. Using my mental health module as a template, we put together a six-week module in sexual health and started delivering it to transition year students in St Benildus in 2017.

Everything was trial and error from the start, but we agreed that nothing would be off the table. If the students had a question or an opinion or an observation to share, we encouraged them to speak up. I wasn't going to be attending PT meetings or sharing their opinions with staff members. We weren't there to judge or criticise or stifle any conversations. All views were valid, all voices equal. If there was a difference of opinion in any area we just sat back and let them debate, hoping these conversations would continue long after we had both left the classroom.

The approach Elaine and I take isn't particularly revolutionary. Instead of judging the students for their ignorance, we prefer instead to help them out. We create a classroom environment in which everyone feels comfortable and from there people get to ask the questions they want answered. I would have loved a class like that when I was their age.

Before I appeared on *The Late Late Show* in 2019, I wrote a column on consent for the *Irish Times*. In it I recreated a classroom conversation on the subject with sixteen-year-old boys, trying to accurately reflect the kinds of questions and opinions they come out with. Most responses were encouraging of the work we were doing, but some of the reactions to the article caught my eye. Several people said they were disappointed, dismayed and concerned by what they read. They seemed to have been expecting a far higher level of understanding of consent and the issues surrounding it from a group of people who had never had the opportunity to discuss it before.

Many readers were shocked by these teenagers' reactions to hearing that a drunk person can't give consent. The students grapple with how this knowledge should be applied to real-life situations, a complex question that so many people are reluctant to explore. Again, there was an expectation that these young people should have had all the answers, when they'd never had the chance to ask any questions.

I can't even remember some of the sexual experiences I've had, never mind being able to recall how consent was negotiated in any of them. I was drunk much of the time and have had countless experiences of unsafe sex. But, by April 2019, I was talking to Ryan Tubridy on *The Late Late Show* about the classroom condom demonstrations Elaine and I do with 'little plastic penis things'.

Following some of the publicity around our classes in St Benildus, the Archbishop of Dublin's office contacted the school to say it had an issue with us discussing homosexuality and contraception. Some people have strong beliefs that safe sex shouldn't be part of sex education, which is a bit like sending young people to a driving school that forbids seatbelts.

As for the reference to homosexuality, I'd love to introduce the Archbishop – or anyone else for that matter – to my sister Anna and tell me if they see an unfit parent or a deviant sinner.

Anna told me she was gay in her late twenties. She had never spoken the words out loud to anyone before. She said she had been trying to outgrow the feeling for over a decade, but realised she couldn't. She didn't present it as a positive development. She was crying, telling me she was devastated she had to face up to it. I kicked myself for the times my mates and I would have used words like 'fag', 'queer' or 'bender' in front of her. Why did I have to choose those words?

For a spell, Anna's hair was falling out from the stress of it all and she had to wear a wig. I had never considered how traumatic the process could be for someone.

In May 2011 Anna moved to Brighton as she felt the culture there would be more accepting and open for her to be herself.

So when I was asked to campaign for a Yes vote in the marriage equality referendum in 2015, I didn't hesitate. I found it bizarre to hear some people say that gay people should be denied their rights – they were talking about Anna, one of the soundest, kindest, funniest people you could meet. I posted a video saying it was wrong that only one of my sisters had the right to marry the person she loved. I would never have thought I'd have something to say in a referendum campaign, but it was tough to watch people feel empowered to speak publicly about the reasons they felt she shouldn't marry. Three months after the Yes vote, Anna married Laura in Brighton. Thirteen months later, she gave birth to their son, Ryan.

—

I blanked all the details of what happened in court during the trial of Paddy Jackson and Stuart Olding in 2018. Most people are familiar with the allegations and the outcome of the trial, but sex, consent, respect and alcohol were the central themes. It was an entirely different landscape from the circumstances of my abuse, but the legal process was a little too close to home. I didn't want to see what it's like to be a complainant. I didn't want to know how hard it would be to share the details of those experiences publicly and have some legal professional do their best to tear me down. And then for the case to be effectively tried again on loop on Twitter and other platforms, with anyone and everyone commenting on every detail. I couldn't have put myself through that, even as recently as 2018, though there were plenty of times I wanted to put my abuser through that.

After the Belfast trial, I did a podcast with Sinead O'Carroll on consent with Second Captains where I spoke about the sexual health module. It's the most listened-to podcast we've ever done. I went on the *Ray D'Arcy Show* on RTÉ to discuss some of the issues raised in the case. It's been a long and winding journey for the guy who introduced himself to a woman he'd already slept with. That guy, it turned out, had a lot to learn, and I wonder how much different things could have been if someone had taught him.

There's a saying in recovery circles that, no matter how far down the scale you've been, you'll realise your experience can still benefit others. Stories are worth sharing, memories are worth repeating, no matter how difficult or embarrassing they are to recall, because somebody might take something from what you say. That's part of my motivation for writing this book. We'd learn a lot less about life if none of us shared our experiences, but the topic most people would prefer to avoid chatting about is sex.

Sharing details of my sex life in earlier chapters was not for the sake of it. I didn't write those things in order to shock, upset, amuse or impress anyone. I wasn't trying to settle scores or paint myself in an undeserved, flattering light. I wanted to highlight how unusual it is for someone to chat openly about sex, something that so many people struggle to do in any way. It's one of the biggest barriers to getting people to have meaningful discussions about consent.

Maybe if that physio had been respectful of me and my body when I was fourteen years old, I wouldn't care so much about this topic. Maybe if I hadn't learned about sex and relationships from professional footballers, I wouldn't be as passionate about the merits of proper education. And maybe if I wasn't a recovering alcoholic whose sex life had been soaked in alcohol for so long, I wouldn't see the need to promote responsible drinking to young people now. Either way, I've found myself doing a job that, for some reason, means a lot to me. But discussing sex and young people is like walking through a minefield, with ethical, moral and legal issues galore. There's potential for an eruption of some sort, no matter what you say. And as I illustrated in my column about discussing consent in the classroom, one of the trickiest issues to explore is the impact of alcohol.

If you focus on alcohol after there is an allegation of wrong-doing following a sexual encounter between two drunk people who have little or no recollection of how they behaved, you'll be accused of victim-blaming, which I fully understand. This is why these messages have to be delivered long before anyone is being called a victim and someone else is being called a perpetrator. This isn't an area where being wise after the event is any use. These aren't the kinds of lessons you want anyone to have to learn the hard way. Educating people on the dangers of excessive drinking is always better to do before they make decisions about getting drunk.

At the start of our modules, students are concerned about how consent is defined in a courtroom, but by the end, they're learning about how it's negotiated in the bedroom. Consent is about communication. It's about knowing for sure that you and your partner are on the same page. You can't do that if you stay silent. You can't do that if you've no vocabulary in this area. You can't do that if you've been led to believe sex should never be discussed. And you can't do that if you've drunk so much you can barely speak.

What I didn't say to Ryan Tubridy that evening on *The Late Late Show* was that our condom demonstrations come with a twist. We bring in specially designed goggles for the students to wear after they've had a few attempts. The goggles have been modified to simulate the sensory experience of being under the influence of alcohol and various drugs. It's a far more useful teaching tool than trying to describe how everything changes when you're drunk or high. It also happens to be one of the most enjoyable ways you could possibly spend ninety minutes.

It's a modern twist on the age-old message about drinking responsibly. Rather than wait to shame young people when they get things wrong, we prefer to help them do the right thing before they even try. I don't know if I would have heeded such warnings if I had heard them when I was sixteen. Unfortunately, alcoholism isn't something that can be taught out of you by a teacher who says the right thing. One thing is clear, though, young people can discuss sex and sexuality in a way that was unimaginable for my generation. It's up to us adults to stop feeling so awkward and join the conversation.

Epilogue

I used to have a recurring dream about playing for Ireland. In my view, my eighteen minutes in an Ireland jersey don't really qualify me to be described as a former Irish international. In my dream, I am getting ready to correct that. I will play for Ireland again and be a legitimate international, somebody who doesn't always have to justify himself.

In these dreams, Giovanni Trapattoni is the manager. I'm not sure why, although I'm sure there are various ways to interpret this. Maybe he represents a father figure. Perhaps he is a version of myself I would like to be more often – assertive, straight-talking and to the point. In my way of thinking, when Trap appears in my dreams, it's probably just Trap.

The dream usually goes the same way. I have spent some time criticising him on television, but for some reason Trap overlooks all that and calls me up to play for Ireland again. In the dream, I never get to make my return but the focus is always on how I should handle it the first time I meet him.

For twenty-five years of my life, my dreams revolved around playing for Ireland. I dreamt of it as a kid and then, when I became a professional footballer, I would wonder exactly how it would go when the chances of it moved from probable to possible to sitting in a meeting being asked how many tickets I wanted for the World Cup Finals.

But the reality is, those eighteen minutes against Russia were all I got. They represented the turning point in my career. I played on for another eighteen months or, at least, I took another eighteen months to retire but, in many ways, that was the night my dreams ended.

After I retired, I spent a long time wondering what it would have been like if I'd had the career I was supposed to have. I dreamt then of playing for Ireland as I had imagined it as a boy when I stood on the terraces at Lansdowne Road, or when I watched Ireland at the rehab centre in November 1989.

I had never really believed people when they told me I could make it all the way to the top, but then, when my career ended, I started to believe everything they had said. It became part of the cocktail of resentment and regret that took hold in the years following my retirement. My anger turned inwards. The dreams I had were gone and, now that they were behind me, I took them all at face value. The stuff I had dismissed at the time as beyond me now became part of the rage I had towards myself. My body had denied me the chance to play in a World Cup. I would have been a Premier League footballer if I hadn't been so weak, so prone to injury, so frail. The fantasy became a parallel reality I'd missed out on. The life I was entitled to was the one I mourned.

Now I see things differently. Now I realise I *did* have the career I was supposed to have. That was it. No matter how often I thought about it or tried to will another one into existence, I could not change the facts. I could not rewrite history.

I took some of this shame into my career as a pundit. Who was I to offer an opinion on players whose level I'd never reached? I found another way to be hard on myself. Another way to put myself down.

The sense of awkwardness I felt on the RTÉ panel as the goal-scorer in the U-18 European Championships third-place play-off doesn't exist anymore. I can sit beside Liam Brady or Damien Duff and I'm no longer concerned that my career didn't match theirs. If it comes up, I can laugh at it.

Working with Second Captains has also been one of the most rewarding aspects of my media career. The idea of not taking it all too seriously lies at the heart of that group of lads. They can manage to be more insightful about sport than anyone else, yet laugh about it too.

In other areas of my life, it's been harder to be free of regret, anger and a desire for things to have happened another way. I have tried to work to quieten that part of my mind so I can find some peace, and writing this book was part of that process.

The idea of training as a psychotherapist took hold when I sat in therapy myself and began to wonder what it would feel like to sit in the opposite chair. I felt there would be a sense of satisfaction in helping people the way the therapist had helped me. But that also opened me up to the idea that I needed help. The methods I had used to survive for thirty years weren't working.

There is a line in *Seinfeld* where Jerry says that breaking up with someone is like knocking over a vending machine: 'You can't do it in one push. You gotta rock it back and forth a few times and then it goes over.' I think coming to terms with yourself is a bit like that, too. There are days when it seems like everything is falling into place and days when it can all be overwhelming.

But I don't believe I would have addressed it at all if it wasn't for what I did on one day: 22 August 2011. The day I stopped drinking was the day I could truly begin to repair all that had been damaged. I didn't know that at the time. I thought I was stopping drinking and nothing else, but I was doing something more important, something that fundamentally affected how I approach life.

Without therapy, I might not have got there, but all the therapy in the world wouldn't have helped if I had still been dealing with the weekly collection of shame and regret that is a standard part of the life of an active alcoholic. Once I cleared that away, I could handle other things.

My friends from my teenage years are still my friends. Everything has changed between us and in other ways nothing has changed. I needn't have worried that a sober me would have no place in the group. I just needed time to adjust to my new position. In 2017 I attended Hicksy's wedding in Las Vegas and really enjoyed it. The following year, we all went to the Altogether Now festival for the whole weekend.

In April 2019, McGrath, Ste and I took the boat to Holyhead to watch Liverpool play Barcelona in the semi-final of the Champions League. It was one of the most adrenaline-filled nights in Anfield's history. I didn't need to run for the exit as I had at Croke Park during my early days of sobriety. I had no fear of where the occasion would take me, so I could enjoy every second.

I was adamant there would be no stag do ahead of my wedding, so Kitt arranged for a group swim in the Forty Foot instead. These were the occasions I thought would be beyond me, enjoyed with people I feared would drift away.

I don't go to pubs for the sake of being in pubs, but if there's a reason to be there, I no longer have any reluctance to go. This was not what I thought my life would be like when I quit drinking.

I taught my final class at St Benildus in May 2019. Myself and Elaine plan to take what we've learned teaching the sexual health module and deliver consent workshops in schools around the country. During the last mental fitness class, I spoke openly for the first time to students about being a recovering alcoholic. Instead of discussing addiction or problematic drinking in an abstract way, I was comfortable speaking about my own experiences without feeling ashamed.

But there was one aspect of my life I thought I would never face. I had one secret I felt I would always be wrestling with, caught between the need to tell someone and the terror of how they'd react.

The abuse I suffered is not my shameful secret anymore. I don't go shouting about it out the car window as I drive along, but the people I love – my wife Fiona and my family – know about it. It is not something that gets in the way of our relationships like I always thought it would. It is part of who I am. Getting sober has allowed me to deal with it and, most important, to go easy on myself for what happened.

During the course of writing this book, I wondered whether I was finally ready to press charges. I've been adamant for years I would never do it, that the personal cost would be too great. However, I also swore I'd keep this secret from everyone around me. Things change. Perspectives change. I've changed.

I imagined the ordeal of repeating the details over and over again during the process, but I also imagined the backlash from people if I didn't. *Your silence is keeping a predator on the streets.* As keen as I was to avoid either scenario, the decision was taken out of my hands in July 2019 when I learned he was dead.

If I had to go easy on myself about the abuse I suffered, I also had to do so about so many other aspects of my life. Learning to live a fulfilling life has been the most unexpected benefit of being sober. I thought my life was over when I stopped drinking, but in many ways, I had just been living the same day over and over again. Actually, maybe it was three days: the day I was drunk, the day I was hungover and the day I recovered. Rinse and repeat.

Everything is different now. Life is simpler and it is better.

—

Ten years after my benefit game at Millwall, I stood in the same spot in the lounge in The Den where I felt I had been close to bursting into tears on that day in 2009.

This time, Millwall were about to play Brighton in the FA Cup in March 2019. I had been asked to speak before the game about what I'd done with my life since I left the club. I talked about training to be a psychotherapist to a room full of Millwall fans. I spoke without any sense of awkwardness or hesitation about how it had helped me. I met up with old teammates and friends from the club. We reminisced about the old days without succumbing to nostalgia. Some fans were kind enough to tell me how much I meant to them – the old 'You facking IRA cunt' abuse is long forgotten. The fans are the same as they have always been; it's me who has changed, which is why I can now appreciate them for who and what they are. At the end of that day, I flew back to Dublin to prepare for another week seeing clients.

—

I would not have the relationship I have with my family and I would not be married to the woman I love if I was drinking. Fiona has never seen me drunk. Given the calamities I'm still prone to – like setting fire to spaghetti, twice – she's pretty grateful that she doesn't have to deal with a drunk version of me.

We got engaged on Christmas Eve 2018, fourteen months after we first met. A few days after our engagement, we got another dog, a cavapoo called Joey – I've had many dogs, but this is the first time I've got one with someone else. Despite everything I thought I would think in such a situation, I had no doubts whatsoever when I proposed. Everything I once thought I had to keep hidden in relationships, I had revealed early on. I told her I was in recovery, I told her I had been abused. There is no invisible forcefield around me that keeps her – or me – at a safe distance. Fiona knows everything about me.

Actually, that's not true. Six months after we met, Fiona told a friend that the team I had played for when I was a footballer was called Wanderers. I'm not entirely confident she would know their name if I asked her today. But she knows the important stuff and she knows how I feel about her.

We got married in May 2019. I thought I was prepared for the day – and I was in every sense, except the most important one. The emotion was overwhelming. Anna was my best man and she made a speech which perfectly summed up every moment of our lives and why I've been lucky with my family, in ways I once couldn't have imagined.

And it was a day when I felt lucky in so many ways. Lucky to have my family, lucky to have my friends and lucky – although that word doesn't begin to describe it – to have Fiona as my wife. Through the years of cynicism and self-destruction, I never felt there was a day like that waiting for me, mainly because I didn't believe there was a woman like Fiona there for me. For the old me, there probably wasn't, so the statement of love we made on that day also underlined how everything had changed.

To see my mum so happy on the day meant everything. Once again, she didn't cry because she said that if she started she wouldn't stop, but without her love, without her presence, none of us would have the bonds we do.

At one point in the day, I saw my dad heading out of the garden where we were celebrating. He was followed by my nieces and nephews who were enthralled, as I had been, by the promise of magic.

The relationship I have with my dad today is something I couldn't have imagined. On the day I called Dad to tell him I had stopped drinking, something changed in our relationship. The truth is, the change in him had been there before that if I had looked for it. It was there when he texted me on the day I retired and it was even there when he showed up to watch me play and never offered a word of criticism.

My dad had four kids and a drinking problem by the time he was thirty, but by the time he was forty, he had to find a new version of that relationship with drink and with his family. My parents' marriage didn't survive, but he was trying to find a new way of living. When I started to do the same, the change in our relationship was down to a change in me.

Most of us become more understanding of our parents as we get older and reach the age they were when we thought they had all the answers. When we realise we now have none, we become a bit more accepting of them as they are, and as they had been.

When I stopped drinking I began to wonder what it must have been like for my dad when he quit. He had a wife, four kids and a nine-to-five job back then. He was thirty-eight when he packed it in. I had never considered the hassle he must have had from his mates back then, too. All I had to think about were the dogs, Frank and Paddy, and some media work. I had all the time in the world to attend meetings and therapy and then I came home each evening to a quiet house.

I started to think how tough it must have been for my father to find time for everything when I was a kid. No wonder he didn't make my matches.

I was a kid, I can't be hard on myself, but now that I'm not a kid I don't need or want to be hard on him either.

The enormity of recovery and what it entailed was staring me in the face when I started getting sober. The man in front of me was a complete transformation of the one I had known when I was a kid. It was time to cut him some slack. It was time to let go of some of the memories and feelings I was still holding on to. The better approach would be to acknowledge that I'd had an in-house example of the power of recovery and growth all along. What was possible was not an abstract concept. My dad had been showing me for over twenty years at that point. It was time to open my eyes and appreciate that.

As a kid, I had an idea of a relationship with my dad based on fantasy. He would see me playing football and everything would fall into place. But now we have a relationship – a friendship – that I'm not sure I would really have understood. For the first time in my life, I look to him as an example of what I can be.

I know now that he had never seen football as a way of connecting. He was proud of me and he cried when he saw me play in England, but being a footballer was not who I was, it was what I did.

That's why his text when I retired resonated with me and why I kept coming back to it in the years after retirement. I didn't have to be defined by what I did. He knew that. It took me longer to realise it.

My dad was my hero once. There was a version of him I always wanted to walk through the door. These days, I know which version will walk through the door when we meet and it's the version I idolised as a kid.

I heard someone say recently that if you want a happy ending it depends on where you stop your story. I turned forty in January 2019. I had reached an age teenage me thought would never happen because I expected to die long before then. I marked the day with a swim at the Forty Foot with Fiona. One other person was with us: my dad. As Fiona and I went into the water, he was as playful and mischievous as the father who would do magic as we climbed the Sugar Loaf. I had one of those feelings where I thought that, at this moment, everything was in the right place.

I'd chased that sensation on a football field and I'd pursued it through drink and drugs. As we went for a swim on a cold January morning, it was both mundane and special at the same time. The stuff I thought was beyond me, the everyday stuff of relationships and real life, are now possible. The ordinary has become extraordinary.

—

When Mick McCarthy was named Ireland manager in 2018, I began to have a similar recurring dream to the one I'd had for many years. Unlike Trap, Mick is known to me. He has been my manager and, as he demonstrated when he sat through three interview attempts on *The Player's Chair*, he is a man of tolerance and patience.

My dilemma in this dream was whether Mick would allow me time off on the Monday to see my clients in my practice. How would I tell him I was delighted to be back in the Ireland squad and then, in the next breath, ask him to let me go and do what matters most to me these days? I'm choosing to interpret this dream as a sign that my priorities are different now. The importance I attached to football has faded. In its place there is a fulfilment I never managed to achieve as a footballer.

The dream never reaches the point where I have to tell Mick I'm flattered by the call-up, but I won't be at training on Monday. I wake up before that happens. I don't dwell too much on what it all means. Dreams can be interpreted anyway you like.

Reality can sometimes be harder to understand. Reality can be painful, troubling and overwhelming, but ultimately the real world is more rewarding. Reality is where it begins and ends.

Resources

Rather than end this book by listing off the people who have helped me, I'd prefer to highlight some organisations that can support people impacted by the issues I've written about. They all have very informative and helpful websites, and I have provided some of their contact details below.

One in Four is an Irish charity set up to support adult survivors of child sexual abuse: (01) 662 4070.

The Rape Crisis Centre has a national 24-hour phoneline set up to support adult survivors of childhood sexual abuse: 1800 778 888.

The CARI Foundation provides therapy and support to children affected by child sexual abuse: Lo Call 1890 92 45 67.

Samaritans have a free 24-hour number that you can call from any phone: 116 123.

Barnardos runs several parenting courses, including drug education programmes for parents: www.barnardos.ie.

For help with alcohol and drug dependency issues, speak to your GP about services in your area. They will inform you of any self-help/ support groups in your locality, details about treatment centres and detox programmes that might help, and general information about the type of supports that are available.

Alternatively, if you know someone who has stopped drinking, and it is something you would like to do, discreetly approach them and see if they can assist you in doing the same.

For more formal supports, each of these organisations has a national database of counsellors and therapists who could help:

- Irish Association for Counselling and Psychotherapy (IACP)
- Irish Council for Psychotherapy (ICP)
- Irish Association of Humanistic and Integrative Psychotherapy (IAHIP)